Dance and Magic Drama
in Ceylon

by the same author

DANCE AND DRAMA IN BALI

To the memory of

HUGH NEVILL

Contents

✵

7

Illustrations

9

Illustrations

I owe these photographs to the courtesy of the Archaeological Com-
mission of Ceylon: 3, 9, 40, 41, 46, 47; The Ceylon Government: 4,
5, 6, 8, 10, 11, 12, 49; The Indian Section of the Victoria and Albert
Museum: 31, 33, 34; The British Museum: 20, 21, 32, 50; Mr.
Webster (University of Ceylon): 13, 14; Mr. Weerawardane: 7, 15,
16, 36, 37, 38, 39; Madame Ina Bandy (by the kindness of Mr. Lyn
Ludowyk): 42, 43, 44, 45, 48; Mr. Delaphilla: 17, 18; Nos. 19, 22,
23, 24, 25, 26, 27, 28, 29, 30, 35 are by me.

Preface

During my first short visit to Malabar in the early spring of 1935 I was roused one day from a brief siesta on the raised loggia in front of my peasant house by the noise of a car pulling up with a screech outside the stile which served as a front gate. It was a police officer (or was he a philosopher?) who had taken the trouble to come quite a distance in a jolty car to give me some good advice and find out a little about my movements. I tried not to show my dismay at this dusty incursion, and we settled down to talk. He had read, he said, in some newspaper that I intended to 'do' all India in a year and to write a book about all the dancing. I hastened to reassure him, and if he should chance to have come across my book *The Other Mind*, he will perhaps realize that I do not regard it as possible to make a complete study of anything in a year, or even in many years. He may of course attribute my slow pace to his admonition; it is even possible he will think I have overdone it by spending seventeen years over an introductory study of life and dance in one province alone of the great sub-continent of India.

Some fruits ripen more slowly than others, and my long sojourn on Bali with Walter Spies, most gifted and most beloved of all Europeans who have elected to make Bali their home, was a stage in the ripening. I might plead that the present volume is also part of the same Indian opus; for in spite of the apparent accessibility and even modernity of present-day Ceylon, it is I think just as fascinating as India. There are the magic drama and other rituals in the mountains round Kandy, the last royal city of Ceylon, where every rock is stamped with a heroic memory out of a mythical past; and the exorcistic *balis* and *devol maduwas* of the south coast, which have progressed so discreetly that every precious superstition remains intact, indissolubly woven into the Buddhism which is supposed to have superseded them.

It was a happy coincidence that *Dance and Drama in Bali*, first published in 1938, should have emerged from an overlong *Winterschlaf* in time to welcome its offspring, or should I say its ancestor? For *The Other Mind* is the record of a journey backwards in time, a journey upstream as it were, into a startlingly beautiful and sometimes alarming jungle of magic; a more difficult journey perhaps than that which Walter and I took together in *Dance and Drama in Bali*. For him the completion of that book was the end of an undertaking; he had lived too long in Bali to suffer transplantation, and was eager, I think, to get back to what was after all his life's work and that in which he most excelled: the pictorial re-creation of the Balinese scene, transformed but not falsified by his extraordinary imagination. Even if he had survived that last sea-journey to further internment in British India—he perished almost before it had begun, by a Japanese torpedo—I doubt if he would have wanted to start afresh. He had built himself a house in Bali long before I had even dreamed of its existence, and he had studied every aspect of that extraordinarily varied and richly gifted island. By disappearing without trace Walter has become a legend, and will live for ever in the faithful affections of the Balinese, a culture hero, who will come down once a year with their ancestor gods from the Gunung Agung (the Great Mountain) to dwell for a week in the house-temples, and celebrate the mystery-cycle of the *Ramayana,* a date which roughly corresponds to our Festival of All Souls.

But I, with whom Walter shared his long experience, had already paid two visits to India when *Dance and Drama* first appeared, as well as to other countries of the Far East whose culture had been fertilized by the religion and art of India. I felt I must go more deeply into the origin of those epic themes which in every country took on a new shape according to the soil. I had to go further, and I had to go alone.

When filling in the forms for an International Congress of Folk Music in Brazil I was delighted to read the question: Can you read and write? I can fortunately read quite nicely and was of course once taught to write, but there are few now who would take the trouble to decipher my untidy script. And the question was I fear only meant for poor immigrants to Brazil, who though often much more gifted no doubt than the congress members would have been swamped in an ocean of dreary words, as I was myself. Yet I confess that some of the people I have found most interesting on my travels could neither read nor write, though they were far from illiterate, their memories being stored with music and stories and great names. It may be that the refinement of movement and dazzling invention which characterized the Balinese peasant communities, who for the most part could neither read nor write, will survive their initiation into the path of progress. I have no idea. One appetite begets another, and it is not very likely that the possession of cars and motor-bikes and cameras, and the impact of industrialism will help towards artistic creation. Perhaps my Malabar visitor has also moved with the times and finds a year's study almost enough. But I sincerely hope not, for it is only out of long meditation and experience that beauty is born, and the power to express it.

I cannot agree with the learned Dr. Raghavan, professor of Sanskrit in Madras University, who was kind enough to review *The Other Mind* in the *Journal of the Folk Dance and Song Society*, that it is necessary to display all the learning one cannot help acquiring in the course of one's travels on the written page; but I prefer the rebuke of so learned and kind a man to the praise of an American journalist, who by emphasizing certain inconveniences during one of my most fruitful visits in South India seemed to me to insult the hosts who so wonderfully entertained me at Ambalapuzha, where are some of the finest dancers and musicians and the greatest living teacher of *Kathakali*, Kunju Kurup.

I will not deny that I enjoyed the government car which the same young American was so good at procuring through his influential connections, and kindly shared with me. I somehow never inspire official confidence, and it was only at Trivandrum, after many inquiries of which I confess I was rather ashamed, that a government car came along; though I hope it raised me a little in the estimation of Dr. Poduval, whose archaeological museum I so much appreciated.

To return to Dr. Raghavan's criticism of levity. I fear he will find the present volume even more informal than the preceding one. It is not my aim to instruct people in the intricacies of classical dancing in India or anywhere else in the world. There are far more scholars than poets and I must leave it to the scholars to instruct, while I go ahead with my poetry.

One critic was of the opinion that *The Other Mind* was full of 'chaotic irrelevancies', but admitted that by degrees one might discover a clue to the labyrinth. There certainly is one, and if by my seeming irrelevancies I have helped a few *aficionados* to find their way, and also entertained them, my labour will not have been in vain. I am not at all good at being learned, but everything I speak of I have seen with my own eyes and felt with my own heart, and so I have set it down, like other informal travellers of the past who with varying success recorded their travels.

To write a book, like living, is to incur far more obligations than one can ever hope adequately to discharge. For research of the kind I have undertaken, especially if one is alone, involves the help of many more people than it is possible to thank individually.

Besides my generous long-term hosts, Ignatia and Leston Mendez, the famous de Silva family at Kandy, Dick and Sheila Pieris, and Harry Pieris at Kurunegala, there were many brief oases of hospitality which I shall never forget; Mr. Delgoda of Kekewatte near Ratnapura took me in and gave me delightful instruction; Dr. Nell was always ready to help, and if only I had then inquired about Hugh Nevill would certainly have been able to tell me something about that wonderful man whom no one else is old enough to remember; the dance-teacher Sederaman who gave up much time to instruct me in the texts of the *Kohomba Kankaria*; the kind and learned patriot Mr. Dolapihille, who told me much about the headsmen of Kandy, before and after its capture by the British, and conversed with me on many matters equally fascinating. I have acknowledged elsewhere the kindness of Mr. G. L. S. de Silva[1] of Ambalangoda who prepared for me a programme of the *Kolan* I saw there and, unbeknown to me, paid for my lodging at the rest house. Also of Bishop Lakdasa de Mel, who so kindly redeemed his promise of help, by paying for the *Kolan,* and invited me to stay at Kurunegala on my next visit.

It was in a note to an anonymous preface to an 1818 edition of Robert Knox's *Historical Description of Ceylon* that I first met Lord Valentia, who was cited as an authority for a marriage custom of the

---

[1] All de Silvas seem unusually kind.

Kandyan kings which seemed to me then so strange that I was inclined to think Lord Valentia had been invented for the occasion. The British Museum catalogue had no record of the name, nor indeed had the London Library. But the librarian, Mr. Davis, after falling into a kind of momentary trance, pounced upon Debrett's Peerage and produced Lord Mountnorris, Viscount Valentia, who in the years 1802–6 voyaged and travelled to India, the Red Sea, Abyssinia and Egypt, and fortunately for us kept a diary during the whole of that eventful period when the peaceful trading of the East India Company was giving way to forceful persuasion. There was always some justification for interference, because there was always some injustice to be righted, some cruelty to avenge; and 'rounding off the empire' by one righteous little conquest more was surely as wholly beneficial to the conquered as it was convenient to the Empire Builders. Lord Valentia was the guest of Lord North, one of the most just of British Colonial Governors, and naturally took the point of view of his host, that the bloodshed involved in the 'rounding off' though wholly regrettable was not of our choosing. One is hardly free to hold one's own views if one is the privileged guest of a governor-general.

Besides keeping a journal, Lord Valentia also kept an artist secretary, Henry Salt, two of whose admirable drawings I am able to reproduce.

Probably no one will ever write again those living documents of beauty which we destroyed in the process of 'teaching lawless men to become obedient, inhuman men to love, and savage men to change', which seemed then sufficient justification for our ruthless struggle for an economic empire in the East. We are just beginning to learn something about these strange and beautiful patterns of life; and to know that the lawless men had laws of great complexity, and a strangely civilized code of love.

What are we going to do about it? Is it too late for us to learn? I am sure it is not. But I think we must first walk awhile in the wood where things have no name. Do you remember the sad and lovely episode in *Alice Through the Looking Glass*? I shall venture to quote it entire, and not moralize about it, though I have an idea that it has a moral, and that it is an important one.

15

'Just then a fawn came wandering by. It looked at Alice with its large gentle eyes, but didn't seem at all frightened.

' "Here then, here then!" Alice said, as she held out her hand and tried to stroke it; but it only started back a little, and then stood look-ing at her again.

' "What do you call yourself?" the Fawn said at last. Such a soft, sweet voice it had!

' "I wish I knew!" thought poor Alice. She answered rather sadly, "Nothing just now."

' "Think again," it said, "that won't do."

'Alice thought, but nothing came of it. "Please, what would *you* call yourself?" she said timidly. "I think that might help a little."

' "I'll tell you if you'll come a little further on," the Fawn said. "I can't remember here."

'So they walked on together through the wood, Alice with her arms clasped lovingly round the soft neck of the Fawn, till they came out into another open field, and here the Fawn gave a sudden bound into the air, and shook itself free from Alice's arms. "I'm a Fawn!" it cried in a voice of delight. "And, dear me, you're a human child!" A sudden look of alarm came into its beautiful brown eyes, and in another moment it had darted away at full speed.'

Introduction

My first visit to Ceylon was in the spring of 1935, as the guest of Malalasekara, one of its foremost Buddhists; a learned and most intelligent man, whose immense energy of mind and body made him a stimulating but never fatiguing companion. His hospitality was due in the first instance to his friendship with one of my sisters, through whose introduction he extended it to me, and showed me Ceylon in a way that I could never otherwise have seen it. Many things which I then saw I did not altogether understand; but a fairly full record of them in my diary of that year throws much light on what I have subsequently seen, and I believe that I saw then the best performance of the masked play, *Kolan,* though I was at that time very vague about names, and had no idea that I was ever likely to regard my Ceylon experiences as having anything to do with Indian dancing. It was not till I was collecting the material for a book on the dances of South India that I came gradually to realize the close cultural link between India and Ceylon; and at last my Ceylon material proved so important, that it had to overflow into a separate volume.

At the time of my first visit I had not even begun to collect material for *Dance and Drama in Bali,* and all my experience was in the form of first impressions.

I knew of course that Ceylon was the Lanka where the mighty demon Ravana held his court; whence the Monkey General Hanuman rescued Sita, Rama's wife, after she had been carried off into captivity. It is less material to know the story of this great epic in Ceylon, for though Nature has it in remembrance, no existing native drama is built on it;[1] unless one considers as I do that the *Kohomba*

[1] I need only allude in passing to a Tamil version of the *Ramayana,* which Hugh Nevill studied in detail when stationed in Batticaloa. It was played entirely by the Tamils of the east coast, and a fragmentary form of the same drama is still performed by Tamil fishermen who play in the open air on a circular stage. I have only seen them at the Arts Festival in Colombo in 1949 (see Chapter VI). This drama seems to have a parallel in the *Yakshagana* of Mysore, a country cousin of *Kathakali.*

Kankaria, that great magic drama of the Kandyan country, is part of the same cycle.

I knew little about Kandy then, except that Robert Knox had visited it in the seventeenth century, during his many years of semi-captivity in Ceylon after the shipwreck of his father's boat. His account of the *Perahera* is one of the most vivid we possess, and his knowledge of the language is said to have been unique. Of the terrible facts attending the occupation of Kandy by the British in 1803 I at that time knew nothing at all, and have only recently read the details of it in the diary of the young British officer to whom was entrusted the odious task of heading a punitive expedition. His orders were couched in such vague terms that the young officer of twenty-four who had to carry them out was bound to be inculpated if anything went wrong. It is a dreadful and humiliating story of incomprehension and waste, which for days haunted my imagination, as it clearly haunted the dreams of Captain Johnson for life, and prompted some excellent advice on the subject of dress in the tropics, especially if it is one's object to be as inconspicuous as possible; and also about the urgent need of learning the language of the country one is called on to 'pacify', let alone to govern.

The excitement of discovery is a purely personal matter, and not always easy to convey. But my first experience of Kandyan dance was so exciting and on such an unusual occasion—an out-of-season *Perahera* to celebrate the Silver Jubilee of King George V—that I will quote a few of those first impressions, which however ill-informed, were certainly more vivid than those I received from my first stage performance in 1948. My small-scale *Perahera* was of course nothing in comparison with the magnificence of a more recent one, which celebrated Queen Elizabeth's visit to Ceylon, when elephants were multiplied, an extra octagon built,[1] and Kandyan chiefs, secular and religious, vied with each other in worshipful homage. But how

[1] This octagon, I imagine, was somewhat like the magnificent, solid-seeming tabernacle erected in the west end of Seville Cathedral to serve as a fourfold altar during the weeks before the Easter Day withdrawal of the black veil from the High Altar. It was only at the dismantling of the tabernacle that I realized it was a magnificent pre-fab. Recently, in an eighteenth-century exhibition in the Kunsthaus, Zurich, I saw depicted in an anonymous painting of the Piazza of San Marco, an even more elaborate pre-fab, made, I believe, of thin wood—a kind of two-fold Inner Circle, containing shops, with all sorts of imagined treasures, as in a glorified Marché aux Puces.

delightful mine was, with no *défenses d'entrer*, nor any of the *pezzi grossi* who swarm about the honeypots of royalty. The best treasures, one sometimes feels, fall to those who are looking for nothing in particular, like that fortunate Chinese gentleman of the fourteenth century who, sailing in a boat between Galle and Colombo, the territory of Adam's Peak, and then as now a famous place of pilgrimage because the rock on its summit bears the imprint of Buddha's Sacred Foot, found so extraordinary a treasure that he was moved to write a long, old-style poem about it. One of the most famous of Chinese calligraphers also commemorated the find in a poem which he preserved in the Hall of Gentlemen, as he called his School of Calligraphy.

It is said that the imprint of Buddha's Sacred Foot is reflected in the transparent sea at some distance from the shore. It was not this, however, but something more tangible, which Mr. Ya-Tuan swore to having met with as he sailed along.[1] 'The moon was shining as bright as day, and the sea was smooth and waveless. The water was so clear that one could see to the bottom. I got up and walked about on deck, gazing down the while into this submarine world. There I saw a tree-like object swaying gently to and fro. Pointing it out to the sailors I asked them whether it might not be a piece of transparent coral. They said "No". Is it the shadow of a *sala* tree in the moonlight? Again they said "No". So I bade one of the boys dive down and secure it. He did so and it turned out to be something soft and slimy, which however became as hard as iron when pulled out of the water. I took it in my hands and examined it. It was barely a foot in height, and the tips of the branches were curled into knots. On each branch, wonderful to relate, was the bud of a pink flower. Some of these had already opened of themselves, and resembled a tree peony, while others were half-open and appeared similar to lotus buds. The sailors brought candles and crowded round to look at it. Then they began to dance about in their excitement, laughing and saying: "This is a

---

[1] Save at dawn, when few tourists are awake, the holy mountain is veiled in mists of sanctity. It was at this hour of sunrise that Henry Salt, Lord Valentia's artist-secretary, made the drawing here reproduced. A mysterious phenomenon may also be seen at sunrise from Adam's Peak, of which I have seen a photograph in Traut's *Ceylon*. A young Army officer, Captain Thomas Skinner, made a drawing of it a hundred and twenty years ago, and his description is so vivid that I shall quote it in an appendix at the end of this book (p. 219).

red agate-tree in full bloom, truly a rare product of the seas, of which marvellous reports have reached China. We have sailed these seas for more than forty years, and never found a specimen before. And now to think that you, sir, have found one; why, it is something you come across only once in a thousand years." '

As it was only six hundred years later that I first visited Ceylon, I could not hope to find another agate-tree in full bloom, and indeed I did not. I would of course rather have brought back such a treasure than any number of notebooks, and one can imagine how lucrative it would have been! Nor had I the possible qualification of looking for nothing in particular. For, on my way back from a journey of many months in the Hinduized countries of the Far East, and fresh from the *Kathakali* of South India, I was definitely in search of something in particular. First, the scenes of Sita's captivity, and of the tragic climax of the *Ramayana*, that great Hindu epic, which sup-plies the themes of countless dance-dramas, and the motifs of so many temple sculptures and paintings. I had also heard rather vaguely of magnificent dancers to be seen at Kandy, the highland royal city of Ceylon, whose only contact with Europe had been as members of a very superior German menagerie in the early years of this century.

It was during my first drive to Kandy with Malalasekara, in the spring of 1935, that I came upon one of those scenes of the *Ramayana* of which I spoke just now. My delight in the landscape of Ceylon is unbounded, and the magical associations of those strange rocks give them a fascination for which I can hardly account. On this May Day in 1935 we set off very early, before it was fully light, and climbed continuously among the paddy-fields which seemed to me less beauti-ful than in Bali, on account of their greater monotony of level and shape. As we mounted higher, and the ground became more and more uneven, a greater variety showed itself, though I do not think they ever quite reach the architectural beauty of the Balinese *sawahs* with their superb and elaborate patterns. But the setting could hardly have been more lovely of those paddy-fields, surrounding small soli-tary pagodas among groves of trees. The bare hilltops and downs covered by tall, coarse grass, which at a distance looked as smooth as golden moss, lend a lovely wildness to the mountains, and the road, one of the most winding I have ever been on, coils so persistently upon itself that one has a feeling of climbing up the giant tree-trunk of silver grey which rises from the precipitous wall of a ravine. For at each bend it reappears and never leaves us, till at last one looks down on its wide lovely, cedarlike foliage; broad spreading boughs, covered with green serrated leaves, almost like mimosa, upon which great white flowers recline. Having to find a name for it I called it for a long time *Amherstia Splendida,* till I reluctantly gave up this name on seeing the real *Amherstia,* with its curious wax-like coral flowers in the Botanical Gardens of Peradeniya.

The small hotel at Haputale, 4,583 feet up, is perched on a cliff, looking over a vast horizon to the sea; mist or cloud-shadows half veil the blue peaks which rise out of the plain like huge rocks out of the sea, reminding me of the strange vision of Soracte, as I once saw it from the summit of Monte Terminillo just before the sunrise. Later one could see the long line of surf upon the shore. Bare peaks and rocks and emerald slopes were bathed in exquisite light above a tumult of lower hills and bright red earth. Tea-plantations, incomparably more beautiful than in Java, rise almost to the top of the mountains, while flat-topped espalier-trees, grown for shade and leaf-manure, rise like greyish mushrooms above the dark polished green of the tea-plants; and deeper grey rise the great dark rocks among them.

And now at last I became conscious that every signpost pointed to Ella! Who or what was Ella? How could I guess that Ella was our goal for other reasons than its incomparably situated rest-house? At every turn of the road the beauty increased, till one would have been well content to have no definite goal. Yet in the end, towards sunset, we did reach Ella, and it was truly one of the loveliest places in the world.

In front of the bungalow a garden full of flowers leads on to a grassy promontory. On all sides the valley drops away, and a stream falls below over a smooth bed of rock; the most enchanting *sawahs* I have ever seen feather the steep slopes with bright green plumage, like young apple-leaves or the vivid brilliance of the inner birch bark. The setting sun shone full on these narrow, feathery curves of green, but even when the sun left them they seemed to retain their brilliance. On either side of the valley rocky mountains framed but did not confine the vast horizon of the plain, from which emerge strange and lovely shapes of jagged hills, like rocks under the sea, their peaks lit by the sunset. And, strangest of all, Ella, the loveliest valley in the world, was the very place I most wanted to see, the site of great Ravana's last retreat.[1] There is the cave where he hid his treasure—was not Sita the best part of it?—on the face of the mountain, easily accessible, if only the brushwood were cleared away; but into which no wise man would dare to force an entrance. In this stream he bathed, and his demon face looked out from the rocky promontory which guards the valley. Sometimes it is said, one can see him draw deep yogic breaths, proper to one who would have conveyed the mountain on which Siva and Parvati sat enthroned, to Lanka, that he might save himself the exertion of a daily journey to Kailasa to pay homage. But the effort necessary for uprooting Kailasa made it shake so much that Parvati clung to Siva for safety. Such insolence could not go unpunished, and one flick of Siva's toe sent Ravana, like Lucifer, hurtling down to Hell. But the great magician Ravana was beloved by Siva, for he was also a rare musician and patron of the arts. Not only was he re-called, but he was presented by Siva with a sword of silver.

It must have been design on the part of my Buddhist friends that I should arrive in Kandy at the very moment that this exceptional *Perahera* was to take place. It was here on the 5th May 1935 that I saw my first Kandyan dancers, and my diary of that date reveals my delight as well as my lack of preparation.

'We went about 6 p.m. to the Temple of the Tooth, hoping to meet some of the dancers before the Procession got going. They did not come, but we saw a familiar stick-dance done by boys in the grounds of the main *devale* (Hindu shrine) and on the grass facing the *devale* from which the Chieftains were to issue, men with great coiling bracelets and shoulder-pieces, naked torsos, white skirts and magnificent leather waist-belts, danced superbly to the accompani-ment of singing and tumultuous drumming, with wild motions of the head, splendid leaps and crouching and circling movements in-volving the whole body. Elephants were gathering from all sides, fifty of them at least, large and small, with mask-like face-hangings. The

[1] Appendix II, Hugh Nevill's description of Ella.

procession started from various points at once, and we watched it slowly defile; group after group of headsmen and temple guardians in their wide brown berets, close-fitting and spreading out in a kind of circular brim, like the Spanish beach hats of a few years ago. Men carried flares of copra in iron cages, and a rickshaw followed somewhere in the rear of the procession with a great sack of spare fuel. Slowly the elephants moved forward, some with golden howdahs on their backs, carrying relics. The leader of the procession sat on a huge elephant, reading a manuscript; groups of dancers dressed in varying degrees of splendour, and many small boys were interspersed among the slow stream of headsmen and elephants, who halted frequently while the dancers and drummers worked themselves into a frenzy.

'I hear they have a number of *wannams* or modes of song, descriptive of animals, which are danced and sung against the complicated rhythms of the drums, the object being to give a stylized rendering of the characteristic movements of the bird or animal represented. Some of the drummers in a gradual crescendo of rhythm themselves break into dance, with widely turned-out knees.'

In the days following this first exciting experience I visited a famous dance school near Kandy, and learned a good deal more about the content as well as the technique of the dances.

The friends with whom I was staying in Kandy, a most sympathetic Scotch woman married to a Sinhalese Buddhist schoolmaster, who lived in a bungalow above the lake, with a superb view of the mountains, were good enough to arrange a special demonstration for my benefit, in the open air outside the school boarding-house. This was one of my most delightful experiences during my first visit to Ceylon; but a further detailed description would be out of place here. It will be found on p. 25.

I must now move forward about thirteen years, to the date of my second arrival in Ceylon, and explain how it was that I went to Ceylon at all, when my purpose was to study the dances of South India; above all, how it was that my first objective was Colombo.

Ram Gopal, the famous Indian dancer, was an admirer of *Dance and Drama in Bali,* and had communicated his enthusiasm to a friend of his in Colombo, Ignatia Mendez, who wrote to me before I left England, expressing the hope that I would regard her house as my home if I ever should visit Ceylon. I had not at first intended to do more than go to Ceylon some time after my Indian journey was ended. But I received a letter from Ignatia in Bombay, which decided me to make all haste to get there. She wrote that a friend whom she described as the 'Walter Spies of Ceylon' was shortly leaving for India with a group of Kandyan dancers, who were to restore the Buddha relics in the Temple of the Tooth in Kandy, to Sanchi in North India, and that if I wanted to see them I must come immediately. I somehow had a picture of the best Kandyan dancers lost to sight for ever on a world tour, and made all haste to reach Ceylon before they started. It was not of course the 'Walter Spies of Ceylon' who was to take the dancers, as his work in the Tourist Bureau claimed him, but the idea that dancers should form part of this religio-diplomatic mission was certainly his, and he had brought them from Kandy, and accommodated them in a hall which by great good luck was only a stone's throw from where my hosts lived. Here, he felt they would be better fed than in their own villages, and no doubt he was right. I was eager to see them and their benefactor, Fred Fogl; and with the kind connivance of a German doctor in Bombay, telescoped the two compulsory cholera injections, of which I now heard for the first time; and took the first available plane to Ceylon.

Sequel to the 'out of season' Perahera of 1935

7 *May.* In the afternoon I visited a village about eight miles from Kandy where I had heard there was a famous dance-school. This consists of a fairly large barn, with palm-leaf roof and a very uneven earth floor, not even covered with cowdung, which after treatment makes such a beautifully smooth surface and is absolutely without smell. Bamboo poles support the roof. Here the dancers were assembled; three in their gala dress, which consists of circular silver tiaras, hung with small silver plates and coinlike ornaments which shake and tinkle; and surmounted by a separate silver point, attached to a zedi-shaped headdress which confines the hair. Their naked torsos are enclosed in a sort of bead harness with a daisy-like pattern, the petals raying out from a collar round the neck, and the whole fastened behind. This is a most charming decoration. The skirt consists of voluminous folds of white plissé stuff, falling in flounces

below a wide silver-studded clasp. From this dangles a wide sporran-like ornament, studded with silver buttons. Beneath the flounces hangs a white sarong—loose in front and wound tightly round the legs behind like trousers. Ankle-bells are attached to a leather or metal ring which falls over the foot, and is caught over one toe. Ear-ornaments of silver project from the sides of the face, very large and embryo-shaped, like the design on cashmere shawls. Above the tiara five narrow fluted silver shafts, like organ pipes, rise to join the top-knot. From this topknot a long narrow strip of embroidered stuff, practically a ribbon, hangs down to the small of the back. Another man wore only a white cloth, very gracefully folded and attached round the waist by a red bandanna scarf, over which hung a silver chain, folded many times round the waist. He was accompanied by several small boys in similar skirts, but wearing only the bead harness. He had a white turban, with a long flap of the stuff falling over in front. A group of small boys also danced, one of them extremely well; the others were evidently learning by imitation.

The barn grew darker and darker; only the silver headdresses and discs which ornamented the belts and aprons, shone as they danced. The tiara consists of about eleven separate plaques, which form a crest above the forehead. Lamps were brought and dimly lit the gloom. Children and village crowded round. We leaned on the bamboo rod which serves for the small boys' exercises, precisely as in a classical ballet class.

9th May. After seeing them again yesterday, I begin to have some idea of the subject as apart from the technique of the dances. They came up in the afternoon and danced till dark in the open shed or kalari above the school boarding-house. A graceful elderly teacher, with charming, alert face, was giving the boys a lesson. He danced markedly on the outside edge of the foot, as in *Kathakali*. He has a very muscular and sensitive instep, and a good voice. He sings a phrase which the boys imitate in all pitches. He does not correct their steps; they learn by constant imitation, as everywhere in the East where I have seen dancing. They danced with the metal rings called *pantheru,* resembling a tambourine, but without the parchment, changing rapidly from hand to hand, and whirling them in the air; also with the bright-coloured hour-glass drums.

The *wannams* are eighteen, mostly referring to some animal, horse, snake, elephant, etc. The subject for each *wannam* is very faintly adumbrated in the dance. There are certain snake-like movements, suggesting *mudras*, with the hands; also an elephant-step, with trunk movements, resembling *Kathakali*. The hare and hawk seem the most characteristic. It seems to me that this style of dancing is more like decorative art, as in tapestry. The animal named forms a very small feature in the design, just enough to distinguish it from others. But the decorative design, the arabesque, the foliage and flowers run wild over all the dances. The same energy and vehemence of technique seems to be displayed in all. The *tala* however is different. The rhythmic scene is the most elaborate. It is either given by the dancer to the drummer or by one of the drummers, who are the teachers, to the dancers; and by syllables as in all Indian dance-schemes. These rhythmic patterns are exceedingly fascinating. Each phrase is rendered in an immense variety of ways. Many of the poems refer to moral precepts or comments. 'How strangely men behave; how far they are fallen from virtue. How the gods must laugh when they see their behaviour.' The dance which follows will be apparently indistinguishable from a quite different theme. One represents the episode in which a certain woman tries to bring the Buddha into ill-repute by pretending that she is pregnant by him. Sakra takes the form of a rat, and devours the stuffing with which she has bulged out her clothing; and the Buddha is vindicated. In the dance there was no apparent hint of this episode; the drama survives only in the name; as for instance in some of our own folk-songs. The technique is magnificent, and the whirling and circling jumps equal to any I have seen. There are none of the side-to-side neck movements, though of course the head is enormously involved; no special facial expression, and only vaguely generalized movements. Enormous velocity of movement, much wide-knee posing, lovely *namaskaras*. The dances fall into phrases and grow in impetus, with a wild crescendo, and the most thrilling accellerandos of the same *tala*. A marvellous interchange of force and lightness, perfect poise of body and absolute control by the principal dancer. In the most intricate passages he is still controlling the drummers on whom his dance depends.

CHAPTER I

Arrival—Looking Back

1st December. An emerald island suddenly emerged, floating among cloud-drifts. The sea looked fairly calm, though herds of small white horses pranced upon it. The descent to the Colombo air-field was most lovely, circling slowly above neat villages enclosed in palm-trees and glittering tropical foliage. The recent rains (that chronic retarded monsoon which always comes as a surprise to habitués of the tropics) accounts for the flooded fields everywhere, both here and on the mainland, adding greatly to the beauty of the landscape. My second Ceylon adventure had begun.

Scarcely emerged from the clouds, I saw a swarthy Hawaiian beauty in golden sari, and gold sandals, with abundant black hair hanging loose, evidently on the look-out for someone. Her exuberant air, huge liquid eyes and expression of enthusiastic kindness, marked her at once as Ignatia Mendez, the friend of Ram Gopal, whose warmly worded invitation, couched in terms of tried affection, had already greeted me in Bombay, where she had even had the kind thought of sending a friend of hers to meet me at the air-terminus; as if divining that a little cheering would not come amiss; though she could hardly have guessed that I had just lost my tortoise-shell framed spectacles on the T.W.A. plane, and that my carefully labelled luggage had gone astray.

So this was Ignatia! Her notepaper was stamped with the famou dancer's image in Nataraja attitude against the rays of the setting sun. This I supposed at the time to be only an innocent vanity, but I was to learn that her adoption of Ram Gopal's image was no presumptuous identification of herself with him; for a *rishi*-horoscope had linked their fates thousands of years ago. They were destined to play a common part in the service of Siva, Lord of Dance.

Thus it was that I, a friend of Ram Gopal, was received by Ignatia as his Angel or Messenger, and by her husband, who accepted every, thing that came to him through Ignatia, as a blessing from God; for they are devout Catholics, like so many Sinhalese, and equally devout believers in omens and magic.

I was swept off to the customs and quarantine, but thanks to Ignatia's efficiency and her husband's position, I was passed through with exceptional speed, and joined the two Mendez outside. Leston Mendez was of a still darker complexion than Ignatia, and the photo, graph which appeared next day in the *Ceylon Daily News* shows him smilingly in the background, while one of the greatest of Kan, dyan dancers, Guneya, accompanied by his small son, offered me a bouquet of lilies, which I was assured was his own idea, while Ignatia looked on with unassuming vigilance.

When all the formalities were over and the press photographers satisfied, I was whisked off through torrents of rain to Colpetty, the suburb where my hosts lived, in a spacious and airy house, sur, rounded by luxuriant foliage—palm, banana, champak, hibiscus, canna and every variety of flowering shrub; whose only drawback is that it is on the highroad from Colombo to Galle, and the traffic from an early hour is incessant.

But I could not do more than take in the spaciousness of my sur, roundings, while changing for the show arranged for that very evening by Fred Fogl. I must admit that Ignatia's analogy with Walter Spies was a singular one; for Fogl, however great his industry and excellent his intentions, could hardly compete with that brilliantly gifted artist, painter and musician, to whom every visitor to Bali must acknow, ledge a debt of gratitude and whose legendary charm and overflowing fantasy will surely inspire many a tribute.

Lionel Wendt, a Burgher[1] like Fogl, founder and endower of the 43 Group of modern Sinhalese painters, had a more obvious resem, blance to Walter Spies, for he was like him a fine musician and photographer; of his creative gifts I cannot judge, as he died alas shortly before I arrived in Ceylon. He is one of the people I should most have liked to know. His interest in Kandyan dancers must certainly have gone far beyond their photogenic character. But he

[1] As the Sinhalese-Dutch are called. As a rule they rank high in enterprise and intelligence.

did not in any case come into Ignatia's ken, and I only even heard of him when I got to know his friends, after I had been some time in Ceylon.

The only person to whom Ignatia's analogy might with justice have applied was an Englishman named Hugh Nevill, of the Ceylon Civil Service: a man of comprehensive genius and vast energy, for whose memory I have a peculiar devotion; for he was an artist as well as archaeologist, zoologist, ethnologist, linguist and collector, and was excited by the same things as make my own heart beat faster: by legends and landscapes and new discoveries in the realm of tradition. His collection of bronzes, ivories and masks forms, together with that of Sir Stamford Raffles, the chief treasure of two departments in the British Museum: the Oriental Antiquities and the Ethnographical.

The *Taprobanian*, by which Nevill is best known in Ceylon, is a mine of Sinhalese and Dravidian folklore and original research. Like Walter Spies, he did not reach the age of fifty. He died in 1897 and I do not even know for certain the place of his death. Like Spies he was interested in every form of life: insects, shellfish, orchids, birds, beasts and men. Perhaps the analogy ought to end here, for Spies was cer-tainly one of the world's most imaginative painters, recreating the fabulous landscapes of Bali with a mysterious sympathy, and the in-evitable magic of a Prospero. Between Nevill and Spies lay a whole epoch of pictorial experiment. But there is a curiously interesting pas-sage in the *Taprobanian*, telling how, in order to arrive at an under-standing of a highly coloured image in a *purana*, Nevill would attempt to put the poetic description down in paint, and then interpret it in his own way. For it was his conviction that early history was solely pre-served by pictures and bas-reliefs, under which, at a later date, a name came to be written, or a poem was made. How I wish we had some of these paintings, besides the few beautiful line drawings scattered through the *Taprobanian*.

There is so much to say about Hugh Nevill that I must leave it to another place. I have perhaps already digressed too long in the effort to find a credible parallel in Ceylon to Walter Spies of Bali; and must now join Ignatia Mendez and Leston in the violent thunderstorm which hurled us along the road towards the hall where the dance display was to be held.

It is clear that Ignatia has implicit faith in Fred Fogl, and is en-chanted by his ideas. She had sent me to Bombay a preliminary notice of tonight's performance, in which it was promised that a real cobra would appear on the stage during the cobra *wannam,* and that the swan *wannam* would be danced to the music of Tchaikowsky's Swan Lake. I did not ask Ignatia's opinion on this, as it fortunately never hap-pened, and may only have been a newspaper man's foolish joke.

Fred Fogl's new dances, the *Bo-tree* dance and the *Butterflies,* were not, I felt, successful, and did not seem to appeal to the dancers, whose ensemble was bad. Certainly the lack of freedom in the arms, which were held high above their heads, in a rather stiff position, impeded them. The Butterflies were preceded on to the stage by a horde of small children, boys and girls, who had no idea of dancing, and had to be hustled off as quickly as possible. How different was their reception, I could not help thinking, from that of the fictive birds and butterflies who danced at the opening of the Empress Akikonomu's spring devotions[1] which were so lovely that everyone wished they might go on for ever. Those dances too were 'new', but devised by young noblemen who were steeped in the musical traditions, the poetry and religious ritual of the court, which was as essential a part of the education of a gentleman, as it still is in Java at the court of the Sultan of Djokyakarta.

Kandyan dancing can never be other than magnificent when per-formed by Guneya and his pupils. But like Flamenco it is somewhat limited in scope, and even the best dancers cannot quite overcome the disadvantages of a stage. For so much is lost of significance and beauty when exiled from its natural setting of foliage and flickering lamps and the crowd of villagers who seem so essential a part of the per-formance. Their spiritual participation is as valuable an element as their physical presence is delightful to us as onlookers. For they know the poems on which the dance is based as well as they know the ani-mals represented in the dance.

On this particular evening the opening invocation was a disaster. Two rows of motionless boys, whose eyes roved helplessly over the audience, stood sloping slightly inwards with joined, raised hands, dressed in unfortunate pink cloths, while the soloist performed his

[1] *The Tale of Genji* by Lady Murasaki, translated by Arthur Waley, Book III, Chapter VI.

dance which, impressive though it was, seemed too long for the occasion. All the animal *wannams* were most beautiful: horse, rabbit, peacock, tortoise, monkey; especially Guneya's Tortoise and Horse. His nephew, Heenbaba, of whom I later saw a good deal, visiting him in his home and being introduced to his family, is also a remarkable and exciting dancer.

The procession of masks would have been more impressive if the small boys who wore them in succession had had any idea of the demons they were exhibiting. The drum rhythms for all the dances were extraordinarily varied, as also the melodies. There were fantastic whirlings as of Tibetan devil or Dervish dancers, extraordinary leaps off both feet at once, and breath-taking turns in mid-air. Here for the first time I read and recorded the name which was to become almost an obsession during my months in Ceylon, a kind of leit-motif of this book—a bore to my best friends, and the confusion of false pretensions.

I did not then inquire what the *Kohomba Kankaria* was doing in this programme, for I was utterly unaware of its existence till that moment, or of the impropriety of including in a mixed stage performance the culminating magic drama of the Kandyan country, which gathers up so many of the magic threads that run through the extraordinary folk-lore of Ceylon.

I admit that I enjoyed most of all the '*Ves dance Kohomba Kankaria*' which displayed the Kandyan dancers in all the panoply of their glorious headdresses and silver ornaments, whether or not they ought to have been worn on this occasion.

During the interval Guneya came down from the platform and prostrated himself before the Governor-General, Lord Soulbury, as well as before various Sinhalese grandees. I heard afterwards that several overlords were present, on the look-out for any remission of the homage traditionally due to them, and to add a prostration to the Governor-General was a charming courtesy on Guneya's part.

Fogl and another young man whose name I have forgotten, came to supper after the show. Fred Fogl makes a sympathetic and modest impression, which latter I had hardly expected, as I always expect impresarios to be rather vain. He is a small, wise-looking man, clearly an enthusiast, and genuine in his wish to raise the status of the dancers;

though there is perhaps a certain amount of personal ambition in his wish to take the dancers all over the world. He is fortunate in persuad-ing Guneya, to my mind the finest of those I have seen, to join him in this trip to India, to restore the Buddhist relics to Sanchi. However much I deplore the uprooting I owe to it the opportunity for a much closer study of the dance rhythms than I should otherwise have had; for the reason given above. The drum rhythms are extremely varied, the syncopations particularly subtle. There are frequent changes of bar time, and counterpoint of feet against the drum beats.

4th December. All this I appreciated much more today at the house where the dancers lodge. It is a kind of club called Caldecott House, in which Fred Fogl and a friend give lessons in ballroom dancing to young Colombans after office hours. Fogl insists that the dancers are undernourished in their own villages, where they work for an over-lord, and no longer have land of their own. They are, he says, now a despised caste, and are no longer called on to dance, as in old days, before the king or his representative. He promises me all his notes about Kandyan dancers, of whom there are, he says, several thousand, by no means all equally good, in the scattered villages of the Kandy region. I saw some superb dancing during today's practice. The rhythmic shape on which the *wannams* are built is very various. The dancer's rhythm is certainly extraordinary, and I admire more and more their astonishing strength and flexibility.

Malalasekara came in this evening and talked about his family. He is the same as ever, though increasingly authoritative. He collects folk-songs officially, and says the Veddahs[1] no longer exist. Fogl says the official cars never penetrate the jungle, and so are not in a position to judge. But Dr. Spittel and Mr. Nicholas, who are very much in a position to judge, confirm Malalasekara's view, in so far that scarcely a Veddah is now to be found who is not mixed with Sinha-lese by marriage.

5th December. This morning we drove through lovely enamelled lanes, abounding in almond, hibiscus, *waringin*, palm, with many rampant creepers between the flooded fields, which made the vast lakes I had seen from the air.

We lunched in a pleasant rest-house, above a swirling, turbid river,

---

[1] Aboriginal race of Ceylon.

Waterways on the south coast
Drawing by Henry Salt

Adam's Peak
Drawing by Henry Salt

From Viscount Valentia's *Voyages and Travels to India, Ceylon, etc.*

Sigiriya

Mountain district in Ceylon

crossed by a ferry which had to make elaborate evolutions in order to reach the opposite bank. We watched the slow and fascinating pro-gress of a car being taken over. I was twice to cross by this ferry later on; once to a most remarkable *thovil*;[1] the second time with Malala-sekara, on the very last day of my stay in Ceylon—an occasion which I remember with peculiar pleasure, for it was then that I began really to appreciate the quality of his mind.

On the way home we passed a house standing back from the road, and a little above it, from which came laughter and talk and the sound of a drum, such as I had heard and seen once years ago when visiting a fair with Malalasekara, on the way back from some Vesak celebra-tions, where the delicious fantasy of the village decorations, even though paper is now generally substituted for coco-palm leaf, cer-tainly put the town ones to shame. These were tawdry and often hideous, with large scenes from Buddha's life, executed with a vulgar glitter and ugliness, unredeemed by fantasy of any kind, and only too obviously European in inspiration. Here too were the large square Chinese lanterns, with designs cut out of white parchment with flut-tering fringes. Inside, a circular erection of sticks and string, to which paper figures of animals, monsters, dancers and others were attached, was kept turning by the heat of a candle, and by its light one saw the shadowy forms move round.

The gay little circular paper caps, decorated with *naga*-hood plumes and reminiscent of *kolan* masks, are so much prettier and more decorative than our silly party-caps. At this charming spring festival where pilgrims are fed, no animals are slaughtered, and no one treads on anyone else's toes, *rabana*—drumming always plays a part. On the occasion when I first saw and heard it, outside a house in the jungle, men as well as women took part; but I fancy this is unusual. The *rabana* is usually played by women only, quite a number sitting on the ground, and holding a kind of conversation, often satirical in inten-tion, a succession of improvisations of a gossipy character usually associated with women. On the present occasion five or six women only took part. The *tala* (tempo) was not always set by the same leader, but varied in a kind of gay rivalry, as in the extraordinary dis-plays of dancing and drumming in many Kandyan ceremonies. It is

[1] A ceremony of exorcism.

essentially a domestic entertainment, interspersed with much laughter, but the virtuosity of these amateur drummers was amazing.

In the *Journal of the Siam Society*, published by Luzac in 1924, there is an article by René Nicolas on the Siamese theatre, in which he describes a dance called *raban,* which may or may not have some connection with the drumming described above; there is no account of the accompanying music.

On this first Sunday drive with the Mendez the occasion was a wedding, and the wordless dialogues of the *rabana* probably contained many allusions and jokes which escaped us altogether. There was plenty of laughter anyway, and the musical, wordless gossip was almost as much appreciated by us as by the delightful group which had gradually collected round the drummers, consisting of various members of the family, and neighbours who kept dropping in. The cottage was prettily decorated with tinsel flowers, and we drove on with a pleasant sense of jollity shared.

On the way back we visited an old friend of Leston Mendez, a rich and popular man, whose wife, though a devout Buddhist, had gone in largely for purification and propitiation ceremonies. When she died last spring a big *bali* was held—a 'rich man's *bali*' with every possible accompaniment of figure-moulding in clay, and astrological houses built of bamboo and palm-leaf. W. D. Fernando, though sceptical as to the efficacy of such ceremonies, promised, at Ignatia's instigation, to put on a 'rich man's *bali*' for my benefit and the possible benefit of his rheumatism. Who knows? It *might* help it, and could hardly make it worse. This *bali* never took place, but a humbler *bali,* to which I was invited near Matara, a rare spot for such ceremonies, certainly lacked none of the necessary ingredients, and was a sincere expression of belief in the supernatural.

W. D. Fernando told how the English planters used to go out with ropes and lassoo the peasants for forced labour in the tea-plantations. It no doubt seemed quite a good joke to these unimaginative creatures to catch a few niggers, as no doubt they regarded them, by the same means as they employed for catching other wild animals. But the Sinhalese peasant, accustomed to work on his own piece of land for a Sinhalese overlord, was not at all amused by this primitive joke, and could not be persuaded to work as a slave. Cheaper labour had to be procured from South India, so that satisfactory profits could be shown. (Ceylon is now independent, but Tamil labourers still work on the tea-plantations and live in what are called the 'coolie lines'. It was frequently explained to me that these are an improvement on the slums of Madras from which they come.)

Later in the day I called on Fred Fogl at his government office. He promises me all his notes, and is arranging various programmes and dances to be seen in the villages. He seems of the utmost generosity. I hope he is in a position to implement it. His programme includes a few days' visit to the jungle.

There is, I gather, a tendency among dancers to break away from their dependence, and take up another profession, such as carpenter, etc. But since dancing became compulsory in schools, the mass of boys, one can well believe, are rather bored. If a dancer shows conspicuous talent, he is sent to India, preferably to Santiniketan, to study, and returns with his ideas considerably *embrouillé*. Not that this really matters very much, but it tends towards an amateurish attitude, which is always bad in the arts because it leads to superficiality, and a mixture of styles, which I cannot think good except on a basis of real knowledge and understanding.

There are a few, very few, dancers of the first rank left now in the villages. Guneya is certainly one, Ukuwa another, and Lapeya, who is perhaps older, and certainly more difficult to contact, a third. Guneya's nephew, Heenbaba, is exceptionally gifted, and there are probably others, unknown to me, since I left Ceylon at the end of 1949.

The *wannams* never seem to have been mentioned by earlier travellers, but whether this means that they were not performed earlier as dances, or that the travellers were not interested in them, who can say? Possibly, as in the case of the Balinese *Kebyar*, the texts of which were recited long before an expressive dance solo was made of them by the great dancer Mario, the *wannams* were only sung, which is how I first heard them performed in London years ago by a Europeanized Sinhalese singer, to piano accompaniment.

5th December. I watched today the foot technique of the dancers at the *barre*, and took down the steps as far as possible. The knees are much bent, and turned outwards in the fifth position—the basic position of

Siam, Cambodia, etc. There are twelve basic rhythms, and each has a variation which chiefly consists in adding one or more beats, and elaborating the steps or introducing a turn. The variations are very subtle; there are also many lighter steps on the ball of the foot.

This afternoon I drove with Ignatia to the new Buddhist temple of Kelaniya, on the Kelani river, which flowed past the rest-house on Sunday. The temple was destroyed by the Portuguese almost entirely. The dagoba, however, is old, and some of the ceilings are very beautiful. Some murals are also of the same period, and by far the most beautiful. For the most part, the temple was entirely repainted and sculptured by one monk—an extraordinary feat—in traditional style. Some of the sculptured figures are casts, but I found it difficult to distinguish one from the other. The moonstones, as the semi-circular stone thresholds are called, are very beautiful and certainly original. Traditional technique lends a certain dignity even to the paintings. We passed several poor but pleasant villages; on one side ran the swift river, which people were crossing on a ferry-boat so narrow that there seemed no room even to stand. But they were packed in as successfully as sardines in a tin, and a projecting gunwale balanced the boat. This is supposed to be a cobra district, and it must certainly be malarial.

I remember of this drive particularly a beautiful peasant girl in a cottage doorway, and the grouping of palm-trees waving in the breeze at Mount Lavinia, Colombo's most 'posh' hotel, to which the outward bound British colonial who has to spend a night in Ceylon is driven as a matter of course; it is still thought rather eccentric, I am told, to wish to see more of Ceylon than the interior of this big hotel, to which all one's British shipmates are at once conveyed; so that one need not mix with 'natives' at all. I know of two who violated this taboo, and thoroughly enjoyed themselves in consequence—a very English professor of Oriental History on his way back to Burma, who took the night train to Polonnaruwa and spent a glorious day among the ruins; and the wife of a Hong Kong business man, who hired a car and drove with her young daughter to Anuradhapura, finding it really too boring to be British all the time, on shore as well as on board a P. & O. Darkness fell, and a long line of breakers fretted the beach.

6th December. Guneya danced a series of *wannams*: lion, horse, nay-yadi, an ecstatic dance of great beauty: the cry of the kirala, a small bird; and the *sera wannam,* showing the bobbing of the teal's head while swimming. They are not all imitative, though some are more so than others; such as the hare, tortoise, monkey, etc. The king's walk was very fine, threatening and arrogant; but also smoothly royal and full of grace.

To the museum library, where there is abundant material about *bali* and kindred ceremonies. I did not then realize that most of the printed material was already in my possession, as it had been given me by its author, a Czech professor, O. Pertold, at an ethnological congress held at University College, London, in the summer of 1935, after my first exploratory Far Eastern journey. Professor Pertold's pamphlets, written in English by himself, were offprints from the Prague *Orientalni Zeitscrift.* It was no doubt my interest in the *Kolan* masks which illustrated his lecture, that led him to offer me those pamphlets, and to inscribe them with my name and a courteous greeting; for I had then nothing to contribute to the subject. It was not till the autumn of that year that I returned to Bali for the long sojourn of which *Dance and Drama in Bali* is the record. And it is only now that I can draw the full value from his admirable study, first published in 1930 but collected at least twenty years earlier. Now that I know a little more I should so much like to meet him again, and also to read, if it has been trans-lated, his account of a two-years' stay in Ceylon, written in Czech. I remember that Professor Pertold was rather shocked by the irregularity with which I wore my congressist's label; without it I was of course unidentifiable. The only other thing I remember about that congress was a very lively lecture by Professor Starkie on gipsy music, illus-trated by his own admirable fiddle playing. This lecture was certainly an *acte de vie,* while Professor Pertold's was more learned than lively. Yet his three paper volumes, illustrated by all the Sinhalese masks and their whereabouts, are one of my most treasured possessions. When, towards the end of my stay in Ceylon, Fred Fogl produced his promised notes, it was the typed text of Pertold's pamphlets that he gave me!

This afternoon I visited the sub-director of the Colombo Museum, Mr. M. D. Raghavan, who gave me his booklet called *Folk-plays and Dances of Kerala,* which contains, among others, a first-hand description of a festival seen in his youth,[1] which fills an important gap in my own experience. Mr. Raghavan was described to me as 'our ethnologist', so when I heard that he had not yet succeeded in seeing a *bali,* I was quite alarmed, as I thought my own chances must be small. But when, towards the close of my stay in Ceylon, I accompanied him to a singularly exciting *thovil* he seemed to take so little interest that I could not help certain reflections on what time may do to one's sensibilities.

The director sent down word that he would like to see me before I left. He is a Trinity man and a biologist, son of the historian Sir Paul Pieris whose translations from Portuguese accounts of Ceylon are justly famous. I gather that there will be no difficulty in obtaining permission to photograph the masks, most of which are now not visible, owing to structural alterations. In the event, however, this permission was never given.

7th December. I was invited today to tea with the Museum Director and his charming wife. The director did not appear, but I met his brother, the gifted modern painter, Justin Deran`yagala, whose dislike of Fred Fogl's undertaking was expressed with characteristic but unnecessary violence. I dislike as much as he does the attempt to impose a feeble *idea* on the virile purity of Kandyan dance. But I think more dramatic treatment of some of the *wannams,* especially when the theme is dramatic, as in some of the *Jataka* stories, might be rather amusing, especially if undertaken by a choreographer who was himself versed in the magnificent and often subtle technique of the Ves dancers. Most of all one hopes that the glorious gift of rhythm and design which seems inherent in these dancers will be brought again to all the crafts of village life, once so flourishing in Ceylon.

9th December. I spent a long morning with Guneya at Caldecott, and saw many dances. His energy is terrific. He was bathed in sweat after his tremendous dancing: elephant, king, Vishnu, etc. I begin to follow the different subdivisions of the dance, the alternations between calm and floreated action.

The industrious Fred Fogl, whom I had asked something about

---

[1] Quoted on page 51 of *The Other Mind,* a study of life and dance in South India, published by Gollancz in 1953.

shamanism in Ceylon, had looked it up in Chadwick and told me
it existed in Siberia and Central Asia!

10th December. Today was fixed for a *Kohomba Kankaria* at Kurunegala; but when we called by appointment to fetch Fred Fogl at his
office, we heard the ceremony was postponed, as today turned out
not to be auspicious. It seemed a little odd that this was not known
beforehand to Fred Fogl. Meanwhile a telegram arrived from Matara,
in response to a notice in the vernacular press, asking for information
about any forthcoming ceremony which it might be possible for me
to attend, and inviting me to a *bali* in the country a few miles from
Matara tomorrow. So we invited Fred Fogl to go with me; for
Ignatia cannot go herself, and I shall need an interpreter. It was a
brilliant idea of Ignatia's to ask the editor of the principal Colombo
newspaper to put in this notice, and produced some most valuable
responses.

A story is told about Bertrand Russell's experimental school, in
which a child, probably his own, jumped down from the mantelpiece,
and hurt himself, after Lord Russell had promised him he would come
to no harm. When he reproached his seemingly heartless mentor, Lord
Russell is reported to have said: 'This, dear child, will teach you never
to believe what you are told.' This is possibly sane advice for a diplo-
mat, but I am incurably trustful, and had I not put faith in what Fred
Fogl told me, I should have been the poorer by many strange experiences. I had been supplied by the *cognoscenti* in Bombay with introductions to those they called 'the right people'! I did not make use of these
introductions till much later, because I realized that I was already
pledged to those who might be, in their eyes, the 'wrong' people; and
I soon realized that 'rights' and 'wrongs' cannot mix. I should have
done no better if I had at once presented my introductions. For the
'right people' had either never heard of the *Kohomba Kankaria*, for
instance, or would not have shared their secret knowledge. It will presently become clearer why Fred Fogl's promises could not be fulfilled
by him, however excellent his intentions, and all the things I learned
in the process of discovering why. As an interpreter he was of the
greatest help.

CHAPTER II

With Fred Fogl to Matara—South Coast Activities

11th December. The drive was extraordinarily beautiful, for the most part at the very edge of the sea, with a golden beach, fresh water lakes and salt lagoons and great rivers flowing into the sea, just as Viscount Valentia describes it in his journal of 150 years ago, with the difference that instead of bridges by which to cross the water, he and his secretary, Mr. Salt, went by boat. To Salt we are indebted for the charming picture of this boat in which they and their palanquins were carried across to the other side, formed from three native canoes fastened together with a platform over them. The British governor, Lord North, had given orders that every attention was to be paid to the noble lord, and he was consequently honoured with an awning of white cloth, a mark of distinction reserved for His Excellency and the King of Kandy. It transpired later that Viscount Valentia was an invalid, so it is possible that this very special attention was not wholly a tribute to his rank, though a three-year Grand Tour of the East, accompanied by a private secretary who was also an expert draughtsman, showed him to be a man of considerable wealth, as well as of unusual tastes.

'The posts which sustained the awning,' he writes, 'and the railing that went round the boat, were fancifully ornamented with young leaves of the coconut, split into pieces, which had altogether a pretty effect. The river was clear, and the bank covered with jungle to the water's edge. The country the whole way was undulated, and occasionally broken by the most picturesque rocks; the vegetation as rich as ever, and the sea was constantly close on our left hand'; for Viscount Valentia was travelling towards, not, as we were, away from Colombo. 'When it was dark they made torches of the dead branches, or rather leaves, of the coconut; these burned with rapidity and brilliancy and had a beautiful effect, when reflected from the closely woven roof of lofty coconut-trees under which we were travelling.'

I must here take leave of the noble lord for the time being, and continue my humbler but freer journey in the opposite direction.

About a mile before reaching Galle, we passed, close by the sea-shore, a small house which seemed to be full of people. In front of it stood a kind of cradle, square like a child's bed, made of banana stems and decorated with young coco-palm leaves. This represented a bier, and in it lay a man at full length, wrapped in a red cloth, with a lighted torch in his hand. His duty was to recite a number of *mantras* calling on the devil who had possessed a woman, to come out of her and enter him instead. The woman lay crouched on the floor of the house, with a small child on her lap. She had been badly frightened during the night by a fearful devil whom she had met on the sea-shore, when she had gone out on the beach at 2 a.m. The devil's name is Maha Sona Yakka, the one who haunts lonely beaches, and is liable to bring on any disease. He was all in black, and held two torches in his mouth, from which blood dripped continually. On the spot where she had seen this devil a *maduwa* had been erected; square, and about fifteen feet high with a cupola-like top on which offerings were to be laid. It was made of the stems of banana, which are extremely strong, and decorated, like the bier, with hibiscus and palm leaves. The bier also had a central erection of hibiscus, young coco leaves and candles, or rather slender torches dipped in coconut oil. Several torches were also stuck about the bier. While we were there a cock, which lay in front of the bier and would later be sacrificed, was taken to the woman to be consecrated by her touch; and the man on the bier, the scapegoat, stretched his hand above his head to be touched by the woman, presumably for the same purpose. From time to time the pot holding the torches not yet lit was carried to the woman, who touched it with both hands, after which it was replaced.

The woman's family belonged to the *dhobi* caste; but many people who would not otherwise have mixed with them were there on this occasion, even including Muslims.

The climax would of course be at night, with the slaughter of the sacrificial cock, the transference of the 'possession' from the woman-victim to the professional scapegoat, and his subsequent release through trance; and finally with the beautiful bonfire when the offerings and the *maduwa* were burnt together on the sea-shore. All we saw of these later operations were the tattered fragments of the altar as we drove home next day from our tryst with Kalu Kumara somewhere beyond Matara.

I tried in vain to take some photographs of this first small *bali* (each has its own special interest and singular feature, and the very humility of this, my first *bali,* endeared it to me). But my camera obstinately refused to work. This was alas too frequent an occurrence to be attributed to demonic intervention; a little first aid from Fogl when we halted for lunch restored it to tolerable health.

The drive became more and more beautiful, and we had difficulty in choosing where to halt for lunch. But the imminence of rain forced us at last to decide on a sheltered beach just beyond Galle. Here we ate the delicious sandwiches provided by Ignatia. I never tired of watching the immemorial sea life of Ceylon: the fishermen drawing up their nets into a long line, the sailing-boats, the outriggers and catamarans, with their palm-leaf shelters against the rain; a solitary figure standing in mid-sea on a bamboo erection, very lonely and dark and graceful above the water. Here and there a few scattered rocks, minute islands out at sea.

Beyond Galle a tremendous storm overtook us, which began with slow huge drops while we lunched. Soon the road was flooded with reddish water, just as Valentia saw it nearly 150 years ago. The shore was in places almost covered with a wonderful trailing creeper with huge convolvulus-shaped blue flowers, which we call Morning Glory, and the French Volubilis, possibly after the Roman city of Volubilis south of Moulay Idris, the most holy city of the Arabs in Morcco, where I saw it first in its greatest profusion, growing among the ruins.

We passed several Buddhist temples, generally up a flight of steps. The houses on the shore became more and more primitive and beauti- fully grouped as we neared Matara, with steep, sloping palm-leaf roofs. The bigger ones, like the Buddhist temples, were built on high terraces with mounting steps.

Then came wilder jungle, and lonely stretches of coast, till we turned inland from Matara to find the village near where the *bali* was to be held. As we drove through rice-fields and brilliant vegetation towards the blue hills, the country became every moment more beautiful, and the dignified houses of red earth more charmingly primitive, till we reached, all too soon, a country market at a crossroads; this was the hamlet of Attaduwa, and our destination.

We alighted and walked along a path of bright red earth, a narrow track only, between the paddy-fields. Winding up through rich vegetation with here and there a few houses in the trees, it seemed to have been newly hewn out of the red rock, which sometimes rose like a cliff on either side.

We came at last to the eminence on which our house stood, exquisitely situated among coco-palms, banana and bamboo. A wide terrace in front of the house was roofed with palm. An orange-tree grown over with betel-leaf creeper hung above the little alcove prepared for us; a very vivid heart-shaped green leaf and one green orange were a constant source of refreshment to me during the sometimes tedious hours of the long ceremony.

Beyond the terrace was a palm-leaf *maduwa* or pavilion in which sat many people, naked to the waist, working at the decorations, which were indeed lovely—a basket bordered by banana stems, with curved openwork leaves stuck round; another that looks like a crown of curving feathers surmounted by a flower; bunches of thin plume-like coco-palm shoots whose ends are singed in a flame to stiffen them, hung about. But what at once struck us and remained one of the most interesting features of the ceremony, was a large oblong frame of banana stem, enclosing a clay relief, on which a boy was working. It represented a pregnant woman, with small elegant head, emerging from the jaws of a cobra-headed demon. It was being traced in black paint by the squatting boy, bending completely absorbed in his work over the scratched lines of the design. At the stage when we arrived only the figure with one arm was complete. The body was still grey clay. Then we made out two cocks' heads, and between the children's feet two small goats' heads, bearded. The cobra head is gradually emerging; the headdress and ornaments are now clear, splendid in design and decorative treatment; and the cobras' heads superbly coloured. Throughout the night the young man painted away, till

43

there finally emerged a magnificently coloured relief, the woman's body covered in a red *sari,* with a small design in gold. The woman's face was yellow, the demon's hands dark blue, as also the heads of the two children, mask-like in their abstraction. These seemed to hang over the woman's arms, but were, I suppose, embraced by her. The bearded goat seen at the foot of the left-hand child is the steed of the devil Kalu Kumara, the Black Prince. The demon's dark blue hands met over the woman's stomach, and two others were visible, also dark blue, with the nails clearly defined. The woman wore great round earrings. Behind her arm was seen that of a small child holding a leaf in its hand.

All through the night I kept thinking of the artist working by the light of his torch, and summoning with his nervous hand legendary figures from his fantasy, traditional, yet always susceptible of individual treatment in details. When finished he would stick threads and tufts of coco-palm all round the frame. The maker of the image is a young man of twenty, belonging to the potters' caste, which ranks low in the social scale. He has made about a hundred of these figures, of course entirely without a model, save in his own trained and remarkable memory. The design was entirely his own. In the morning the image was obviously cracked, which I hear is done on purpose.

The *naga*-headed pot with many spouts, which appeared later in the proceedings, will be broken, I gather, on the head of a buffalo when the ceremony is over, and the fragments carried away by the stream.

Kalu Kumara, the Black Prince, was the very demon who had frightened the woman on the sea-shore at 2 a.m. on the same day. The legend is that he became a demon only after his arrival in Ceylon, infected perhaps by the Yakshas whose native home it was. His holy mission was to protect Buddhism, bringing with him a branch of the Bo-tree. But Kalu Kumara was fond of women and, forgetting his holy mission, joined the Yakshas. Lurking by the wayside, he met Giri, a passing woman. He grabbed hold of her, and put her head in his mouth, and she became known as *Yaksha Giri.* They lived together as man and wife, and the children hanging over her arm were begotten by him; the cock would be sacrificed to feed him.

Anyone whose good fortune it has been to have an old-fashioned Nanna, must surely have heard her sometimes say: 'You look so good, I should like to eat you!' After which she would cover you with kisses. Probably now this would be thought to savour of cannibalism, and such a Nanna would be instantly dismissed. The incident of Kalu Kumara's substitute for a kiss is I believe sometimes represented in devil-dances, not only in the *bali* images.

I will not try to arrange the extraordinary experiences of this night in a logical order. Things happened one after another and I noted them as they came, but I cannot claim to have put down everything. My 'field-work' is apt to be somewhat desultory, for my attention wanders if I am bored, and I cannot pretend to have been equally interested in all that happened, and most probably did not grasp it all. Often quite a number of things were going on at once, and I must certainly have missed some of them, even with Fogl's help. But as every ceremony of the kind follows a more or less prescribed plan, the reader will find much more accurate descriptions in Dr. Wirz's exciting and scientifically sound book, *Exorzismus und Heilkunde auf Ceylon,* the accuracy of which is vouched for by Dr. Sarathchandra in his admirable study of the folk-dramas of Ceylon.[1] This certainly ought to be sufficient recommendation, for Sarathchandra is no amateur in such matters, but a very cultivated native of Ceylon who *par exception* has not spent half his life in Europe!

The farmer's daughter, on whose account the *bali* was held, was sitting on the ground in a corner of the loggia, behind a curtain held up by little boys. She remained completely immobile during most of the ceremony. She was in an early pregnancy. I did not discover whether any alarming symptoms had made themselves felt, or whether the *bali* was held merely as a precautionary measure, to ensure a happy delivery. Her name was Aturaya. We were told it would not be proper to speak to her, which was rather a relief.

Among the dancers are several different castes. The two main castes are *Goigama*, tillers of the soil, who are high-caste farmers, and *Bera Vayo*—the drummers. They also make decorations, polish furniture, etc.

Crowds of little boys with heavenly faces collected round the

[1] E. R. Sarathchandra, *The Sinhalese Folk-play.*

maduwa; old men too, of course; one so old that he could no longer even help in making the decorations. These dear aged creatures have a quite peculiar charm and a beautiful refinement. Their place in the community is assured.

Proceedings. Offerings to *Kalu Yakka*. Rice must be put into the pot by the patient, and cooked by a special man who must be clean and tidy. He also prepares fish. This work is regarded as low-class, which means, I suppose, suited to a low caste. Sea fish, the flesh of elk, deer and goat may be eaten, but not beef or mutton or pig. Vegetables of different kinds are cooked by the same man. For each Yakka an indeterminate number are offered. Besides Kalu Yakka there is Riyakka (a dwarf fond of blood), Sunniyakka (who brings on colds, chills, etc.), Maha Sona, who was beaten by Godinberaya, and his head damaged.

The drummers are now seated in the *Mal Maduwa* (the flower pavilion). Through the *Mal Maduwa* one sees a flickering light of torches in the *maduwa* where the dancers are dressing. The torches are made as usual of rag soaked in coconut oil. There is a whistle called *wasdanda*, used in 'calling for devils'. Devils may take the form of dog or bull or other animal. As yet it has only sounded once, but will be blown seven times. A long cloth is held out by an old man, while the dancer winds it round his waist above the short, scarlet, gold-fringed skirt which hangs over his long white *dhoti* or body cloth.

A bright light flashes, called *kile*. After the devils have been summoned they will be asked not to leave too soon; i.e. before they have finished their work.

The other *maduwa* is called *Sunni Anvidiya*; in it the devils are assembling. Offerings are now placed on stools in front of the screen hiding the patient—rice and flowers. Two torches are set up in pots, and a man with a torch which he keeps twirling moves to and fro with uneasy steps in front of the offerings, chanting. He is summoning the devils. The man who swings an incense-bellows is the one who cooked the offerings. The uneasy chanter has a strange face. I watched him preparing the offering-bowl.

As usual many odd people stroll casually about. About seventy sticks support the *Mal Maduwa*. For a really big *bali* 100 sticks may be used. Women are now collecting behind the patient. The man who cooked the offerings is quite impassive. Now an old man with a drum has seated himself opposite us, and beside him is a small boy in a green crown, green bodice, and red sash above his flounced white ballet-skirt.

Another small boy has now risen from the ground, and dances with bells on his feet and palm leaves in his hands. The chanting man holds his whistle across his torch like the hilt of a sword.

The *mantras* are all derived from Buddhism.

At intervals the chanting man whistles, and abuses the devils, or rather challenges them. This kind of abusive challenge was a most striking feature of the *Baris Gedé* (great Baris) in the island of Bali, where one leader so infuriated his followers by taunting them that on one occasion they actually retaliated by using their spears in earnest, and his body was said to bear the marks till he died. In *Dance and Drama in Bali* under *Ritual Baris* there is a description of this strange and beautiful ceremonial fight, in the village of Sanoer by the sea, and a photograph which shows the superb passion of the leader.[1]

A great flame is made, with loud cries, in the face of the patient as the screen is withdrawn. The *Kattadiya* (exorciser) is charming some water; turmeric and sandalwood are put into it, and it is sprinkled over the patient.

A dancer, with a crown, and holding a torch, with shoulder ornaments, short bodice and white belt like a cummerbund, calls again on the devil; the small boy begins whirling; the *Kattadiya* whistles and waves the torch before the offerings. The small boy whirls at intervals. The young woman sits impassive; the drums are terrific, with many cross-rhythms: a deafening tumult. Thick smoke rises from the incense bowl: people stroll about and refreshments are brought. Again the whistle sounds.

(The ceremony should take place five or seven months before the child is born.)

Now the patient touches the offerings; grown-ups kindly push children out of the way in order that we may see, and then stand in it themselves!

The dancer shifts continually in quick two-time from one foot to

[1] Facing page 64 of *Dance and Drama in Bali*, republished by Faber & Faber in 1952.

the other, and advances to the offerings; then circles with the small boy, who with wide knees sways continually. The patient sits patiently and rather pitifully on her bed.

We had a little talk with the village headman, an intelligent young man named H. N. Francis. He is in control of one square mile of country; a village of 1,600 people, and 386 houses. He is responsible for the schools, also for police duties, excise and revenue.

'Will the *Kattadiya*,' asks Fogl, 'allow me to take down what he intones?'

A. The *Kattadiya* will under no circumstances allow anyone to take down his *mantras*.

(It would indeed be difficult, as his sentences are quite unintelligible to any but himself, and frequently interrupted by a prolonged Ah-aa-ah or Eh-a-eh.)

Q. Why does the patient not wear any jewellery?

A. It is bad for her to wear jewellery, because owing to the presence of metal, the spirits do not like to approach.

Q. Why does one of the *Kattadiyas* have two half-moons of soot and coconut oil underneath the lower eyelid and above it?

A. These are called *Andun*.

Q. Why the dancing?

A. The devils delight in the sound of drums, and are ever happy watching the dancing of the sorcerers.

The second sorcerer has no torch, but holds a bunch of palms in each hand, called *chamara*. Feathers of the *sabada*-bird are represented by tender coco-palm leaves cut in shreds, about fourteen inches long, and held in the middle: about twenty-four in each hand.

Q. Why does he hold these feathers?

A. Because he cannot dance empty-handed. They are only for decorative effect.

The artist, torch in hand, has now begun the painting of his image; the drums here reach a maddening point, and the *Kattadiya* yells. Old faces, fringed in white beards, gleam out of the darkness, full light falls on the pregnant image.

Now an old man, uncostumed, begins to circle among the dancers, chanting, with a bunch of palm-strips in each hand. Another costumed *Kattadiya* begins to dance with him. Now he is dancing in

Avenue in Peredeniya Botanical Gardens

Elephants bathing

Sinhalese girl plaiting palm-leaves

front of the drum. He is becoming quite an important personage, and seems to be dictating to the others. His dance has become quite striking. He seems to adjure the costumed *Kattadiyas*; I hear he is a volunteer.

9.30. Three decorated little convex-shaped spiky offering-trays, called *ayele,* which I had seen being prepared on the chest of a man lying on the ground, are placed on a bench, and rice and vegetables are placed in them. The cock stands quite impervious to what is happening beside the three *ayeles.* They are now taken to the patient by the man who cooked the food. Into them the patient puts betel leaves and flowers. Then, as in the first case, she puts her hands on them, thereby asking the devils present to intercede on her behalf, and remove the spirits from her. After one and a half hours of dancing, incantations and drumming, these suddenly stop, and the *pideniya* is offered to the patient, who touches it and puts copper coins and betel into the *ayeles.* Then she touches them three times, and the offerings are taken away. She has now offered them to the devil with a view to soliciting his help in removing any evil spirits who may still remain in her.

Two circular stands are now brought to take the place of the first offerings. These are made to Giriyakka and Sunniyakka. The cock is brought in and stood under the Giriyakka offering. As before, rice, vegetables, meat and spices are put on the offering stands, which are hung with streamers of coco-palm, and to each of which a torch is attached. The cock, his feet bound, totters rather miserably about, and cannot sit down.

The whistle sounds again. I am comforted by the orange-tree above our heads, which is overgrown with betel leaves.

The image now has black hair and a scarlet and black crown. The outline of the body is quite clear in the torchlight. The artist is painting somewhere by the feet.

Now three torches are stuck in each of the offering-stands, and more lighted torches are placed on the offerings. As in the former case the two offerings are touched by the patient and taken away.

The *Kattadiya,* undressed, carrying the wand and a rolled mat, advances with his torch towards the patient and retreats again. He chants and moves uneasily from foot to foot. He throws down his wand and mat by the cock, and does a wild torch dance, whirling and scattering sparks. The cock is absolutely immobile, and the patient too just gazes. The crowd has become dense, at every angle of the enclosure. Beyond the offerings I see now a yellow band below the scarlet of the demon's headdress. On going to examine it I find the scarlet and yellow are the demon's eyeballs and eyelids. His lips are scarlet above his huge teeth. Snakes' heads are delicately painted in on his headdress; also the cocks' heads. The body is becoming scarlet, the hands blue; blue also are the faces of the children.

And still the artist works on.

9.45. Now the *Kattadiya* lies on a mat and is covered by a white cloth which the pregnant woman had made into a ball, circled round her head and thrown to him. It is with this that his body is covered. The three *ayeles,* with offerings in a canoe-shaped vessel with bristling plumes, are placed on his breast, and a tall torch is stood beside him. The *ayeles* are taken up in turn, censed and replaced. The recumbent *Kattadiya* continually moves his legs under the sheet. The man lying down is also now an offering. He recites continually, holding the *wasdanda* (demon-whistle) in his hand. He rhythmicizes the *mantras* (spells) with his foot under the sheet. The man squatting beside him fans the fire-pan.

He whistles again. The cock is now a part of the *pideniya* offerings. An endless stream of *mantras* flows from his mouth. Coins are counted out. The old man who is our informant is now charming water with an areca-nut flower.

The cock is lifted up and circled round the head of the prostrate man. The *ayeles* are moved further and further down his body till they rest almost on his knee. His right hand, holding the torch, turns anti-clockwise. A quick rhythm is sung to soft drumming.

10.10. The *ayeles* are removed and presented to the patient who puts coins and betel into them. They are then replaced.

The *mantras,* we are told, are made by hermits. It is the sound, not the meaning of the words which counts in the *mantras.*

The *Kattadiya* rises from his mat, rolls it up and carries it off. The *pideniya* are removed; only the cock remains.

The artist still paints by torchlight behind the hedge of bodies.

10.30. Four dancers now appear: one is a tall old man with a kind of white cloth hat framed by a high brim of coloured tinsel. All have scarlet cummerbunds, short bodices, necklaces of beads, white skirts. The tall old man wears a stole of palm-slithers.

Three fat torches are held together in the hand of one of the *Kattadiyas*. Their eyes are curiously blackened. Bunches of palm-slithers have the effect of demon-nails, as they are waved by the small boy who continues to dance very actively.

All are now dancing in front of the *mal maduwa*.

Now torches are distributed to all, the floor is pounded, the cock removed.

A whistle is several times repeated, twice over. Now all wear palm stoles. The drummers stand—excited, the dancers whirl in and out of the flower-tent. Each now holds a torch in his hand.

All offerings other than the cock have now been removed to the *puranapala*, where the devils have also repaired.

Now they form together a mad circle. The drumming becomes deafening, the dancing vertiginous; the child in particular whirls furiously.

The cost of a *bali* ceremony is based on the wealth of the man who orders it. For performances outside the *Kattadiya's* area the charges are levied in accordance with the distance, on a basis of transport plus retaining fee. The cost of this ceremony, together with all the decorative work and the several *maduwas*, would be 40 rupees, i.e. about £3, including three drummers and six dancers.

Now all issue in turn from the flower-tent, with a tremendous twirling of torches, scattering of sparkles and flames. The old man dances as if possessed in front of the drums. The dancing is done, as it were, to the intention of the drums. The drum rhythms are wild and broken. The dancer squats and trembles. The ground is covered with flames and sparks; frantic dances and frantic drum rhythms. Crouching, with knees spread wide, the feet interpret every small note of the drum beats, while the drummers watch the feet of the dancers. This interchange in dictating the rhythm became later very familiar to me in every first-class *bali* or *thovil*; above all in every *Kohomba Kankaria*, which is a sort of signature-tune of this diary!

The great Indian *sarod*-player, Ali Akbar Khan, and his tabla-player recently provided in London a magnificent example of this alternate leadership; and the same thing might also be seen between

Shanta Rao and her singer, though here perhaps it was the dancer who dominated the fantastically beautiful counterpoint, one of the most exciting experiences one can imagine. The occasional and most beautiful breaking of Shanta into song, which my friend Richard Buckle, usually so perceptive, found 'unpleasing', was an additional delight to musicians and musical ballet dancers.

To return to the *bali* at Matara. The dancing was strangely impressionistic, yet always gave one a sense of frustration; it never reached full abandon.

Again they dance in a circle; one holding a cloth and palm-stole above his head. The little boy is extraordinary in his whirling acrobacy, with deep body-bendings, till he almost touches the ground.

The oldest drummer joins in the incantations, while continuing all the while his vigorous drumming.

They move in a rapid succession of steps in and out of the *Mal Maduwa*.

The dance floor is never without an animated dancer, whirling or leaping to the throbbing of the drums.

The cloth which has covered the *Kattadiya* is now presented to the patient, who touches it; and the central dancer throws it over the *Mal Maduwa* so that its top is covered. The cloth too is an offering.

(All the cloths worn by the dancers during the ceremony, together with their jackets, are supplied by the local *dhobi,* and have to be returned to him. The cost of their hire varies; this time it would be altogether ten rupees. The *dhobi* hires out his client's sheets for this purpose, and naturally has to wash them again before sending them back, so that a delay in the return of one's laundry suggests that a *bali* or *thovil* or *devol maduwa* has taken place.)

The host invites selected guests to partake of food at intervals during the night. Betel is served all round; so is water from time to time.

The drums beat furiously three times. One dancer puts four torches inside his bodice, takes a great handful of incense, dances violently with it, and then in a great burst of flame explodes the incense, amid vertiginous rhythms and whirling. The flame-dancers advance towards each other; the rhythm grows slower; waving their torches, they loudly chant. The frenzy reaches the point of possession, then subsides. The drummers seem to be going mad. The small boy continues

52

to dance indefatigably in the background. Without a torch the old drummer begins to shout, and overshouts everyone. He is about seventy, the boy-dancer ten. Now they jump and step in a slow *staccato* rhythm. The bells are on one leg only, attached to a kind of puttee. The oldest dancer goes round intoning a chant which all take up. The others go about collecting coins, which douceur indeed they deserve, but to which we were not allowed to contribute. Now they are dancing and singing in honour of their *guru*.

A new phase opens with short rhythmic phrases of praise to distinguished people in the village. The master of the house gets some splendid somersaults of praise. The dancer receives money and shares it with the drummer. There is a brief dialogue; rhythms are given out by syllables; every moment the rhythm changes. Each verse is followed by a dance rhythm. The small boy, who is the son of one of the drummers, does a fantastic 'dervish' dance, while a pulsing drum rhythm never ceases. The footwork of this child is amazing; since he began to dance hours ago he has never ceased for a moment.

Incense dance. The old man dances with the incense pan, whirling it above his head.

Mace dance. The eyes are blackened so much that the dancers appear to wear great black spectacles.

It is impossible to convey the variations of these stupendous drum rhythms which if one only tells about them sound rather boringly the same, I fear.

The incense is used, as in the island of Bali, to send the dancer into trance. He was at last carried out and laid on the ground and fanned. He turns his head from side to side. He was, they said, in the power of the *mantra,* not possessed by any devil. He went into trance by his own agency. After enchanted water has been sprinkled on him he recovers.

The patient now retires. It is midnight. There is an interval, during which we go to look at the image, now decorated with flourishes of palm leaf, stuck all round the frame. The artist could not, he says, tell the story of Kalu Kumara on flat paper, but only in relief. The richness of his invention, within the limits of the tradition, is really wonderful.

I walked outside the enclosure on to a terrace overlooking the rice-fields through foliage of palm and bananas, their leaves exquisitely outlined. The moon rode high among light clouds. In the distance I saw a torch moving along in the world of men—a reminder of the lantern which 'interested the sight' of Gerard Manley Hopkins. The *bali* figure is lit by torches and leans against the wall.

12.30. A new part begins. Unfortunately not so very new, as it is the same torch-dancers. They have now only white handkerchiefs on their heads. The third, who went into trance, wears his crown. The other crowns are hanging above the picture. The crowd has cleared considerably; in fact only a few are left. The drums sound like an explosion of firearms; they create the illusion of shots, when accom-panied by flame-throwing torches.

The dancers whirl the torches round behind their backs. (*Bali*-ceremonies can take place on Friday, Saturday or Sunday, and during any but the full moon. They must, however, be timed to agree with an auspicious hour for the person concerned.)

The torches when not in use are stuck into the banana stems which form the wall of the enclosure.

Now the torches are abandoned and dancing is henceforth done with tufts of palm leaf in each hand. A small boy in a check kilt collects the torches from an old man, and sticks them about the flower-tent.

The whistle sounds again. There is a dance with an offering from which two torches protrude. This also is offered to the devil. This vessel is called *potalé*. It resembles one I saw in the museum, and is made of mud covered over with coco-palm leaf. Thin spikes of areca-palm stick out from the central orifice. Tall areca shoots now fill the *potalé*. It must have three cobra heads, seven longitudinal lines, and twelve points.[1]

Mal-bali (flower-offering). Now comes the turn of the crown-like structure on a square frame of banana shoots, which was being made when we arrived. Two torches protrude from it. Stanzas are recited on Buddha's descent to the world, chasing out devils.

The patient has wisely gone to sleep.

Kapuketima, or cutting of threads. The basket, with banana border

---

[1] If you want to wreak vengeance on someone, you have a *potalé* made and take it to the *kapurale,* who attends to the ceremonies in a *devale* (shrine dedicated to a Hindu god). He chants *mantras* and dashes it to the ground.

and hoops of coco-palm leaf round the top, is stood on a stool and censed. Two torches are stuck in the banana border. An address is made to it by a dancer. Then two dance round it with circular motions of the arms, and turning rhythms, while the drummers (now seated) prodigiously drum. Stoles are much in evidence; two are worn by each, one hanging behind and one in front; the dance increases in velocity. They continually approach the basket and dip their bunches of coco-palm leaf in the flame of the torches. To the rhythm of the drums the dancer dips his hand into a bowl and wrings it out. They let their stoles hang over their heads in front, dip them in the basket and rub their hair, which hangs loose, then wring out their hair and do it up in a top-knot. They are two queens washing their hair. At last, after several repetitions, they fling back their hair.

This is really a dance for women which, I understand, is thrown in to appease the devil. Again they violently splash their hair in water, and leaping wildly about, fling off the water. One lifts out a comb made from a banana stem, curved and with teeth. Now each has one, and they dance, combing their hair—their long locks, and loose hairs. All this is done to the rhythm of drum beats. They repeat the action. The drums weave elaborate patterns round their simple action-rhythms. Then each holds a tress of hair, an extra plait, such as the Veddahs wore, according to Mrs. Seligman. This is carefully combed, and the action of combing long hair begins again for a moment to a triple rhythm. But almost immediately the rhythm has again changed. Now the hair is wound in a tight rope, coiled over the head, each with a different style of coiffure. Each has a pin in his hand and fixes it into his hair. Each has a white cloth with which he dances before tying it round his body. They sway from foot to foot meanwhile.

Now they put on earrings. The two queens are called 'riddi bissauw', meaning 'silver queens'. They recite their story as they dance, but it was not alas confided to me. They put on necklaces: the drums are meanwhile somewhat subdued. They sing in unison, but soon break into tumultuous syncopation.

The queens undress. They carry each a mirror of banana stem, beautifully shaped, which shines like ivory. The rhythm of the drums becomes more and more complicated, then stops suddenly, and the dance is over.

Now one dancer, holding a basket on his left arm, starts dancing. He puts the basket on the ground in front of him, and plants a cotton-tree in front of the queen, made from coco-palm leaf, with waving, tall, pointed flowers.

The queen draws a thread from inside the pods and begins twining it. The chant alternates between drummer and dancer. She sways continuously in a circular motion, to and fro, describing the cotton-tree. The drum is subordinate to the long-phrased chant. From this thread is woven a cloth which is offered to Lord Buddha. The buds are opened out into flowers and inside is the cotton thread. Finally she begins plucking the cotton by quick hand movements above the swaying flowers. She chews betel which is part of the act. She weaves. The drum has quick beats for her quick motions. She has made a ball of cotton thread, and proceeds to wind it on the spindle, to make the cloth, to a gentle accompaniment of the drum, with occasional cascades of sound. She teazes the cotton with a comb followed by a short passage of quick and complicated drum rhythms. She threads the cotton ball on the spindle, and unwinds the thread which grows longer and longer, till it reaches above her head. She manipulates the spool with her right hand, and winds the thread round a reel; draws a cloth out of the basket and does passes over it. She is weaving a cloth. The drum continues monotonously. She weaves a golden towel, folds it and places it in the basket. With the torch she does passes over it, and over the two torches in the basket with another torch. The narration goes on interminably.

The other dancers are dressing for the next part of the entertainment. At last she rises and the basket is carried away to the patient who puts one copper coin and betel into it. It is placed with the other offerings.

Indefatigably the same dancer begins again in front of the flower-tent. Incense is burnt under all the *pideniyas*. One drummer beats emphatically and then takes the drum from the oldest drummer, and plays standing, with shrill metallic note.

The rhythm is taken up by another drummer for a few bars; then returns to the first.

Manipulating his coco-palm tresses the dancer sways and whirls before the flower-tent; then, holding the tresses above his head, he beats them violently against each portion of the wall in turn. He has areca flowers on his head, which he offers to each of the seven pillars. The seven pillars are seven queens; seven miraculous queens who could do exactly what they liked! To them are offered the areca flowers. To seven non-miraculous queens will come later offerings.

The dancer's cloth is folded to look like a child. The name of the next act is 'lulling the baby'.

The child is being put to sleep. It belongs to one of the seven queens. It is taken away to be breast-fed and bathed. The mother sits on the traditional coco-palm stool. This has reference to the mother-to-be. The baby is made of a log; its ears are being formed; its face is now washed. It is breast-fed at both breasts. The 'mother' sways in a circular motion all the time. The drum becomes slightly more excited. A doll is now brought out; a nice puppet in a red dress, its arms outstretched towards the patient. It is given a coin.

The rhythm is continuously in triple time. The drumming is very subdued while the doll is carried round collecting.

This man has held the stage alone for over two hours. The doll is now taken to the mother-to-be, who gives more coins. The indefatigable dancer does a wild dance with two palm whisks in the offering pavilion.

A sudden cessation of the drums. How wonderful! Crickets are heard in the silence; birds begin to twitter.

The sixteen masks are now making ready to appear.

Interval. The same dancer recites now in front of the crown-offering, which is being censed, amid tremendous smoke. It stands near the patient, the flame of the torch half hidden by smoke.

The dancer now begins to moan. He has curiously well-defined breasts, and a very strange face. As usual something is being charmed. The poor 'queen' continues to sway and intone, while the drum keeps up a low accompaniment in triple time. The patient, lying peacefully awake now, is being censed.

Long moans of oh-h-h continue.

There is a new offering, with a shovel-shaped wicker tray. One of the miraculous queens went once into the principality of the *rodiyas*.[1] Hence the name of the offering.

---

[1] See *Monthly Literary Register,* 1895–6, and below, p. 80, note.

A jack-tree is brought; its leaves are being plucked. They will be used as cups to put rice offerings in.

The cock reappears. It cannot now be killed for seven days, but it can be tortured quite a lot, as you will see.

Another boy begins now to drum. As he belongs to the farmer-caste, he may wear something on his upper body, which the *berawayo* caste may not. Very unusually the drum now beats in duple time.

4.15. The masks, it seems, really *are* coming at last. The loggia is full of incense smoke. There is much excitement as they arrive, with a great burst of incense. A small one in a huge red mask, with two torches, a red and white cummerbund, two fringed skirts, one above the other, red and blue; black and white puttees with bells. He strides to and fro, screaming and wildly contorting.

A terrifying one comes next, in a green wreath with gnashing teeth, a red bodice, yellow and red fringed skirt, bell leggings, fierce movements and wild contortions.

Another red-haired one, with a bowl and toothy mask enough to frighten the poor patient out of her wits.

Water is still being charmed with torches on the ground.

A demon with terrible teeth and protruding eyes, white cloth, green hair, carries a vase with areca-palm flowers. The patient sits quite impassive. The dance gets more and more frantic, still in duple time.

A man stands holding two torches between the drums. As the mask enters, the drums increase to frenzy. A fearful creature in a *tutu* of coloured fringes is number five; he has a grey face.

Again a tangled red head, so shaggy that it is almost impossible to see the mask. He advances on the patient and flourishes in her face, doing a kicking step the while. Shakes his mane violently with Rangda-like[1] cries.

A green head, with black beard and chocolate face, holds the incense bowl. His protruding eyes seem more terrible as he does his wild dance from side to side.

Redhead carries the poor cock in all positions; spreadeagles it, holds a wing between his teeth, whirls it in the patient's face, almost tears the cock apart in his frenzy. He comes in again briefly, without

[1] Rangda is the witch in the Balinese magic dance-drama Chalonarang.

the cock, and makes his bow, and one fears the worst for the cock, in spite of the promise. However it is shortly afterwards replaced, and a curtain is held up in front of the patient.

The serious child who danced all the first half of the night, sits now at the drum, in a white *dhoti*. A slow halting rhythm, with many floreations, comes from the drum, but I have an idea that it is the drummer in the 'flower pavilion' who is beating it out. Through an opening in the enclosure, one sees smiling faces lit by the torch.

With cries, mask number nine advances to a duple rhythm. Bells are heard jangling on the dance-leggings. The rhythm changes, then returns to the one above; and all the drums together make a great accellerando.

The old man carries a triple torch, and a matting is spread. The next mask is dressed in leaves, with a great black beard and wig and a white belt. He crouches on the ground. The horrible coal black creature breaks through the wall, brandishes his torch and displays his scarlet tongue. Coal-black feathers also surround his face. The curtain is withdrawn, but the patient shows not the least alarm. He staggers malignantly amongst the crowd, then sinks to the mat amid a burst of terrific flame.

Now even the devil seems tired; he uses bad language and throws away his torch. He is breathless, but accepts a new torch, and breaks through the crowd again, among bursts of flame. With shuddering steps he intrudes everywhere, and eats the offerings which pour again out of his mouth. His face is really rather like a curly retriever, which should make him more sympathetic, but somehow doesn't. After prancing about for a while, he again squats, exhausted.

8.30. Offerings are being made to the *bali* figure; torches burn in front of it. A drum beats. A sheet is held up in front of the patient, and a torch lit at both ends.

The eleventh mask has a headdress of coco-palm in high loops. Red flowers representing a tongue hang between his palm-leaf lips, and crinkled streamers from his torch. He also wears a skirt of several tiers of short flounces, and does an excited dance with a torch in each hand. With a handful of incense he dances before the *bali,* which is lit by two torches. The torches are continually re-lit, when, as so often, they become extinct.

The dance is repeated, the dancer going all through the house, expelling devils, particularly from the rooms where the women sleep. His efforts to frighten the patient have been quite unsuccessful. What a pity! Her insensibility begins to jar. His short skirt is made of jack-fruit leaves. I really cannot follow all his shootings forward, wig-rufflings, exhausted collapses, cock-shakings and pulling apart of feathers. Masks always disquiet me, even if I know who is behind them. So, with his discussion of the various parts of the cock, which is certainly very comic for those who understand the joke, I will leave him setting the cock on its feet, ignoring the black man with a stick, a bunch of leaves and what looks like a fresh mask—flat and grey and distorted, with a hideous hare-lip. As in the island of Bali, terror and fun are seldom apart for long. And obviously here fun is an easy winner.

Crows are feeding on the food sacrificed to devils; the *metjaru* of the Balinese.

The patient is touched by the dancer's wand or mace. A lime hangs from a spool on the dancer's headdress. It will be unwound by the patient, and the lime flung at the painted *bali*-figure. The patient accepts the lime. A man unwinds the thread and attaches it to a tree. It falls from the tree on to her knee.

The offerings at the foot of the *bali* are a coconut and rice-pounder; one new and one old pot containing areca-nut flowers. The *Kattadiya* waves his torch against the *bali*-figure, reciting. The patient as always sits completely passive, holding the lime.

How I welcomed the cock's sudden crowing after his dreary and even dangerous night! How did he know that dawn had come, and he could soon be free?

It was time to go. We also were free, and still alive! I took some photos of the celebrants, the family, the *bali* and gave a poor ten rupees to the principal drummer for distribution. I fear this was a minimum donation; but consoled myself with thinking that the *bali* was happening in any case, and not on my account.

13th December. I hear there is to be an Arts Festival at the museum from the 4th to the 11th of February, when there will be a great variety of *bali* and other ceremonial dances, as well as puppet-shows; also an exhibition of lacquer work and other handicrafts for which

Ceylon is famous: masks, ivories, woven straw hats and purses, etc.; the best dancers of the Kandyan School are also promised. Who knows whether the *Kohomba Kankaria* may not find a place? It seems impossible to find out anything about the nature of this dance, which is somehow connected with the Margosa-tree, except that it lasts all night—possibly for several nights; hitherto Fred Fogl is my only informant. Barnett's famous Alphabetical Index to the Hindu gods of Ceylon (based on Hugh Nevill's abstracts of ancient ballads) does indeed list Kohomba, the Margosa-tree, but no more.

14th December. We started at 5.30 for Jaffna, where Leston Mendez has business. It was still quite dark, cloudy and cool—almost too cool. The drive is very long—250 miles—and for the most part through monotonous jungle, crossing some rivers and passing great salt lagoons, flocks of white storks and many water birds; a few parakeets. The most arresting trees were the flamboyant and lovely *surya*-trees with heart-shaped leaves and bell flowers, yellow and soft red, rather the colour of tulip-tree flowers. Also many *waringin*. Many paths led into the jungle but wild animals have become what Ignatia called 'sophisticated', and nothing wilder than a water buffalo showed its head. We met, however, many flocks of goats and kids, cows and calves; in fact, they strayed all over the road.

At a small wayside booth we ate some excellent freshly baked hoppers, filled with honey, and paid the passer-by's tribute at a shrine to some local deity.

Passing rapidly through Anuradhapura I got at that time a distinctly muddled impression; it was evidently once an enormous city, covering a very wide area; the main street is said to have been seven miles long.

Elephant Pass is a narrow road between two huge lagoons, so shallow that even in the middle the water would probably only reach one's knees. The floods had evidently been tremendous over the greater part of the route, after one of the worst droughts on record. It had rained most of the way, but as we neared Elephant Pass, where in ancient days a great battle had been fought, the sun came out and lit the wind-tossed waves of the lagoon, fringed by palmyra palms.

The rest-house stands in an exquisite position, on a little promontory dropping into the lake. The loggia outside the dining-room is only a few feet above the water, and swallows and butterflies so large that they seem like sunbirds flit and dip between its pillared terraces Above there is a similar balcony outside the bedrooms. I have never lunched in a more enchanting spot, or seen a hotel to which I more longed to return for far longer than an hour.

The character of the landscape changed from here onwards, and became more interesting; partly of course on account of the sun which lit the variegated carpets of rice-fields and hedges. The villages too were different, and the people unmistakably Tamil; the women with bright *saris* and bare breasts. The houses had pillared verandas; the carts, laden with *surya* and other leaves for goat food, had large wheels and were open—not with the hoods one sees in South Ceylon. Also, towards Jaffna, and notably after Elephant Pass, the houses stand in fenced enclosures, as nowhere in the south of Ceylon. We drove into Jaffna, a garden city. All the shops have a colonnade outside them, raised above the street, and painted in various colours, pale blue, yel-low, cream; with lattices between the columns which produce a very South Indian effect.

We visited the double-walled fort, which was built by the Portu-guese and continued by the Dutch. Its great gateways and road wind-ing between the walls are very exciting. A moat still full of water also lies between the walls which are of considerable extent; and a grassy road runs quite round the top of the inner wall which is immensely thick. A Dutch seventeenth-century church, solid and beautifully built, is within the inner fort, but rises above the walls. There are various delightful pillared houses inside, with wide grass lawns. It is a most beautiful place.

Having turned down the rest-house in the town and made an appointment for Leston for the following morning, we drove ten miles through delightful cultivated fields and orchards of bright red earth overhung by vast groves of palmyra palm and interspersed with charming lanes and houses. I forgot to mention the picturesque pil-lared market, everything about it decorative and well-spaced; and the Hindu temples, one with a high *gopuram*.[1] The hedges, like the house roofs, were of fan-shaped palmyra-palm leaf, which gave them a curiously flounce-like appearance.

[1] Gate-tower.

The rest-house near the northernmost point of Ceylon is the most delightful imaginable. It faces endways to the sea, so that its loggia is somewhat sheltered from the strong warm wind which seems to blow continually from the Indian Ocean, but still overlooks the sea and the tall white lighthouse. It is shaded by two great trees. A large curving wide stone wall, rather like the cob at Lyme Regis, juts out into the sea and ends in a ruin; a similar curving fragment of wide stone bends towards it from the other end of the beach. This is part of the original fortification built by the Dutch before the fort of Jaffna. There is a terrace which seems to have been once grassed, for trees border it. A pleasant beach of soft pale yellow sand, washed by each tide, lies below. The breakers are huge and magnificent, nostal-gically northern in character and colour; were it not for the warm wind, almost but not quite unimaginable in mid-December.

To the north is a small salt lagoon, and a long stretch of sandy shore on which coco-palms grow in lovely groups, the feet of many of them actually in the sea. They seem to thrive in the salt water.

We walked after supper by full moon along the shore. Massive wide-bottomed boats, with impregnable ribs, lie on the shelving beach.

How beautiful it is! I had not then even heard of the Male Raja, that legendary figure who was to become more real to me than all Ceylon's historic invaders: Tamil, Portuguese, Dutch, British; ances-tor possibly of the proud Veddahs, so sadly fallen from their high estate, but conscious to the last of a racial superiority which even those who looked down on them socially seem to have admitted. It was at this very spot, so they say, that the Male Raja landed, in pur-suit of the wild boar, a god in disguise, who had ravaged his orchard, and enticed him across the sea to cure another prince's inherited malady. The friends with whom I made this journey certainly at that time knew nothing either of the Male Raja or the wild boar, so I will not anticipate the moment when these became so far more real to me than my Sinhalese friends.

The rest-house was spotless, though without linen, and presided over by an exuberantly hospitable Tamil, from whose attentions it was impossible to escape. 'This is your home, not a lodging.' 'It is I who thank you,' with each fresh mouthful we ate. This venerable man ended by being my son! The dinner was certainly delicious, but one was afraid to linger over it, since this also meant the prolongation of our host's protestations. He says he is clairvoyant and reads palms, though not by lamplight, and only on certain days of the week, of which this was not one.

15th December. I woke frequently from too much air on my bed, being only covered by a cotton dressing-gown and a cloth of Ignatia's. The wind blew freshly and I saw the white line of breakers. All night the glorious sound of the sea. . . . I have been out on the sea wall. The sky is laden with brilliant stars. A figure in white, with hair hanging down his back, came out also and stood on the edge of the sea. It was very light, though the moon had long ago set; light from the stars and the intermittent lighthouse flash. But the day is certainly longer here in the north.

We hear the *devadasis* from South India arrive in February and will dance in the Hindu temples in Jaffna. It may be worth while coming to see them. The keeper of the rest-house has promised to let me know.

I visited the beautiful bathing-tank, with steps down into it all round, and the sea flowing over its outer wall. It was built several hundred years ago; a fresh-water spring bubbles up in it and keeps it perpetually fresh. The water was absolutely clear. One solid brown person was enjoying it. The only blot on this landscape is the cement works which lie between it and the rest-house; they certainly are horrible to the disinterested eye.

We had another delightful drive through the orchards to Jaffna, and breakfasted with the brothers Cooke, to whom Leston is hoping to sell his petrol pumps. The loggias in Jaffna, raised above the street in front of each shop and office, under wide eaves, keep the inner room beautifully cool and shady, and give a sense of spaciousness and dignity to the town.

After Elephant Pass rain fell, and increased in violence; Anuradhapura was soaking, but a surprising view of two distant *viharas* (Buddhist temples) rising above the trees was most impressive. Then came a long journey through the endless tunnel of trees, mile after mile. We passed a Buddhist procession, in which were three elephants, the first with a small illuminated pagoda on his back; the other ridden by a few boys. There were drums and cymbals. Little

Start of the procession

Disc balancer

During the *Perahera* in Kandy

boys in white and gold crowns, some dance costumes and banners; women in white carrying lilies; a hideous image of Buddha, etc. Was this a *perahera*? Certainly, for *perahera* only means procession; but I wonder if it was really Buddhist at all.

16th December. A letter from the Madras dance-critic to Ignatia, announcing a dance festival in Madras for the last week in December. Read Pertold at the museum, and begin to get clear about the different parts which constitute a *bali*. Visited a quarter of very small houses in a rather slummy part of Colombo. They looked charming, with latticed windows, once perhaps a rural suburb.

Fogl had arranged a *Kohomba Kankaria* for Saturday at Kurunegala; but it appears there is a still rarer *Devol Maduwa* a short distance from here which we must go to; so the *Kohomba* is now fixed for Wednesday, and Kandy for Friday.

Some of my Matara photographs have come out not too badly, so I feel more confident.

17th December. This evening Fred Fogl came to supper. He is certainly completely wholehearted, but has perhaps no great experience of classical dance. He told me that the Kandyan dancers who were taken by Hagenbeck to Hamburg were billed as Wild Men of Ceylon. When, while rehearsing, one of them lost his cloth for a moment, it produced such prodigious applause that the losing had to become a regular part of the programme. They were so badly paid, said Fogl, that they used to go round the grounds after the show was over and collect butt ends of cigarettes, which they rolled again and sold next day.

18th December. I hear the *devol maduwa* has been put off for a month, on account of the girl for whom it was to be held having begun her periods. (Ceylon is becoming strangely like Bali.) We had meanwhile put off the *Kohomba Kankaria* on its account, and I had refused an invitation to a *thovil* quite a short way off; in fact only just down the street. It was to this that Fogl and I decided to go in the end. It was held in an old-fashioned street, called High Street, just off the modern thoroughfare of Galle Road, but centuries away from it in feeling. The road was of course unpaved, the houses low and charming, rather dolls'-housey in character, and each standing in its own garden. We drew up before a garden, at the far end of which stood a low unlighted house. Could this be it? Peering about with a torch, we found the number, and walked in the miry sand, through puddles under dripping trees to the back of the house, from which came cries and the sound of drums. We entered a rather narrow courtyard, on the right of which was a one-storeyed earthen house with three barred windows. From the darkness of the house, as from a dungeon, shone the bright eyes of crowds of smiling children, picturesquely tiered one above the other.

Along the front of the house ran a raised dais, on which was a bed. A woman sat on it, holding a child on her knee, a sweet placid baby. Beside her, on a jutting ledge of earth, a man, naked to the waist, crouched motionless on his heels. From time to time the master of ceremonies swung towards her a torch, while he recited and swayed.

But the eye was drawn most of all by a remarkable erection at the far end of the court, like a very large old-fashioned fireplace or hearth.

This was the *Torana* (ceremonial screen or arch), entirely built of plantain stems, carved most cunningly in squares, which gave the illusion of tiles, through being delicately painted with flower designs. The *torana* had three pointed eaves, decorated with areca and coconut palms skilfully cut into open starry flowers.

As one's eyes grew accustomed to the darkness one distinguished, behind the *torana,* a sort of shrine in which was a painted image of a wild boar-man, a manifestation of Kalu Kumara, with a boar's head and fat tummy. There were various beautiful little offering-stands about the courtyard, and two in front of the patient, who had been suffering from some kind of nervous disorder. A great jack fruit hung against the trunk; the breadfruit leaves, plantain and coco-palm were lit up by the lamp or torches. The ground was covered with puddles and exceedingly muddy; rain dripped at intervals from the huge leaves.

From time to time sand was sprinkled over the ground churned by the dancers' feet. The *Kattadiyas* dressed up in full view. The flounces of their short skirts were handsomely embroidered with a simple fine design in red, black and white. The fourth dancer was a small boy, more elaborately dressed than at Matara, and the dancing was also superior, or seemed so to me. This was strange, for Matara is supposed to be the centre *par excellence* of devil-dancing. The space was also more limited than at Matara, but the whirling was superb and most skilfully adjusted to the space. Some of the dancing was done almost sitting on the ground between widespread knees. There was an extraordinary variety of figures, some of the best reminding me of the Balinese *baris*. Torches were freely whirled, and later two men made great play with them, rubbing them all over their chests, putting them in their mouths, etc. One used often to see this in Morocco during some ecstatic festival. Unless one happens to be worked up oneself it is not particularly entertaining—in fact slightly boring and unpleasant.

Those present took much more part in the proceedings than at Matara, giving what sounded like three hoarse cheers for the patient each time the offerings were presented to her, and she had been adjured by a *Kattadiya*. There were two drummers; the *Kattadiyas* wore beautifully embroidered three-tiered skirts; a white cloth wrapped again and again tightly round their waists, and a red cap surmounted by palm leaves. . . . A double torch was held by the dancing *Kattadiya*, who moved to and fro in the mud from foot to foot, and never stopped dancing, even when he went to give some command to the drummer.

Torches began to be stuck into the openings of the *torana*; the sick woman, who had so long sat motionless, began to shudder and make convulsive movements of face and shoulders. It was clear that something strange was happening to her. Her face became distorted by a kind of nervous tick; she made curious passes at the priest; then, after having been heavily censed, she got up from the bed, and began to be carefully decorated for the dance by the priest. A kind of harness, or bodice of palm-leaves was put on over her dress; she stepped forward, her hair flying, was touched with the *Kattadiya*'s wand and danced wildly, with contorted face, ineptly at first, then more vigorously, with a rough imitation of the *Kattadiya*'s technique. She was then subjected to a questionnaire from one of the exorcists, who suggested to her the names of the devils who possessed her, and apparently received satisfactory answers. All the time he was questioning her, the exorcist held a wand to her head. She was given a small bunch of areca-palm, and danced into the *maduwa*. Then she joined in the wild dance, from which she was drawn out by the *Kattadiya*, who again addressed her and, supported by two men, she was carried, obviously exhausted, and laid on the bed. Later she looked quite normal, as when we arrived, with a very sweet smile.

The drumming and dancing were really formidable throughout the night; the three *Kattadiyas* and the boy, in a black bodice, finely embroidered, a three-tiered skirt, leggings and bells.

The court was full of people continually on the move. One dancer wore a double stole of coco-palm strips; sparks flew, torches flared. The exquisite flower-motif decorations of the *torana* shone in the fitful light of the resin, which flared up at intervals from the ground, when a stray spark fell on it. Then one of the whirling dancers became possessed; and another sheltered the small boy dancer during the other's madness. This seemed to me a charming touch.

Sometimes the dancers played ball with the torches, and, swinging their heads violently, beat them against the door-posts. Or the principal dancer, having oiled himself all over, would rub the torch on his chest and swallow fire, till his whole body was black with soot. A favourite trick was to fire the chest in curves to the rhythm of the drums. The correspondence between dancer and drummer was really thrilling; the rhythm on this occasion was dictated by the dancer.

We left, one may be sure, long before the end, somewhat worn out. But the people were too absorbed to notice our going. On that one can always count! And still the rain poured down.

CHAPTER III

The Kandyan Dancers at Home

19th December. We set off early to Kandy. The roadside houses as one mounts into the hills are enchanting in the variety of their architecture, and the country extraordinarily beautiful. The journey by train is really more sensational, though one gets a little tired during the four hours (for seventy miles) of perpetually meeting the engine of one's train coiling back on one out of the window. The scenery as one mounts gets continually more lovely; marvellous jungle, paddy-fields, mountain peaks, rivers flowing over smooth slabs of rock, golden pools, waterfalls, then miles and miles of slender woods, almost like England, except for the tree-ferns which suddenly delight the eye. One is reminded of the island of Bali by the narrow paths between the rice-fields, leading to enchanting palm and plaintain groves. But the temples and beautiful villages are missing; only a few dagobas beautifully set.

The Peradeniya Botanic Garden, one of the most famous in the world, is surrounded on three sides by a wide river. The situation is enchanting, high wooded hills rising, not oppressively, from beyond the river bank. There are lovely lawns, and avenues of palm— palmyra, coco and royal palms; above all a wonderful curving avenue of the silver-stemmed cabbage palm, an exciting perspective of silver pillars, crowned by the bright foliage of palm leaves. The spice grove which I remembered with such wonder from my earlier visit, thirteen years ago, seemed to me somehow less impressive now, perhaps be-cause I was not alone; but how lovely the creepers are that form a transparent but closely woven screen as if on a framework of their own stalks; and how curious the cannon-ball tree, that certainly has also a botanical name (!), with a crest of leaves high up, and all down the trunk a close armour of brown twigs and flowers and fruit like small brown cannon balls. The labels on the trees are so covered with damp that one cannot read their names, but there are so many unfamiliar ones that I would certainly not remember them. There are the rain tree, and many kinds of *ficus,* and that wonderful tree which I first saw in the Botanical Garden of Buitenzorg in Java, under which a Chinese boy gave me a Malay dictionary in 1934, and which has a trunk divided into thin stony walls of a lovely reddish silver. It may be that it is a speciality of Indonesia, since this one, *Canaria zeylana,* was evidently a Ceylonese variety. I identified at last the *Amherstia nobilis,* with strange beautiful butterfly-like waxen flowers of coral, with yellow splashes.

We drove rapidly through Kandy, not pausing this time to examine it, and turned up into the hills to the village where Guneya lives, and the whole of one clan of dancers. We left the car, and dived down a narrow path to the clearing opposite Guneya's house, where all the dancers have been trained. One looks down through plantain, breadfruit, jack and palm leaves to the paddy-fields, winding paths and background of mountains. There are four families, all related, now forming this hamlet; all at a little distance from each other.

Fogl disapproved of our straying, as being 'against tradition', as if one could ever hope to be anything else except by chance! So I strolled down towards Ukuwa's house (Guneya's cousin) since Guneya was not at home; and met, hobbling up through the trees, a very ancient man, belonging, it seemed, to the beginning of the world. He had the worried, wrinkled face, with soft inquiring light brown eyes, of an old monkey, fringed by white bristling beard and hair, and he leaned on a stick. One toe was missing, through gangrene of his left foot, evidently dating from long ago. He wore a sort of plaid shawl and was a very moving figure. He was once a great dancer; the teacher of Guneya, and of his own son, Ukuwa. We visited Ukuwa's house, while the old father, who said he was 105, went back with Fogl to await the return of Guneya. These houses are decorated with the skulls of bulls and smaller horned animals. The skeletons are enclosed in painted wood or clay, the houses left as they were. Ukuwa's house was almost like a big game hunter's; in the centre of the room was a tank open to the air, which I suppose fills with water when it rains, and is the bath. Ukuwa was also with Hagenbeck's circus, and has a few words of German. He lived for three years in Europe, chiefly in Germany. He has a definitely Western manner of presenting himself, in that he turns a smiling face on the audience, while Guneya has the concentrated, inward-gazing expression of the true dancer. Ukuwa was dressed in part of the Ves harness, but Guneya in all, with the high-crowned silver hat, with quivering brim of little hanging coins. What seems like a crown is really a hedge of seven upright silver ribs, round a bell-shaped metal crown, surmounted by a glass ball, which is firmly fastened on the top of the dancer's head. The skirt is of luminous white cloth, caught up below the waist into crisp, billowing flounces, and held by a wide belt or stomacher of blue or green or red leather, studded all over with glittering metal discs. Big earpieces, and heavy-looking, but very light-weight bracelets, and hollow anklets, filled with seeds which rattle with a small bell-like sound when the dancer moves, fall over the foot.

Ukuwa danced the *Conch-Shell* and the *Horse,* Guneya an *Invocation,* and both together the *Gaja-Ga.* There can be no doubt, to my mind, of Guneya's superiority. Heenbaba and Somadasa also danced invocations most admirably. There was also a most remarkable drummer; the dancer's command over the drum is authoritative and complete. The drummer had a dreaming face; he was entirely absorbed in the dance, as he stood swaying, the muscles of his back and shoulders violently working. The footwork of the boys and their agility is most remarkable. The old father expressed to Fogl his appreciation of the change which had come over the dancers since they had been in Colombo; he said a new spirit had come into their dancing.

It appears that in the time of the Kandyan kings only seven families were allowed to live together in a dancers' village, so that all might live by the land allotted to them. Each teacher had only so many pupils under his care. Now dancing is taught rather indiscriminately in Central Schools, and the old apprenticeship to one master has broken down. Promising dancers are sent to India to get a smattering of various Indian techniques, which they return to teach in Ceylon. Obviously the right way would be to get teachers from India, and let them teach, each the style of his own school—for no real teacher will pretend to teach any but the tradition in which he has grown up.

Fogl is much worried by the problem of sending twenty-one dancers to Calcutta to accompany the Sanchi relics; he can get no financial support, but has promised the dancers they shall go, and seems to anticipate a world-shattering reception which would prepare the way for them everywhere.

20th December. I dined with Malalasekara, who has a charming house and garden. Four of his six children were present. Chitra, now almost grown up, is a pianist and has won a scholarship at the Royal Academy.

According to Malalasekara, the headsmen are turning against Guneya's group, because they have left their village to settle in Colombo. But I cannot discover that they ever turned conspicuously towards them before. In fact they did nothing at all to encourage them.

21st December. I got from Fonseka at the museum library the name of someone in the rubber control department versed in *wannams*. Quite a lot of problems crop up. When were they first danced, apart from being sung? Were they danced as solos or by groups? Where do they come from?

This morning I went for an early walk in the lanes immediately behind the noisy thoroughfare of the Galle Road. Here are enchanting small rural houses and gardens ending sometimes in a field and a cow, and lovely flowering trees of many colours.

Tuan Bura, a Moslem from the east coast, came with a youngish, gaunt American woman, one of a trio who sing, dance and play the piano, and are persuaded that there is really no difference between East and West. She finds herself very well able to copy the dances and seems unaware that her hard American limbs cannot possibly render the technique of these dances, still less understand their spirit. She does, I believe, a sort of impressionistic hybrid.

Tuan described to us the *asram* of the Maharishi,[1] that fabulous old man of God, who in his old age has become the victim of a horrifying touristic visitation, his genuine holiness being considered in the light of a magnet for the numerous addicts of holiness who have little time to practise it themselves. The Maharishi clearly had had a strong personal vision and sense of vocation which set him indisputably apart for the service of mankind, not by active good works

[1] The Maharishi died last year.

72

as the West understands them, but by communicating what had been revealed to him in solitude. I have heard that he was ready to converse with those who wanted help in the conduct of their life. His help came in the form of very practical questions as to why they had chosen such a way of life, not of advice how to live it. The *Way* each man must discover for himself; but many had not even considered why they had embarked on their course at all, and when for the first time obliged to put the question and answer it, were forced to delve far deeper than they had ever done before into their own nature and motives, and slowly and perhaps painfully to discover a certain emptiness of purpose which turned all the laurels they had won to dust. The Maharishi did not advise or even suggest how to fill the void beneath all this activity; he only revealed it; and that was perhaps enough. Tuan Bura contrasted the primitive *asram* of the Maharishi, which was situated in a landscape of marvellous beauty, with the more comfortable and spacious *asram* of Sri Aurobindo at Pondichéry. This is a much more sophisticated *asram,* and certainly to myself more interesting. I visited it later, and confirmed some of the account given by Tuan Bura. If Sri Aurobindo became a visionary, it was by long study and contemplation, and not by sudden enlightenment that he achieved his vision. I must not linger on the subject of Sri Aurobindo's *asram* here. For it was only some months later that I went there with an introduction to Dilip Kumar Roy, the poet and singer, from Ignatia, who could also boast a personal letter from the Saint himself. Sri Aurobindo had no direct communication with the inmates of his *asram*; all his contacts were through the medium of The Mother, that mysterious French woman who as far as I know alone held converse with him. I never went to a *darshan,* i.e. the yearly occasion on which Sri Aurobindo appeared for one day in public. I heard that the editress of the American *Vogue* flew all the way from New York to gaze on him, sitting in silence beside The Mother, who presumably was transmitting spiritual force to those who gazed. Gifts were brought on this occasion, and afterwards I heard that the single occasion had been multiplied to two, perhaps because Sri Aurobindo felt his end approaching. He died last year. One has such fascinating memories of the *asram* that they must wait till there is time for them to be expanded.

22nd December. We visited Mr. Kottegoda of the rubber control department, whose speciality is folk-songs of the south; he told us quite a lot about the masked plays of that region, performed, he said, chiefly at Matara. The stories he told are those of *Kolan,* precisely as I afterwards saw it at Ambalangoda.

The subject of the first one he described is that of a king and queen who were attacked by a brigand. The queen fell in love with the brigand, and when the king, during his fight with the brigand, fell, with the brigand upon him, and called for his sword, the queen gave it instead to the brigand, who killed the king with it. The queen goes off with the brigand. They come to a river. The brigand says to himself: 'If she so quickly gave up the king for me, will she not much more quickly still give me up for someone else?' And he decides to rid himself of her. He told her he would swim across first, with her clothes and all her jewels, and return to fetch her. The queen undressed, and the brigand swam across, and went off, leaving her half-naked on the river-bank. She digs a hole to hide her nakedness, and gets into it. Two gods look down and enact a parable. One changes into a jackal, the other into an eagle. The eagle drops a piece of meat on the river-bank; the jackal sees it, but in running along sees the image of a dog carrying a piece of meat in the river, jumps in after it and is swept away. The eagle reads the queen a Buddhist lesson on *Maya* (illusion).

Another story is of two peacocks in the Himalayas. The king of Benares falls in love with the pea-hen, and kills the peacock with his arrow. He is revived by some god or other and carried up to heaven. The pea-hen laments for him and refuses to yield to the blandishments of the king.

Kottegoda thinks the *wannams* were introduced into Ceylon by the Tamil kings, and compares them with the texts of *Bharata Natya.* He thinks dance always formed a part of them because the end is obviously intended for dance, and he thinks the fact that they were danced in procession changed their character, and made them rely less on *mudras* and facial expression; but it may be we see now a degenerate form. It seems there was an early Buddhist attempt to suppress devil-dancing in Ceylon, but in vain.

We had called earlier on Fred Fogl, and confirmed the *Kohomba*

Kankaria for today. We were to call for him at 2.30. At about 12.30 a message came to say that it was 'off'. A telegram had just come. I went down to see him at the office, and proposed that we should go all the same to Kurunegala and see what had happened, for this is the third time they have put us off, alleging that it must be on a Wednes-day or Saturday and that several days' previous purification was neces-sary. Fogl was adamant; he absolutely refused to go.

I was, I must confess, extremely annoyed. He promised to come round to see us at 2.15. Instead of coming he sent a very curious and huffy letter to Ignatia, advising us to rely on his 'enemies', and get things done by them. His messenger, a clerk in the office, said that the *Kohomba Kankaria* cost three thousand rupees, and that was why it could not be done!

In hastening to join Ignatia and go to the museum, I fell and bruised both my knees. My unlucky day; the government of India refused a grant of money for which I had never asked; and then my 'offer' to give a lecture to the Ceylon branch of the R.A.S., which was really an acceptance of an invitation, was turned down.

At first it seemed maddening to spend these days in inaction, but my fall brought me somewhat to heel, and I am now content to read the *Mahavamsa* chronicle and note its dance references. The tourist bureau is sending someone round to see me, and Fogl proposes to come this evening.

Cedric Seneratne, Secretary of the Tourist Bureau, called, and we had a long talk about the possibilities of seeing dancing near Kandy. He is a friend of the guardian of the Temple of the Tooth, where one can go and see the prayer and drumming every day. Cedric Seneratne is a friend of Arthur Molamure and Harry Pieris, to whom the painter George Keyt had given me introductions. He knew Harold Acton, and belongs to a set of sophisticated people who are bound, one feels, to be the 'right' ones. We shall see.

23rd December. Looked up the *Mahavamsa* chronicle in the Museum Library, and found few references to dancing, but in the later *Culavamsa* there are a few very generalized references to *mandapas* built for dancers, and certainly a great deal about music for different instruments. I was interrupted in this by the arrival of Ignatia and Will Pereira, reputed a great scholar; he is certainly a man of great refinement and distinction. He lives with his only son of eighteen, who looks much younger and is desperately shy, in a tiny house in a distant suburb. He attributes the cessation of Kandyan dancing to the policy of the British in suppressing the temple schools, and the disappear-ance of women dancers to the bad behaviour of the troops, which led to the rebellions of 1817, 1834, etc. The Dutch, it seems, had been more encouraging to native customs. There was a famous dance school at Dondra, south of Matara. A Dutch captain was once wrecked off the coast, and all the crew and himself were kindly treated and clothed by the mayor of the place. Years afterwards, when his rescuer was head of a famous dance school, the Dutch captain was made governor of Ceylon. The governor sent for him to be brought to Colombo. It was assumed that this was for punishment (what a reflection on colonial government!) so he was brought in chains, until halfway they were met by messengers from the governor, saying he was to be brought in great honour. He and his family were rewarded by substantial grants of land which they hold to this day. The Kandyan chiefs were robbed of their lands by the British, so that the soldiers of the Napoleonic wars might be rewarded. They have never recovered their former position and with them have fallen the dancers who depended on them.

Ignatia and I went with Will Pereira to visit an astrologer who lives at Waters Meet on a mound above the sea, just beyond the fishermen's suburb of Mutwal, where there is an imposing Catholic church of the eighteenth century, with colonnades. The astrologer is very learned in all the Hindu laws of astrology, and a most interesting and lively man. He was at the School of Economics with Firth and Evans Pritchard. He has a great sense of humour. There is a touch, but only a very slight one, of the Serbian prophet Mitrinovich about him in appearance, as he used to be, but nothing of the charlatan. The astro-loger said that when Saturn is rising, proletarianism is in the ascen-dant. He foresees a victory for Communism in about seven years, and finally a victory for Churchill, symbol of Toryism, as Christ is used to symbolise the Church.

He talked about the *rishi*-horoscopes made thousands of years ago, but applicable to people now living. How this is he has no idea; but apparently one of these foretold Ignatia's life with remarkable accuracy, and the people involved in it; the loss and recovery of the Mendez' fortune, her association with Ram Gopal, etc. The astrologer told with what extraordinary accuracy the place of a man in his own family had been foretold, the number of his brothers and all his relations. Identical twins, he said, always have an identical fate. (In the case of the identical twins I know best, this seems disproved.) This astrologer does not cast horoscopes for money, but hopes to secure some *rishi*-horoscopes, and make money out of them in America. Apparently the soothsayer looks at a person's palm and then chooses a roughly appropriate *rishi*-horoscope from his store. It may be partly true, but is seldom altogether so. There is much to be inquired into about this.

We went down a lane to the fishermen's harbour, where once a great river flowed into the sea; there is now a beach and a lagoon with palm-trees. Three Hindu temples form a complex of buildings. There are all kinds of boats and sails drawn up on the grass, which instead of sand goes right down to the sea. It is an exquisite spot. A great globe-shaped wood rises behind. The beach is sheltered by a breakwater or quay made of huge blocks of rock, only roughly placed together, which have to be walked on with precaution as they are very irregular in surface and there are great gaps between them. On the left it is built up higher, so that the great waves which are breaking outside do not come over and drown the breakwater. At the end of this curving quay is a small watchtower, perhaps a lighthouse. There were catamarans, thick planks loosely bound together into rafts, and many unattached planks, almost pillars in thickness; also many outriggers which seem impossibly narrow; one cannot imagine how they are manipulated safely, but I have seen them riding in over the great surface waves near Madras. They have sails, as also have the catamarans. After we got home Kottegoda came and sang some charming folk-songs, and also gave us the names of several more *balis*.

24th December. Christmas Eve. Early to the fish market; two hens were brought to be felt and were immediately sacrificed. The colours of the fruits were lovely, and the passing carts with slim dark bodies, often marvellously posed and poised. Great circular crates full of fowls doomed for Christmas, or families of hens and chicks. In almost every shop, a melancholy radio. We drove through charming though poor streets, evidently dating from the Dutch occupation, with one-storeyed houses latticed, sometimes colonnaded, with raised loggias as in Jaffna.

At 11.30 Peter the cook announced a *thovil* just beginning in a lane near by, and took me there. It was in a bicycle shed. The preparations were not yet finished, palm-leaves were being spliced to make the decorations on the plantain offering-stands. A young woman suffer-ing from fever was wrapped in a clean white sheet and sat on a matting beside a banana-stem stand covered with palm-leaf offerings, hibiscus, areca-flower, incense, a torch. Opposite sat the drummer, and an old *Kattadiya*, also in a clean white cloth, with naked upper body, and an eight-pointed silver crown, with a silver chain looped between each point, danced with special concentration before her in the bicycle shed, with a torch in his right hand and a bunch of palm-streamers in the left. The space in front was taken up by a stand, with the usual palm-leaf decorations; several smaller ones, and one which seemed to be the cot-like coffin in which the exorcist would lie during his scapegoat period. After the old man had circled and twisted in front of her for some time, twirling his torch, swaying be-tween his knees, and touching her with the familiar 'wand' and torch, she fell over forwards and was held up and supported by another young woman and a boy. Her head hung back, propped against the wall, her eyes squinted. I stayed some time, but as it was said to be going on till 6 p.m. I went home for a rest. When I returned at three o'clock it was all over! I hope Toni Mendez has been able to take a photo.

This evening an old friend of the family came to call, dressed in the old Sinhalese style. She was a rather handsome woman, but for two prominent teeth which seem common among the women here; through them she sucked in her breath in a rather disconcerting manner. She talked in so low a voice that I could not hear what she said; only raising it at intervals to discuss some household economy. She is, it seems, very careful about food, but ate heartily of the choco-late wafers. Just as I was looking for an opportunity to make my escape, she suddenly began a fascinating story of how her second husband, who was apparently a very handsome and elegant man, 'bought', by offerings made to the temple, an old stucco tile from a temple in the hills. She refused to travel in the same car with it, and protested against the theft. She would not have it in the house, and as she could not persuade him to return it, it was banished to his office and put away on a high shelf. From that moment everything went wrong. He had continual frights at night, dreaming someone was clawing his throat and threatening to kill him. He did not tell her at the time the cause of his nightmare, but she knew it was connected with the tile. At last things reached such a pass and his health grew so bad that they arranged to take a trip to Rangoon, and booked their places secretly. He seemed to be better for a while, but in Rangoon had another such bad fright that he confessed to her that he was threatened with death and had decided to give back the tile. They gave up the further journey they had planned and returned on a Dutch boat. It was the day of the birth of Princess Juliana's first child, and there was a fancy-dress party on board. She possessed an orange *sari* which she gratified the captain by wearing at a fancy-dress ball. Her husband went early to bed, and when she joined him she found he could not move, and next morning when they landed he was completely paralysed and had to be carried ashore. The tile was returned, but things had gone too far, and he died soon after.

She went on to tell that some months later she woke with a sense of great fright; she could not get better; so at last a devil-doctor was called in who gave her a charmed amulet. At first she refused to wear it; but it was put under her pillow, and when she was obliged to admit its good effect, she consented to wear it. She is a great character; indeed, rather formidable.

No news of Fred Fogl or his plans.

We went to midnight Mass at the church in Pettah where all the poor shopkeepers of the quarter go. It was already very full, though long before midnight, particularly of English sailors, and many babies, who squalled during the whole service, and had, too late, to be removed. It was a rather Protestant kind of service unfortunately, the priest being extremely gloomy and dull. A vast number of communicants; but both singing and organ were vile. Came home at 2.30 to eat a magnificent Christmas cake and drink cherry brandy.

25th December. Christmas Day. We visited Ignatia's convent; the Mother is Irish and so are all the Sisters; all very sympathetic and gay.

The Kandyan Dancers at Home

To the fishermen's beach again; the men were balancing their long narrow canoes and plank-rafts with extraordinary dexterity as they approached them to each other in drawing up their nets.

I finished writing my broadcast, of which Ignatia highly approved.

Tonight the sewer-cleaners, dustmen, bathroom- and latrine-cleaners came, and did a perfunctory dance with drum and pipe.[1] This morning we had seen one painted mauve, with a yellow face to represent a tiger. But this evening they were all in white. They did a small amount of hopping and swaying, but went away directly we gave them something.

[1] These menial tasks are performed by Rodiyas, a mysterious caste of scavengers—of royal descent—degraded owing to the cannibalism of a princess, but proud of their origin and culture.

Kandyan drummers

Pantheru dancers

CHAPTER IV

Monarakande—Bali for Sederaman

26th December. We set off at 5 a.m. Quite dark still and the roads empty, except for a queer group of people walking along with pillows! A cloudy dawn, then suddenly it was day.

Winding gradually up into the hills we passed many houses among the trees, thatched thinly with straw, with the ends left un-trimmed, paddy-fields chiefly under water, with green rice sprouting as we rose higher. They had the varied, patterned, terraced character of the Javanese *sawahs* near Bandung. Sunday markets.

The rest-house of Belihul Oya is most attractive, with a natural swimming pool; a deep, clear green pool among the rocks of the stream which rushes down beside the house. From here on the scenery became ever more exciting. We wound above ranges of hills some-times lost in the clouds, above many tea plantations and grey leafless rubber groves. Then began the lovely grevillea, with delicately ser-rated narrow leaves, and the spreading albizzia, looking at a distance like cedars or Scotch pines, spathodea in glorious bloom, with great orange cups.

We skirted the hills, dipped again, then started rising by hairpin bends to Monarakande, the hill of the peacock, where is the bungalow belonging to W. D. Fernando, who lends it to Ignatia to entertain her friends in. It has a terraced garden with lawns and many flower beds; a rose garden, mauve potato-tree in flower, every shade of tree hibiscus, magnificent canna in great variety. The garden had been rather denuded of flowers for the funeral of a young planter who had died of typhoid in the very nursing-home where his wife is expecting her first baby in a few days.

The house, built originally by Sir Thomas Lipton, is very solid, simple and extremely comfortable. The house is full of magnificent

F

tiled bathrooms, each matching the bedroom to which it is attached. It is a lovely place to play hostess in, and Ignatia does it to perfection. The view is superb, over a landscape of mountains which were hidden in mist when we arrived. The garden drops suddenly to the tea plantations, and cows wander occasionally on to the lawn and remain there to graze.

Across the valley a steep rocky hill leads to Alpine slopes; high up also are the 'coolie lines', and a tea factory. I climbed up through the plantations beside running water, through several 'coolie lines' which are not villages but rows of what look more like up-to-date pig-styes, one to each family, with corrugated iron roofs and cement floor; between the rows, a wide cement-paved street, and a common pump or perhaps a well. Brilliant-coloured *saris* were hanging on the bushes to dry, and women with nose ornaments and necklaces, looking very picturesque and not too dirty, emerged to look at me, so far less orna-mental! They were very courteous and not tiresomely interested, though a group of little boys, who thought I must have lost my way because I was going in the opposite direction from the bungalow, fol-lowed me a little way, hoping to make me realize my mistake. I climbed from line to line, up steep flights of rocky steps; they are built on terraces looking almost like fortifications. The situation is certainly glorious. I was told that attempts have been made to build better houses and introduce sanitation, but without success. It is no doubt more convenient to regard these people as unreformable; but I believe that one of these attempts was proving very successful. On a walk I saw from afar a charming looking thatch-roofed village, as different as possible from the cheerless 'lines'; and found, on inquiry, that this was a village which had been built for the workers in the tea plantations. It may even have had a temple, who knows? It takes some time for slum-dwellers to become accustomed to better condi-tions, and able to use their unaccustomed privileges, whether the slums be in London or Madras. The London schools evacuated during the war had not been famine-stricken materially, no doubt, but the squalor of their accustomed surroundings was certainly no less degrading, and it was only by infinite patience that the unreform-ables were gradually changed from destructive hooligans into co-operative and delightful human beings. Few have enough patience, or enough love, to see the change through, and to discover the creative possibilities in a crowd of starved individuals.

Their employers say they would like to get rid of them; but I wonder! They would have to pay their own peasants more, so salve their conscience with the reflection that these coolies are better paid than they would be at home, and their keep is guaranteed. They cer-tainly live in wonderful surroundings; with the most glorious views in the world. But I still remember that one experimental village which had succeeded, and wish I had been able to visit it.

The clouds lifted, and I had a sensational view of the mountains on the way back; towards sunset, which we sat long watching from the terrace, the peaks emerged one by one, a single splendid rocky mass overtopping the rest. Wisps of snowy cloud hung about the sunset; a silver lake seemed to be hanging high up in the hills. It became quite cold, and we had a fire, and I a hot water bottle in bed, though it was so warm when we arrived that I could not believe it would ever be cold again. The Gotteliebs who manage the estate came to dinner. I had been told he was very small, scarcely four feet high, and pre-pared a tactful reception for a dwarf, dimming my height as much as possible. A giant of six foot five entered. Ignatia's little joke!

27th December. A glorious sunrise, the last crescent of the moon, and one very bright star. The mountains emerged from the mist, marvel-lously clear, though dreamy; and very blue in outline, with faint mists lying between. Though the earth is in general bright red, the hills have a greyish surface, corrugated with green forests. The out-lines of the high mountains are most lovely—one long wisp of snowy cloud simulating a lake. Ignatia told me that W. D. Fernando's wife, a pious Buddhist, for whom nevertheless a magnificent *bali* had been held during her last illness, chartered a private plane and flew above the great Vihara at Anuradhapura when the ruby was set in its summit, and scattered flowers and blessings. This was *mal vu*, for she had, of course, no right to be *above* a Buddhist shrine. There is a small round look-out built by her, in which a lamp always burns towards the shrine of Skanda at Kataragama.[1]

---

[1] In a posthumously published monograph, entitled *Kataragama*, Paul Wirz refers to it as the holiest spot in Ceylon, for Buddhists and Hindus alike. *Kataragama, Die heiligste Stätte Ceylons* can be obtained at the Birkhauser Verlag, Basel, and is a most interesting document.

It is now afternoon, and I am lying under the honey-flower tree. Clouds have covered all the mountains which this morning were fascinatingly clear. I went for another long walk, winding above another valley, and saw the sea glittering along the horizon. The tea-gardens were full of twittering coolies, who keep them in beautiful order, weeding and trimming.

I passed a great rock at a bend of the road, from which a chimney seemed to emerge. Below the rock was a plantation of spears, each shaft decorated by a little bracket from which dangled small bells and discs. A bell hung from the top. There was also a clay jug, in the form of a horned Buddhist lion. When I climbed level with the top of the rock, I saw the chimney was a *lingam*. A group of clay animals, some horned, stood on the top of the rock, looking out towards Katara-gama.

Saw kingfishers, butterflies and many wild flowers—the same as ours, but with a difference. We visited towards evening the tea-factory, and watched all the processes. Most agreeable of all was the scent of the fresh leaves as they lie on their shelves to be dried. The tea is picked over by hand, and the refuse piled into a great heap, which is actually sold and used for tea! We met a crowd of Tamil tea-pickers on the way back. One old woman had lovely gold orna-ments, nose-studs and necklace. Some of the girls were exceedingly pretty.

The mountains which looked so clear and illumined earlier this evening are now completely hidden and towards the east where I saw the sea this morning, only solitary peaks rise out of a lagoon of mist. The great brilliant cumulus clouds must have foretold rain, as it is now coming down in sheets.

A few Tamils came down this evening to the bungalow just as it was getting dark, to show some dances. One was a boy dressed like a girl in a short flounced skirt, and jumper with short sleeves, earrings and necklace, and belled anklets. His hair was bobbed and very thick. He wore dark glasses and was powdered with gold dust. On his head he balanced, very badly, a brass pot with a high erection of paper flowers, conical in shape, on which was perched a paper bird. His face was throughout completely impassive. He did some very elemen-tary dance steps, with balancing arms, accompanied by two drummers with flat, tambourine-like drums. It was a singularly poor performance, but I gave each one rupee. I suppose one would have given a penny in England, but this is Ceylon, and I am researching in 'oriental' dance!

28th December. I woke up in the middle of the night to see the sky full of blazing stars; it had seemed when we went to bed that the rain would never cease.

We started at 5.45. The last slip of the moon was clinging to the great dark orb; only at Fez and Assuan do I remember the old disc so clear. The sky was absolutely bright, though it was scarcely day, and dawn was just beginning. The lunar landscape was marvellous as we wound down and down, endlessly as it seemed, always with a shifting panorama of mountains. After the turning to Haputale began the Patanas: red hills, rolling one after the other, and covered with long coarse grass, which of course in the distance does not show as grass, but only gives a kind of sheen to the hills. We wound down through a much less inhabited region to a military station where during the war was a German prisoner-of-war camp. Some of the country is delicious, and a little like England, with rolling meadows and streams. No tea plantations, but paddy-fields and woods.

Welimada: a rest-house in a charming situation, in a garden on a hill overlooking the village, which never really is a village, but a line of ugly little shops. We wound up a stream overhung by jungle-covered hillsides to the botanical gardens of Hakgala—a most delicious place with lotus-pool and tree-ferns; also an avenue of magnificent conifers. Further along the road is a little shrine to Rama, Sita and Hanuman, above a delicious stream which cascades down rocks over-hung by tree-ferns, dark rocks, in which are curious deep round holes. This is called Sita Eliya—the light of Sita. Here she is supposed to have been kept by Ravana, and in this pool she must have bathed. When Hanuman came in search of her and could not find her, he set fire to the whole place and burned down Ravana's city. Since then the earth round here has been black. It was after the destruction of this palace that Ravana is supposed to have carried Sita away to the cave in the wonderful valley which I had visited with Malalasekara in 1935 on my first journey to Ceylon, and which Hugh Nevill has described so vividly in *Taprobanian*.

Seven miles beyond Hakgala is Nuwara Eliya (Town of Light), a gay pleasant place, and the coolest in Ceylon; still much frequented by the former Empire Builders. It lies at the foot of Pidurutalagala, the highest mountain in Ceylon. Trees and flowers abound on the road thither, and also in the Patana hills; datura, and mimosa of a rather slender species.

After Nuwara Eliya we rose to the Ramboda Pass, and again descended by hairpin bends to the valley, past sensational waterfalls and tea estates. As usual the tea-factory occupied the finest position, but the coolie lines are also magnificently placed; the horrid corru- gated iron roofs and grim partitions make them look more miserable than perhaps they really are. The whole drive was of the utmost beauty, though we passed too rapidly to remember its details. But I was grateful to the Mendez for giving me this opportunity of seeing so glorious a landscape even cursorily, especially as the occasion was of no particular interest to them; as it was to convey me to stay with the de Silvas whom they did not know, in order to assist at a *bali* ordered by his family for a certain dance teacher, Sederaman by name, in the neighbourhood of Kandy; a *bali* unconnected with devil- dancing or exorcism, and therefore one of the few admitted by Buddhism, since its sole object was to bring blessing, and to avert a dimly sensed danger; what particular presage made his family aware of this impending evil, whether it was presaged by the dropping of the dung of cobras, lizards or crows, or by the appearance of a black ants' nest, who can tell? Sederaman had read in the vernacular news- paper Ignatia's advertisement about my wish to see such ceremonies as might be in progress, and had written at once to invite me. Throughout my stay in Ceylon he proved a disinterested and valuable friend.

We lunched beside the river in the Peradeniya Botanic Garden under a *Canaria zeylana,* and I identified a few more superb trees.

We called on Sederaman at his small house up a grassy lane just off the Kandy road, oddly numbered 504/1. He was not at home; his wife only knew that he had gone to 'town'.

I was dropped at the foot of the climb to the de Silvas' bungalow. The Mendez, not knowing them, thought it incorrect to take me up. It is indeed a formidable climb for any ordinary motor-car, high above

the town, scarcely a made road, and with startling bends. The bungalow is in a rather ruinous condition, though the garden is most
lovely, and the ruinous condition is the result of Minnette being an
architect, and in process of rebuilding the bathroom shared by her
and me. Perhaps the corrugated iron roof adds to the air of imperma-
nence. The railway station, which is immediately below the house,
though at a considerable distance, did of course exist when George de
Silva built his house, but the quiet must have been absolute then.
Now quite a lot of puffing and shunting and snorting goes on at certain times; but the view across the valley is glorious, to wooded hills
and one overtopping green peak—which was later to prove my
Philippi.

The formidable George de Silva, of whom I had heard so much,
was at tea. I listened in vain for the malapropisms of which I had
heard so much and which were supposed to denote his lack of
scholastic education! They are a tribute to the invention of those who
had never met this remarkable self-made man, and those quoted were
certainly funny, but they were *not* made by George de Silva. One can
well imagine after seeing him that he would become the object of
unkind criticism, for he is extremely irascible and domineering, and
was surely always in the opposition, when he was a member of the
government, and held in succession various important posts. In the
capacity of Minister of Health, he extended the hospital on a hill
above Kandy, and planned many small hospitals which would certainly have been a boon to villagers who could not make the journey
to Kandy or Colombo. But originality is seldom welcome to bureau-
crats. The Minister of Health was accused of wasting public funds;
and took it so much to heart that the last years of his life were spent
in getting justice done. But London was far away, and though of
course he won his case, it was at the cost of much worry and expense. Meanwhile, his family had to suffer not only the wasting of
his substance, but the irritation of a wounded lion. His daughters
have inherited his toughness and purpose. Mrs. de Silva is vague,
charming and intelligent, and worships her masterful husband, but
one imagines she has a rather tormented time. She is a kinswoman
of Dr. Nell, one of the most learned men in Ceylon—familiar with
every aspect of village life and every corner of the country.

Monarakande—Bali for Sederaman

A message came from Sederaman, while we were at tea, saying the *bali* would begin at six instead of seven, and instructing us how to get to the place; but though we went late it had by no means begun. Minnette, though delighted at the idea of going with me, was never punctual in starting. Rain, rain, rain. We found our guides at a village eight miles away, near which is a dancing school presided over by Sederaman's father. We climbed in complete darkness, by the light of rather feeble torches, up extremely slippery, muddy paths—scarcely paths—and round tree trunks, sometimes so steep that one could only cling like a fly to the face of the bank—through coco-palm groves of which one was only conscious of the tree trunks. First we came to a white house from which, out of a bare clean room, shone a welcome light. But this was the priest's house and not for us. We climbed further, led by a cheerful man who 'talked' French, and contrived to say 'doucement' at every other step, while he propelled one up the slippery slopes.

The rain poured down ceaselessly, and I was frightened lest Minnette should want to turn back even before getting there!

At last we reached the school, a pavilion with thatched roof and open sides (like a *kalari* in Malabar) except at one end where the clay figures had been set up which had been made that morning for the ceremony.

The *bali,* as I have said, was ordered by Sederaman's family to counteract certain dangerous influences which his horoscope showed to be at work. The figures, over life-size, were of Mars, Saturn and Rahu (the eclipse-demon). They are shown in one of the illustrations to Upham's *Buddhism.* The artists who made them were spoken of as 'artisans' by Sederaman in his letter. Mars was by Sederaman's father, who is at once dancer, drummer and image-maker. All the figures were executed with the utmost splendour and variety of costume. They will be kept for three days, then taken into the fields and turned face downwards. The colours are made by the artists themselves out of earth, tree bark, etc. The wood used for the frame of a *bali* image has to be cut fresh and should be cut straight. The clay is mixed with powdered sandal-wood, milk and water, puddled to a proper consistency. When the moulding of the figures is completed they are painted according to the directions given in books. A temporary shed

88

is erected for the preparation of the image. It must be square, its floor smooth as a drum, and purified by coating it with cow dung and sprinkling with milk and water; the roof covered with a white ceiling cloth and the sides with painted cloth. The apartment should be lit with many lamps, and decorated with tender coco-palm leaves, flags and flowers; the ceiling with tender betel and other leaves placed in position at the west end, facing east, and sprinkled with scented oil. *Bali* is a Sanskrit word meaning an invocation, an offering of appeasement, and is used as a generic term for ceremonies which have as their main feature appeals and offerings made to the planetary gods whose influence is prevalent in the life of the person for whom the image is made.

The performers in *bali* ceremonies are known as *eduras* (masters of the craft). They have to possess a knowledge of astrology, as the ceremonies are based on the planetary aspects governing the life of the *atura* (the person on whose behalf they are performed). The *bali edura* should also possess considerable knowledge of the art of moulding and painting the various figures required for the ceremony, and be fully acquainted with the verses and invocations relating to the craft.

At the opposite end from the images was a low seat covered with a white cloth for the 'patient'. Soon he came in, carrying a bouquet of flowers for Minnette and me. This was my first meeting with Sederaman. He is a smiling, open-faced and most amiable man, who cannot really talk French, though he was some years in Paris. He is one of those who went with Hagenbeck to Hamburg. Mr. de Silva tells me that Hagenbeck was an agent in Colombo who stocked German boats with fruit and also collected animals for his zoo; with the elephants' keepers he took over the Kandyan dancers, as another kind of wild animal. I met later a Sinhalese whose father had looked after the German interests at the beginning of World War I, and who has, it seems, a mass of letters from Hagenbeck, which must surely be of considerable interest.

The father of Anura, the little drummer whom Ram Gopal discovered in a London music hall—a dignified man in a splendid black velvet sarong, was introduced. He too had illusions about his languages, having visited Germany, France, Belgium and Italy with the Italian impresario Marinelli. This 'Tourist' troupe performed at the Moulin Rouge on the Place Clichy. The wonder is that they have retained their Kandyan character to such a remarkable extent. I have dealt with this strange episode in an article which appeared first in *Ballet,* and will be reprinted in a forthcoming book of essays.

The 'patient' was covered up in a white sheet, face and all, during most of the ceremony. His little pupils were grouped round his feet, and immediately in front were the eight objects for the warding-off of spells; among which were a tiger's nose bone, a rice pounder on which his feet rested, a coconut, rice, areca-nut flower, and a mat.

Sederaman's father is a magnificent dancer. All the *eduras* were related to the 'patient' in some degree, and all belong, I suppose, to the village of Matadeniya, of which one scarcely became conscious on that rainy night among dense coconut groves.

The first *Kattadiya* entered at 8.30, in an elaborate white turban bound with braid, long earrings, naked body, gold bracelets, a white cloth with red embroidered border and a red sash. There were two of these, one being Sederaman's father, from whom all have learned. Torches now light the figures, and torches are stuck round the frame of plantain. Incense smoke covers the offerings. A third drummer enters, dressed like the others. Cymbals keep the beat, floreated by the drums, with great variety of rhythm and tone. The family sits round the feet of the *atura* (Sederaman), as well as his little pupils. A small crowd collects at the far end of the loggia. The third drummer, to make up for having cymbals instead of a drum, wears more bangles than the others, and a chain of beads round his neck. The dancers vied with the drummers in virtuosity of invention. Sederaman's father made play with a four-pronged torch, in the shape of a Greek cross, which he whirled perilously near the arch of paper roses framing the patient's end of the *kalari.* This paper arch was most ingeniously made in imitation of the beautiful materials which were formerly used. He also at times rubbed his arms and chest with the flame of the torch, but without any sign of being in trance.

The great drumming family is that to which Anura belongs; but for the unlearned it is difficult to distinguish between the virtuosity of the grand old man who was introduced to us as Anura's father and that of Sederaman's father, who is also prodigious in his drumming.

It is said that the first *bali* recorded in the *ola*-leaf books, was under

Parakramabahu VII (fifteenth century) when the Court was at Kotte in South Ceylon. The story goes that Brahmins came from India and made *balis* and collected money which they carried back to Malabar. Two learned Buddhist priests of Ceylon frequented these ceremonies and one of them memorized the procedure and wrote it down. He said to the Brahmins: 'There is nothing wonderful about this; even our children can do it.' And he sent a child to fetch the books.

The *eduras* raise and circle the torches round their heads and the children cry out. Now they wave the torches before the clay figures, addressing themselves particularly to the central figure, Graha-mangale; for this is a joyous ceremony relating to the position of the planets (*graha*). There is a quick ringing of bells and whirling of torches, with answering cries from the pupils, sitting on the ground at their master's feet. Two drummers are seated behind the *eduras,* one on each side.

A sort of swaying dance begins, of the *eduras* with their torches, moving from foot to foot. The dance grows more excited and the torches are replaced by others. They change direction, advancing behind coiling arms, stepping backward, sideways, circling, with many varieties of footwork. Sederaman's father dances admirably; sometimes the lines face in opposite directions, and again they whirl. The clank of the bells never ceases. The old men leap high; an excited phrase is followed by a sudden pause; then continues in a calmer measure, till it again grows to a climax. Now the lines face inwards and outwards, and seem after every three beats to change direction. After another long phrase all kneel for a moment, and again very slowly change places.

Now the bell rings every six beats, while the feet continue the rhythm and the drum floreates.

An attendant changes the torches.

They tell stories of how the torch came into existence, reciting a well-known ballad. And while reciting they never cease to dance and brandish their torches.

They call on the *atura* to look on the clay figures. A swift and diffi-cult dance figure is led by Sederaman's father, while Anura's father drums.

There is a rapid shaking and trilling of bells.

Now two of the dancers retire. The four remaining ones describe very exact figures, with stamping feet and whirling torches. The dancing becomes ecstatic on the part of the old father. The first place is always given to the elders. How wonderfully they dance, with great intricacy of steps and curious posturing! Now each in turn performs in front of the *atura,* leaping and pirouetting.

The elder now leading is a practitioner of the ancient Vedic system of medicine who has retired from dancing but returned to-night as an amateur. He is vastly agile and inventive; every evolution in space seems to be at his disposal. Finally he retires panting, and a younger man takes his place. The measure consists of two continually repeated bars. All the dancing is done between wide knees; very agitated swift spins, high jumps with both feet at once forward and back.

The doctor returns, and serves this time as passive partner to a technically superb young man, who seems to be inciting to even more difficult feats, inventing remarkable combinations of movement, with vibration of the torso, and crossed legs with knees bent. Much of this is certainly improvised, one technical feat leading to another, till there seems no end to the dazzling display of bodily virtuosity. Sederaman senior, holding crossed sticks with a torch at the tip, passes the flame slowly across his chest and arms. Now the other end is also lit, the two flaming torches multiply, now three, now four; still ringing his bell he does elaborate evolutions with the wheeling circle, then hands it to another younger man, who makes obeisance, then dances with frantic art. Again the square forms. The same foot beats the ground three times in swift succession, each time placed at a different angle. This pattern of footwork is several times repeated, then suddenly changed, with exciting effect.

The eclipse-demon Rahu is shown in a female form, with yellow face and body, and long black hair. She has a red halo with flowers round her neck, a green flowered bodice, and stands on a blue uni-corn, a Himalayan sheep.

The *Graha-mangale* is surrounded by astrological figures, all *rakshasas* (demons). Yama Kala stands on a bust of Mahincante who holds an offering pot. Kala, dressed in a green bodice, with a yellow face, holds in one hand the sun, in the other a wooden weapon.

Above is a Naga head; two arms are orange and two yellow; a yellow girdle encloses a red skirt.

Visvakarman's eight upper arms hold utensils for work. He is blue and has a *naga* necklace. He has five heads; four peer out over his shoulder; two long arms, a striped and spotted *sarong*, of yellow, red and blue. He stands on a green bull, more like a dog.

Now a fourth drummer appears. The 'patient' holds a thread tied to the paper arch. It is now taken hold of by the old father, and a hibiscus flower is attached to it. All the dancers bow to each other with elaborate salutation. Anura's father, the master-drummer, holds a thread tied to an areca flower and recites. They all join in at the end of the cadence with a curious tremolo. They stand in two rows facing each other, and chant together. The patient under his cloth sits with crossed hands. Each sound ends with a queer vibration in the nose. The *mantras* (recited spells) are very long and rhythmically as elabo-rate as the drum rhythms. Each takes it up in turn.

Each period seems to be taken in a single breath. All hold bells with a glass bulb at one end. Now at last all ring together, like horses trotting, with bells on their harness. They recite meanwhile with increasing speed and continuity. The glass bulb is held forward in the left hand, and the dangling bell rings incessantly, propelled by the little finger.

The thread, held by the main *Kattadiya*, is censed, the two oldest reciters turn towards the patient, the bells stop, the recitation becomes a gabble.

At this point we were summoned to supper in a small house where Sederaman's old father lives, and were given a beautifully cooked meal prepared by his mother. We fed in a dark little room by candle-light, which I always find so sympathetic. I suppose I should have stayed all night, had I been alone. But as the ceremony was to con-tinue till 9 a.m. next day, I was obliged to yield to Minnette's argu-ments for leaving before the end. We were both wet enough from our previous walk in the rain, and though we felt rather uncomfortable at disturbing the ceremony by leaving, we stole away about half an hour after midnight, plodding in complete darkness down the path and over the tree trunks, made more slippery by continuous rain. As we crept gingerly down the slippery path, it was no longer raining, only dripping prodigiously through the dark boughs.

As we drove home a sort of false dawn lightened the sky.

29th December. I was much bitten by those tiny midges which played such havoc in Bali. The roof is of corrugated iron and towards morning the rain clattered down.

I promised to return to Matadeniya to take some photographs of the dancers in last night's *bali,* and particularly of the astrological images. I could not have Mr. de Silva's car, but it was arranged that Ratnayaka, the Minister of Food, should take me along.

The morning was lovely, but by the time Ratnayaka arrived it was again raining heavily, and after the gentlemen had had their talk, it was too late to think of taking photos. A car was promised for next morning, and I tried to appear duly grateful, though conscious of the disappointment of my hosts of last night, with whom there was no possibility of getting in touch.

30th December. Rain, rain. The car came, and though the light was obviously pretty hopeless, I went off to the village of Pujapitiya, the nearest point for Matadeniya, where Sederaman senior's school is. I recognized the path, which was even more rain-sodden than two nights ago. It is in an exquisite position among great coco-palm groves, above emerald paddy-fields. I hugged my Leica under my mackintosh, but I don't see how it is to avoid being penetrated by damp; I took some time-exposures of the images, also took some of the dancers, who had dressed themselves for the occasion. There was an admirable young dancer in Ves costume, and some little boys belonging to the father's school, which is, I gather, state-aided. One of them was already remarkable for his force and footwork. Two little girls danced, apparently a version of the rabbit-*wannam*, and the boy Nandana did a fine obeisance dance, very different from the version taught by Guneya, in that it was less obviously 'expressive'. This may have been the effect of the difference between their bodies. The images were to be destroyed next day and were already beginning slightly to disintegrate.

On the road back to Kandy I saw an elephant carrying in his trunk a huge bundle of green leaves, no doubt for his supper. He looked like a moving house . . . I never get used to their monumental delicacy.

The road from Pujapitiya is extremely lovely; oh for a ray of light on it!

Arrived home exhausted.

31st December. Still pouring without cessation! The damp seeps into everything; one's clothes feel quite wet, and generally *are*. We went down to the Temple of the Tooth (Maligawa). The morning drum-ming, from ten to eleven, was just finishing. Many women and girls were worshipping. One of the young drummers, by whom I was later always recognized and welcomed with a smile, has a most lovely figure. The temple court is splendid, with much fine carving, and I was delighted by a patchwork canopy of exquisite design and fresh colouring. All the pieces of stuff were made into flowers. In a small shrine I saw a crystal Buddha; the box in which it is kept is of ivory, darkened by age, beautifully carved and decorated with silver filigree. The ceiling was very dark, but I could discern some fine paintings.

We called on the Lay Head of the temple, who promised some dancing and drumming for the morning of the 5th.

Rain! rain! rain! and no precautions against the damp. These people must be as hardy as bears, and as impervious to damp as ducks with beautifully oiled feathers. From mid-day the rain came down in tor-rents, and towards evening it seemed as if the sky were falling, and as if the whole house and hillside must be swept away in the general liquidation. At midnight it suddenly ceased, and the noise of the rain was succeeded by the noise of crackers and ineffectual fireworks welcoming in the New Year.

CHAPTER V

Ves Investiture. Meeting with Wirz, Dolapihille and Others

1st January. I visited the temple early, where drumming and offerings were in progress. Streams of girls, young men and women, climbed the stairs continually, with flower-offerings on betel-leaf trays, and many worshippers were prostrated on the pavement. The drumming is very exciting and beautiful. There are different rhythms for different kinds of service. I must find out how far these are musical phrases, or express different ideas, as I was told is the case in the *bali* drum and dance duets.

Visited the museum, and saw a *Kohomba Kankaria* costume, which is the same as the *Ves* head harness, but apparently without the head-dress. According to the caretaker, it is possible to get a *Kohomba Kankaria* for fifty rupees if one is content with four dancers.

I saw a *Sokari* mask. This is a kind of comic drama, describing the arrival of people from Bengal. There are a few good *bali* and *kolan* masks, and many fine examples of Sinhalese crafts—knife-handles much resembling the Balinese kris, ivories, chessmen, etc. I was taken by the caretaker to see the audience-hall of the old palace, which contains some very fine carving, and much resembles the palace at Mandalay. We climbed over the foundations which are now being excavated.

On my returning to the museum, the assistant curator brought out suddenly a book which they had just acquired, asking if I could read German. It was Paul Wirz's *Exorzismus und Heilkunde auf Ceylon*, which had actually been published in Switzerland in 1941, but only just reached Ceylon, where German is not generally known. I asked if I might borrow it. 'It is not generally allowed,' said the assistant

96

During the *Kohomba Kankaria*

A *Ves* dancer

director, 'but as no one here can read it, I think I might lend it to you for a few days if you will promise to return it as soon as possible.' So with immense delight I carried it off, and all spare minutes there-after were spent in reading it. It is worth getting for its photographs alone. It can of course be ordered through any oriental bookseller. The full title is *Exorzismus und Heilkunde auf Ceylon, Verlag Hans Huber. Bern.*

In the afternoon we drove down exquisite roads, continually wind-ing above the emerald rice-fields, beside the Mahaveliganga, through coco-palm groves, to the spot where the elephants are taken down to bathe. This is a tourist speciality, and several cars of sailors and Indians were drawn up to watch the sight, as well as the elephants and their keepers.

To Nittegama and Amunugama by an immense detour, owing to the broken bridge swept away several years ago by a flood, and since replaced by a footbridge. Saw Jayana, the dancer sent by George Keyt to Bombay, where he studied *Kathakali* and *Bharata Natya*. He is a very handsome man, quite in the *Kathakali* style, with a long mane of smooth hair and well-modelled face. Arranged for a demonstration tomorrow at the dance school founded at Amunugama by Harold Peiris.

2nd January. Someone has come from Muladanda, i.e. J. C. Malaga-mana, whom I was later to know well, announcing an initiation ceremony, *Ves Bandhima* (binding of the headdress) for midday. This was in consequence of Mr. de Silva's asking him to give me notice of anything that was coming on. He was immediately kidnapped by George de Silva, and a long political discussion followed. Guneya also arrived, who was taking part in the ceremony. It seems that this is the *Ves* investiture of which Fogl had spoken and of which one is allowed to see all but the actual putting on of the headdress. We hired a car and went off to Muladanda, which I gather is one of the central schools at which Malagamana teaches. It turned out to con-tain a small Buddhist temple within its precincts. Minnette was also very glad to take part in this ceremony, but she does not much like translating, and is naturally preoccupied with her own architectural work. The drive as usual led past Katugastota, which is on the road to everywhere I want to go to. My camera being out of action did not matter, as I should not have been allowed to take photos. The school is on a little eminence just above the road. We took off our shoes and entered the courtyard. Opposite was the small temple where the investiture was to take place; to the left the dance hall, with open sides, and also open at one end. At one end of the court-yard was the *bhikkhu's* house, and opposite the entrance the small temple where the investiture was to take place.

We were met at the entrance by an old man, toothless, tall and ugly; the father of the boy to be invested.

The temple is very small, with modern decorations; a seated Buddha and two huge painted statues on either side. The walls are painted with ugly *douceureux* modern figures. There is a wide altar-table in front of the small altar, above which sits Buddha. Flower offerings were on it. Two curtains of modern flowered chintz, like four-poster bed curtains were tied to two posts. Adjoining this, to the left, was a small room full of dancers, and the trunks out of which they were taking their dresses. All belonged to Guneya's group. The other boys were dressing themselves, but Guneya himself dressed Sevranga, who when we arrived had only got on the pants and white flounced and pleated skirt, bound round the waist by a wide sash. His long hair was carefully combed by Guneya, who divided his locks while the dancer leaned forward, then tied the bunch up in a peak on his head with string. Round it was bound a red hand-kerchief, making a kind of turban. His bead-harness, belt, shoul-der-caps, bracelets and necklace were put on, but not the ear-pieces. The ceremony of investment is to be held in the adjoining little shrine.

Two more dancers are being vested, kneeling at their little trunks.

The *bhikkhu* (monk) arrives. Two small candles are lit, and the curtain is drawn across the doorway, shutting out all the children who had watched the dressing, but fortunately admitting us, the *bhikkhu*, Guneya and Malagamana, and the temple servant who kept the incense burning. The boy with the red handkerchief kneels in front of the altar, and is given a bowl of flowers to hold. Guneya and Malagamana stand on each side of him. They begin chanting. An alarm clock was stood on the altar, as it is important that the investi-ture should take place at the exact astrological moment, which turned out to be precisely midday. The clock now shows 11.45.

A coconut filled with flowers is in the middle of the flowers on the altar; the light flickers on the painted figures on the wall. Guneya keeps one hand on the shoulder of the initiate, Malagamana holds the headdress, which is presently consecrated.

The chanting is contained chiefly within the range of a minor third and in a slow rhythm, but gives way gradually to a quicker rhythm, and wider range of intervals. The boy's kerchief and hair are unbound and the string replaced by a red cord. Smoke from the altar rises round his grave face. Outside the curtain loud talking goes on.

There are twenty bangles in four sets, wrist ornaments, small tiger teeth amulets. Now with a new chant the headdress begins to be bound on and the little boys press through the curtain. The tension is relieved by a new rhythm. The headdress seems to take a lot of bind-ing. The kerchief is removed and one lock of hair is bound first. Now the front uprights are put on and fixed to a peaked headdress, and finally the whole glittering circlet, which Guneya binds with string.

Two dancers formerly invested were already in full panoply. It is now 12.10. The white cloth covers the initiate completely. He rises and lays his flower-tray on the altar. The drums begin. The initiate is led out veiled to the bo-tree in the courtyard and again enters the temple and makes obeisance. Now the cloth is removed. On each side of the entry is a drum. The *bhikkhu* passes a string round the boy's neck, over the white cloth round his shoulders.

Three *bhikkhus* chant over him; old priests with piercing eyes. We adjourn to the dance hall which is the main classroom of the central school. The three *bhikkhus* recline in armchairs. We are allowed to sit on a bench. There is a general obeisance all round by drummers and dancers. The aged toothless father of the newly 'confirmed' boy makes a particularly low obeisance. The boy is in the middle of the three dancers who are taking part in the performance. All are superbly dressed in dazzling white with brilliant leather belts and 'sporrans'. The oldest of the *bhikkhus* lies back with closed eyes during a long speech by the schoolmaster. The white cord put on by the *bhikkhu* still hangs round the neck of the newly invested dancer. A dog lies peace-fully at the oldest *bhikkhu's* feet. The beams are decorated with paper frills, very tastefully cut in imitation of the costly stuffs that once were used. Alas, they are no longer woven.

The speeches were greeted with applause. I grieve to say that the youngest *bhikkhu* referred to me as 'putting Ceylon on the map' and saying it was everyone's duty to show me as much as possible! Did I not surprise an ironical smile on the face of the oldest *bhikkhu*? I was shocked by this repetition of Fogl's favourite phrase, but hope to live down my disgrace!

The initiation ceremony is clearly over, but the dancing is to come. Fresh obeisance to the priests by drummers, dancers and the newly initiated. Immediately a very stately and impressive dance of invocation begins. They chant while dancing, very slowly advancing and retreating with forceful steps, facing each direction in turn.

The teachers and some of Guneya's group of dancers join in the chant. Again the drums burst out, and the dancers leap into the air. Wide crossed steps alternate with high springs in an orgy of movement. Finally it settles down and chanting begins again. The long streamers wave wildly from the point of the headdress. The initiated boy always takes the lead. He is certainly a magnificent dancer. His springy step and beautiful hand movements, as it were marking time, his syncopations sideways and forwards, his sudden leaps without preparation into a spin are quite intoxicating. Then in one frantic movement his streamer becomes detached and falls off. He is greatly agitated and unable to continue dancing till it has been replaced.

Hugh Nevill suggests that these streamers symbolize the Ganges flowing from Siva's head. They were a royal prerogative, and the *Ves* dancers, being part of the royal retinue, wore them by special privilege, so the agitation of the newly initiated becomes doubly intelligible.

Meanwhile a very fine figure is done by the two outer dancers, who with legs drawn high make terrific circles in the air.

Now the teacher takes a drum. The aged *bhikkhu* smiles gleefully; who knows what his thoughts are? In a slow movement all three together advance very slowly between wide knees and with a great flourish of turning arms advance and retreat. The *gajaga* (elephant) *wannam* is done by all: a very powerful but elusive rhythm with proud trunk movements. The newly initiated boy surpasses himself in energy; his head almost rolls off in the vehemence of its circlings; yet he never passes the bounds of Kandyan stylization.

The dancers now line up facing us, and the initiate gives out a rhythm of syllables. Guneya's two boys know the phrase and lead the flying movements and high leaps. This is a very graceful as well as violent dance.

The hawk (*ukusa*) *wannam* is done next; a winding motion, cautious progress and occasional big leaps.

Now Guneya enounces a syllabary; the dancers follow the rhythm exactly and the drums follow them. What is this fluttering of fingers? (I am told this is one of the first dances in *Kohomba Kankaria!*)

Then comes a slow, almost hesitating progress round the room, broken by leaps from two feet at once. Now the winding begins again with a tremendous crossing of legs. Sometimes they seem like whirling dervishes. Another very elaborate syllabary is enunciated by the teacher. The syncopations among the quick notes are extraordinary, and certainly altogether beyond my power to suggest in words.

At the end of each dance comes the *adau*, a kind of *sembah* (the Javanese stylized salute or obeisance). It seems that *adau* originally meant 'somersault'. This leaping with legs crossed must be extraordinarily difficult; such combination of power with lightness and swiftness of step is hardly to be seen elsewhere.

The old *bhikkhu* lies easefully in his chair watching the dancers. How strange is his heavy somnolence in face of those whirlwind spirits of the earth, their beautiful bodies gleaming with sweat, their glittering eyes and glances!

The old *bhikkhu's* fat dog strays on to the dance floor, quite in the spirit of Bali; and is pulled back by the younger priests, not at all in the spirit of Bali! And here I speak, of course, of the island of Bali.

A diversion is caused by a speech from the old father of the new *Ves* dancer; after which the action goes on again, with a series of whirlings. A vertiginous syllabary is enunciated by Malagamana for the drums. Presents are now given to the newly invested Sevranga by the priests, Guneya, Malagamana and ourselves.

Coiling arms seem to be a speciality of the Initiate. His undulating body and pointed hand take the shape of a cobra; at last with a great leap he is stretched on the ground, and sways from side to side, searching for prey. (How I should like to see him in the Balinese dance

Kebyar.) This dance is repeated in the air with wild ecstasy, and a series of dervish whirls brings it to an end. What a magnificently virile display! Just now it seems to me the finest of all I have seen.

Directly after the *Ves Bandhima* ceremony we drove to Amunu-gama, for the dancing arranged by Jayana, George Keyt's protégé, who had been sent by him to India to study various forms of Indian dance, I think only in Bombay. Jayana affects the appearance of a *Kathakali* dancer, with a mane of smooth hair. The mane does not make the Nayar, and I have an idea that Jayana has rather lost his way among so many alien influences. A family came from Kandy to watch the demonstration, which was not very impressive. We saw two *Ves* dancers; one of them, Rajapaksa, is extremely 'expressive', in fact violently over-expressive, with fine technique, no doubt, but unrestrained, and with such facial distortions as to make one quite uncomfortable. We at once thought he had been abroad, and learned what Europeans expect of a wild Sinhalese. But he has actually never left Ceylon. I can imagine that in a *perahera*, with all the noise of drumming, the elephants, the splendour, he might appear quite in the picture. But I did not really like him. He seemed to lack the restraint which is always in Kandyan dancing, in spite of its turbu-lence.

We were shown two small boy pupils who danced with great abandon and sang frenetically. One was like a large frog, and extra-ordinary sounds issued from his enormous mouth. But he has vast energy and no doubt will be excellent in time. It is no use starting off with restraint. There were about six girls who had only learnt six months, and were hardly yet interesting. Their rhythm was certainly very good; but the attempt to adapt the real Kandyan dance to girls does not seem to me very hopeful. Shanta Rao, who is in every way a phenomenon, and who has a magnificent dynamism which would surely in the great days of Vijayanagar have placed her among the royal Amazons, is the only dancer who could certainly master the Kandyan technique, and who did, in fact, win the highest praise from Guneya.

There was a long harvest dance, in which the song was obviously Sinhalese, but the figures, I think, Indian. It is in any case very laudable to get these village girls dancing again; and no doubt with time they will learn again the dance ballads collected by Hugh Nevill, such as the Water-pot dance (*Kalagedi*) and the comedy *Sokari* for which I saw a mask at the Kandy Museum, and find among the Nevill MSS in the British Museum in an amusing abstract.

The famous drummer Suramba refused to drum, because he hadn't his dress with him, and was in a dirty vest. Why I never discovered. He sat on the dais at the end of the hall and played the *tabla*, while his baby sat between his knees and toyed with cymbals, and moved to the movement of his father's legs. This is of course how Balinese babies learn to play and dance. In this quarter Sederaman is regarded as a dangerous innovator! I really don't know why.

It was a glorious evening, very fresh and clear, with marvellous stars.

3rd January. We drove up to the Tipperary tea estate, one of George de Silva's. It is in a marvellous position, overlooking ranges of mountains and oceans of bamboo, *waringin* and every variety of palm. The garden also is enchanting, all among the rocks, with many flowers, and there are green meadows under the rubber-trees. One looks down on emerald terraced paddy-fields. A cloudy but brilliant sky.

Went to a *pirith* in the evening—in this case the hallowing of a new house by Buddhist priests. They had brought in a brass model of a dagoba some sacred relics from the temple, which, to the concern of the occupier, they left there all night. There was a vase of coco-palm flowers, looking very much like ears of corn, and a thread which I saw later being unwound; it was attached to the relic-pot. There were also palm-leaf fans on the table, with ivory or tortoiseshell handles, with which the priests fanned themselves now and then during their chanting, waving them towards the worshippers who sat on the ground. When the new house is finished, which is being built by Minnette, there will be a two-day ceremony.

4th January. Early to the museum, not yet open. So I went to the library on the lake and read the *Culavamsa*. Found by chance a pamphlet on the *Plight of the Kandyan Peasantry*, by Albert Godamunne. I returned to the museum but was not allowed to take photos of the masks without a permit from the director of the museum at Colombo. The curator took down the names of those I wanted photographed.

I then went off to Pavilion Street in search of Mr. Godamunne, whom I discovered in his office. He received me very kindly and gave me his lecture and pamphlet on the Kandyan peasantry. More important still, he introduced me to Mr. Dolapihille, who, he said, knew more than anyone about Kandyan dancing and music, and about Ceylon in general. He is a mild, very gracious, middle-aged man, to whom I took at once, and arranged to visit in the afternoon at Meewature on the Gampola road.

Dolapihille lives in a little house which he built himself, on a small hill among trees, and in a garden, opposite the weaving school of Meewature. He was waiting for me in his garden. His house, not yet finished, is built in old Kandyan style, with fine solid doors and windows. I had a delightful time taking down his stories about the Kandyan aristocracy, *bandaras, Kohomba* and *Ves*. He is certainly very generous in giving me the benefit of his knowledge. He seems to me one of the nicest people I have met. I daresay very nationalistic in feeling, at least while the English were here, and resentful of the people of Colombo who, having done much to destroy old Ceylon, are now madly trying to infuse new life into it by introducing all sorts of alien influences.

Exquisite sunset. The gramophone or wireless which has been driving us mad for days during the celebration of a Muslim wedding somewhere down near the station, stopped abruptly this evening, after Minnette had rung up the police for the *n*th time. No doubt the wedding was over!

5th January. I returned today reluctantly Paul Wirz's extraordinarily interesting book on Exorcism in Ceylon, which has the most wonderful flashlight photographs of *bali* ceremonies, and many stories. One, I notice, comes from the Tamil romantic epic[1] about a woman whose bracelet resembled that of the queen, and who was obliged to sell it in order to supply her dissipated husband with money. The queen's necklace had been stolen or perhaps fallen into the water, and the jeweller reported that he had an identical piece in his shop. Though the queen did not recognize it as exactly like her own, the husband was impaled. His wife sought for him in vain and at last found him dead. Her vengeance was bought off by offerings. She is Pattini Devi,

[1] *The Silapaddikaram*, translated by Rumachandra Dikshitar (Oxford University Press).

104

and her husband Polanga Gurunanse. This story is curiously enough the subject of a coconut contest, *pol-gahanava*.

How odd it seems to re-read these stories as I then took them down, before I knew the whole of this strange and fascinating epic in its various versions. The Sinhalese ballad version told in Nevill's *Taprobanian* and in his MSS abstract of the ballad, is full of the strangest magic, and certainly more exciting, as well as more imaginative; in fact a terrific story of humiliation, lust, vengeance and magnanimity which reminds one somewhat of the happenings in Mazendaraan in Firdausi's Persian epic of the *Shahnameh,* where the demon king, to evade defeat, turns himself into stone.

The drums were beginning in the Maligawa Temple; girls, women and children were passing up the steps to the shrine of the Tooth with their offerings; till the wide silver table became heaped with flowers, frangipani, etc., and the scent was overpowering but ravishing. The frangipani flowers with their golden pistils are like huge wild roses. The movement of the worshippers is fascinating. The crystal and jade Buddha in his ivory and gold shrine is singularly lovely, as if illumined from within. *Kavi* reciters sat in an alcove of the Tooth-shrine, on the ground, and drummed and sang. The court was in session, and we heard that the Chief Judge would probably not allow dancing in the temple. A note was sent and he graciously gave his consent. Meanwhile we were shown 'authentic relics of the Buddha' found at Taxila by Sir John Marshall. They were curiously higgledy-piggledy: a bit of bone, a coin or two, all wrapped in loose fragments of cotton wool. The bronze vessels were wonderful; also a most beautiful gold tray, set with jewels, and a plain gold bowl with a lid. There were jewelled boxes for betel and areca nut, and a broom said to be made of the king's hair (in which case the king was a horse!)

The brass bell containing the relics is most lovely, and exquisitely jewelled. Cat's eyes are a favourite stone, and also the Sinhalese sapphire. The great doors were unlocked; their massive padlocks needed turning many times before the bars would open. The dagoba, containing a Buddha made of precious stone, and the Tooth itself, were hung, like a dancer's body, with wonderful jewelled embossed ornaments. Precious stones in abundance; huge amethysts, rubies, sapphires and the setting always extremely lovely.

The king's French brocade coats were all there, given in offering to the Buddha.

The dancing was not particularly good, but the setting was most lovely. More dancers introduced themselves as just returned from England! There followed the usual question: Did I talk German? After which the matter lapsed from sheer lack of vocabulary! They danced in a sunny court, Ukuwa exerting himself particularly, and there were some very fine moments. The problem now arises: If the *Ves* dancers wear masks, *when* do they wear them?

6th January. The day of the return of the Sanchi relics to India. In the morning I called on Seneratne and found he was in hospital with mumps, but saw Hulugalle, chief of the Information Office, and found him very sympathetic to the idea of *Kohomba Kankaria*. He recommended seeing Sir Richard Aluvihare, Chief of Police.

Fogl had gone off on an expedition down the Mahaveliganga at Christmas and has only just begun to collect money for sending the dancers. He says the religious feeling of Ceylon should oblige them to send the dancers, and at the same time 'fears the dancers will steal the thunder of the relics!' They will certainly be imposing, but it seems unlikely any money will be raised for sending them.

I saw the relics start from the museum in a shrine on a motor-lorry, while a loud-speaker brayed a speech. No elephants as advertised, only motor-cars, so the procession passed very quickly, and by the time I reached the jetty the proceedings were almost over. The dancers had performed at intervals along the route, and were now assembled on the edge of the jetty, among many Buddhist priests. The relics were already in their casket on the launch that was to take them to the steamer, which one saw trimmed with white sailors, who stood, like angels, all along the edge of the decks. A loud-speaker brayed without ceasing, sometimes in English, sometimes in Sinhalese, the voice actually coming from one of the priests; and they surrounded, I discovered, a reliquary. Was this also one of the Sanchi relics? The harbour was gay with boats, and launches left continually taking sightseers out. A big barge filled with noisy European children, went off screaming and cheering to see the relics start. Every plank and crevice of the harbour was covered with people watching the departure, mostly dressed in white.

7th January. I went early this morning to Caldecott and saw a magnificent display of dancing by Guneya and Lamuwa, the famous teacher from Kurunegala; also of temple drumming by a young man from the Maligawa, which was really quite extraordinary. What eloquence in the drums!

This evening I received an invitation to a film of Rodin, shown by Harry Pieris, secretary of the Forty Three Group. My atrocious memory for names was responsible for my not having realized that one of the 'right people' to whom I had been given a letter of introduction in Bombay was known to me from as long ago as my first visit to Ceylon in 1935, when I met Harry Pieris, then a young man studying painting in Paris, with a young Javanese friend. I think Malalasekara introduced us. I recall the almost nostalgic pleasure with which I saw again the delicate darkness of an Indonesian skin, after a month in South India.

Directly Harry Pieris heard from George Keyt or Martin Russell that I was in Colombo he sent an invitation to the film show. I at once took a great fancy to him. He is a very dear person, though slightly vague, and, as I was later to discover, extremely contrary.

Aloy Pereira, who takes, I believe, remarkable films of wild animals, and also has two films of the *Perahera*, was to show us one. But for some reason his film, which began with scenes from the Zoo, never got going. Unfortunately I did not meet him again, or have another opportunity of seeing his wild-life film; which I regret much since seeing in *The Observer Annual* of 1953 some remarkable photographs taken by him in the Animal Reserve at Yala.

I heard too late that the Director of Archaeology is taking some French ethnologists or archaeologists from the Musée de l'Homme on a five-day trip to Anuradhapura and the other ruined cities of Ceylon, and hoped I might be included in the party. But I am supposed only to be interested in dancing, and the learned director appears to have feared I might have begun to dance among the ruins!

8th January. I saw Vikramaratne at the Museum Library, known as 'Pandit' by Ignatia, a minor official, who is also preparing a book on *bali* ceremonies, and who was always most kind and helpful.

Called on Sir Richard Aluvihare, Chief of Police, a Kandyan who has also put notes together about dancing, and seemed inclined to be helpful about my seeing certain things, so he will possibly do something about it. If he persuaded the Ministry of Information to put on a *Kohomba Kankaria,* as he seemed to think would be possible, it would indeed be much.

Visited Kapukotuwa at the Ministry of Education, which was buzzing with small officials, all in a state of dither at the bare idea of a visiting card being handed to the Minister while someone else was in his office. He was very sympathetic; had studied Kandyan dancing himself for ten years, and wished to introduce it in its true form into schools. But he says they will have none of it, and only want 'oriental dancing', i.e. Indian? and sackfuls of Kandyan musical instruments lie, according to him, stacked unregarded in one of the offices.

Malalasakera called and asked me to lunch with a landowner near Ratnapura, with whom he hopes to arrange some dancing.

Read Hocart's *Temple of the Tooth.* He makes the interesting sugges/tion that the Tooth relic may have belonged to a Yaksha, as its great size suggests. 'The term Yaksha has come to refer to spirits on the whole evil; but in early writings they are not always clearly dis/tinguished from the gods. A fairy is spoken of as a "daughter of the gods", and addressed as "Yaksha". Even Indra, whose dwelling is in the sky, is addressed as Yaksha. The Buddha himself is described as a Yaksha. Yakshas figure so largely in Buddhist legend that one suspects that Buddhists were largely recruited from Yaksha wor/shippers. And it is a fact at the present day that the Sinhalese villagers in the jungle are simultaneously Buddhists and Yaksha/worshippers. Hence the conflict of two traditions: one which regards the Yaksha as a deity of the infidels and therefore bad, and the other which still reveres them as the ancient gods of the race, and uses it as a respectful title.'[1] Hocart remarks that in the Pacific today the same process can be observed; 'devil' and 'demon', introduced by the missionaries, stand for *evil* spirits, among whom are included the honoured ancestor gods, while the indigenous terms *atua* and *kalou* are applied to the Christian God and the native gods identified by the missionaries with the devil.

[1] Hocart, *Temple of the Tooth in Kandy.* Memoirs of the Archaeological Survey of Ceylon. Vol. IV.

I had tea with Arthur Molamure, at his sister's house. He is the brother of Mrs. Deraniyagala, a charming creature and excellent musician. Molamure has a wealth of knowledge. He told me many interesting things. It was, it seems, only in 1917 that temple dancers and *pantheru* and *udekki*-drummers took part in the *Perahera*. After this innovation the *Ves* costume, which used to be confined to *Kohomba Kankaria,* became the preferred costume of every dancer. There has been, he says, a gradual deterioration in the classical art, and introduction of acrobatics and sensational spins, which of course always formed part of the *Perahera,* as far back as Robert Knox (seventeenth century), but certainly were not classed as Kandyan dance. He seems to think that imitative animal *wannams* are an importation from India; it may be so, for in the *Bharata Natya Sastra* commentaries they certainly appear.

There is a Sinhalese book on dance technique, and many texts possessed by dancers, who guard them as jealously as do the great Indian gurus. They are a sort of family heirloom. They no doubt contain priceless information for those who know how to use it.

Molamure kindly promised to show me the 'pure' tradition in drumming and dancing; it did not unfortunately get beyond a promise. I gathered that Jayana had returned from India with long crimped hair like a *Kathakali* dancer but little else of India. He could only have a superficial knowledge, culled in Bombay. I remember, however, that an indulgent headmistress allowed me to take a class in Greek conversation, on the model of the Perse School, when I was myself only at the learning stage. I suppose it was very frivolous of her (and of me), but we all enjoyed it and it certainly brought some of those lovely words to life. If Jayana is a good teacher, it really does not matter so very much that he had not been long enough in India to complete his qualifications. Most important is that he should be able to infuse an eager spirit into his pupils, and the desire to learn more than he can teach them. And of course one assumes that he will go on studying himself under one of the great Kandyan teachers. An early frolic is an excellent thing, provided the teacher is dissatisfied with his own knowledge.

The word *Vesmuna* applies, says Molamure, to the transformation of the dancer when his part takes possession of him; not to a real mask put on the dancer. Never, he said, did the *Ves* dancers wear masks; these were only worn by *bali* (devil) dancers, or in *Kolan*.

9th January. Arthur Molamure came at 9.30 this morning, and we talked about *Ves, Kohomba Kankaria,* the *Wannams,* and their relation to each other. Molamure agrees that the *Wannams* came from the texts on which *Bharata Natya* is based. He also thinks that the animal miming came from Malabar, not as I had imagined from things seen in European circuses. Perhaps he is right to associate it with the bird-imitations of solo *Kathakali,* introduced by Gopinath, rather than with anything seen in Europe; though it is possible the acrobatics which seem a new feature were picked up, say, in Hamburg, where, in the sailors' town by the docks I have seen the most astonishing feats of acrobacy by Chinese, Arabs and Africans. There is a quality in Eastern acrobacy which is far more akin to dancing, and into which their dance breaks quite naturally. The scene where Monkey steals the peaches, as acted by the Pekin Opera, for instance, is certainly astounding as acrobacy, but so delicately conceived that one at once feels these mortals to be gifted with divine powers of transformation which our heavy flesh and bone pant after in vain.

This afternoon, just as I was fetched by Harry Pieris's car at 4 p.m., it began to rain, and has continued getting heavier ever since, till now, 10.15, when it has long been a hopeless downpour. Harry Pieris lives with his mother in a charming bungalow in a garden full of lemon-trees, a rarity in the tropics. His mother made the house out of several cottages abandoned during the air-raids. The garden is particularly delightful, with ripe lemons looking in at every window, and sunbirds darting among the flowers. Harry has some fine copies of frescoes and photos of sculptured dancers from Embekke; also an old wooden Buddha and two fine small bronzes. I injected the virus of *Kohomba Kankaria* into him and left him muttering that magic word, which till a few weeks ago no one in Colombo had heard, but now is on everybody's lips.

10th January. Met Fogl, elate from having sent off twenty dancers to India. He promised to come at 6.30, but did not.

Lunched in the town with Malalasekara and the landowner he had spoken of from Kekewatte, a village near Ratnapura, who is more devoted to dancing than to the management of his estate; and not dancing only, but every form of Sinhalese handicraft. He has a school of handicrafts. He at once invited me to stay in his house when I go there, and to spend two days, being shown dances, and taught about the music.

E. A. Delgoda grew up at Hiramandagama near Kegalle, of which his grandfather was chief headsman. During the holidays he spent his time in studying music, and learned all the folk-songs of Ceylon. He learned dancing and drumming. Wherever he went he took instruction. He travelled about collecting music. Whenever he heard of a good book on music, he went in search of it whatever the cost and difficulty; he is indeed the principal authority on this art today in Ceylon.

Under the Portuguese and Dutch, there were still Sinhalese kings who encouraged dancing in their palaces. Every evening there was a performance in the dance hall. But after British occupation this came to and end.

In 1933 Delgoda started a school for various arts, including music, mat-weaving, pottery, carpentry, carving, lacquer, cane-work, coir-work, ivory, brass, spinning and weaving. He ran it for some years at his own expense; after years of agitation he succeeded in getting it registered and getting help from the government in the payment of salaries. At first teachers were got from various parts of Ceylon, but now they are all teachers trained by Delgoda. I shall describe my visit later to this remarkable and devoted man.

I went to tea with the Mendez at Steward House. It is a very spacious bungalow in the old Dutch colonial style, which is certainly the best that has ever been devised. The house stands a good way back from the Galle road, with an immense and very beautiful garden, emerald lawns, wonderful trees, shrubs and flowers. The garden at the back of the house goes right down to the lake, and a canal runs outside its furthest hedge. From the lawn on a clear day the dome of the town hall stands just to the right of Adam's Peak. It would no doubt be more correct to say that it is only on such a day that the solemn presence of Adam's Peak makes itself felt. Many orchids grow in the garden, and a hedge of hydrangeas and ferns encloses the kitchen quarters. Everything is beautifully shaped and designed. There is a wide loggia behind as well as in front of this lovely house, which has many affinities in Moedjo-Moedjo where I spent so many happy hours in Java with Claire Holt and Shutterheim and Bimbo, Claire's small monkey. It is not nearly so large, but quite as beautiful and far more sumptuously furnished. The house is full of wonderful old Dutch furniture, of splendid woods, embossed with silver and brass. Above the doors are open-work carved windows so that the air may circulate. The proportions are perfect, and the space, especially the apparent height, in this seemingly low and modest house, is most astonishing. The taste of the present owner is shown by the fine new bookshelf and cupboard made of very dark rose-wood, with the wonderful artistry and perfection of finish which the native craftsman still possesses. There seemed to be various empty suites beside the one lived in by our host, whose name, occupation and even nationality, I entirely forget. I fancy he was Dutch. I remember, however, his handsome Boxer dog, and above all the exquisite green parakeet called Creaky, after the sound which it makes most frequently. It has a lovely scarlet beak, and ring of scarlet round its neck, and there is wonderful shading in its exquisite turquoise feathers. When it looked into my hand mirror, it murmured, not at all creakingly: 'What a beautiful bird'!

11th January. To the Archaeological Museum to ask some questions of Paranavitane. He was not forthcoming, but recommended M. D. Raghavan, for the origin of names in dances, and Ratnasuriya for literary references to dances. I saw some archaeological photos, and went to look at things in the museum. There are some remarkable fragments of sculptured dancers in purely Indian style. I then asked permission of the director to photograph masks in the museum. It seems, however, to be a rule that no one may take more than five photographs of masks in the two museums of Colombo and Kandy combined, and the negatives have to be left with the museum. As a matter of fact the museum masks are not so very remarkable. I fancy those at Stockholm and Copenhagen are far better, and some at the British Museum which form part of Hugh Nevill's fine collection of Sinhalese treasures but which are, alas, stowed in old packing cases in the basement, where the dust of ages settles on them. For they are too late in date to interest the head of the ethnographical department, and yet cannot be classed as Medieval Antiquities. Yet there is a gallery

Painting of a *bali* figure

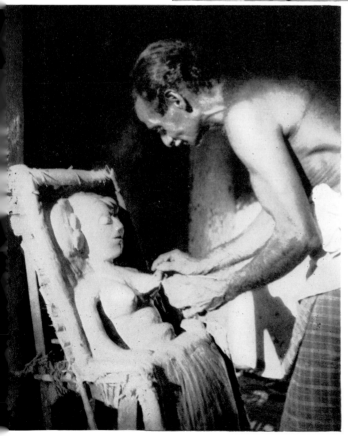

A *bali* figure being
modelled

Early morning after a *bali* ceremony

where things are shown for their beauty alone, since Otto Samson from the Hamburg Ethnological Museum, whom the war drove to our shores and we had the sense to use, dug out so many treasures from the heaps of junk collected by missionaries and placed in that wonderful Exhibition Gallery in the north wing, which is perhaps the most worth visiting for the common man of any in the museum. Would not that be a good place to display those treasures?

CHAPTER VI

Visit to Embekke, Gadaladeniya and Lankatillaka — Degaldoruwa, Dr. Spittel, Delgoda, Polonnaruwa

13th January. I went early to see Ratnasuriya, professor of Sinhalese at the university.[1] He is very charming and very modest: brought out an imposing array of charts for checking up references to cultural matters all through Sinhalese history. He will gladly supply literary references to dancing. There is a record of a king's day, with all his pastimes, which should be very interesting. His view of the *bali* ceremony of exorcism is that it is a relic of a much completer and more conscious ceremony. He compared it with certain rituals described by Madame David-Neel. The whirling dances—now performed haphazard—undoubtedly stem from a dance ceremony more like a dervish dance, in which the whirling probably had a cosmic significance—or in any case was designed to induce a state of superconsciousness.

Took bus to the Fort to buy some new shoes, and then a tram to the market, on my way to the Dutch church of Wolvendal, where in the abandoned churchyard are still some splendid fragmentary tombstones with mutilated scutcheons of animals at least as odd as the 'heathen' gods, and with touching Dutch inscriptions to the dead.

Last night's decoration in the Moslem streets of the Pettah, consisting of gay paper trees stuck up all along the route, and innumerable small streamers—blue, pink, white, green, quivering on wires across the streets, and forming in perspective a gay and airy roof—were not damped by the rain which had fallen heavily since early morning. I

[1] He died a few years ago and his widow, now re-married, is warden of James Pieris Hall at the University of Ceylon, Peradeniya.

visited also the Hindu temples in these small, noisy thoroughfares, loudly braying with Sinhalese radio, alternating with Christian sermons in English. The temples, with fantastic façades piled with grotesque gods and goddesses in painted stucco, are columned and dignified inside. The floor was a small lake, and the dampness was increased by the wet-cleaning which was in progress. Saw some lovely figures of boys, as usual, and many exquisite pictures of green bananas and orange coconuts framed by the palm-leaf covers of the bullock-carts. A man, naked to the waist, old and ragged, wore a large crucifix over his grey shirt.

To tea with Harry Pieris; a cosy personality, with whom one feels at once at home—knowing his friendliness to be entirely sincere.

The weather is now brilliantly fine again; all trace of rain has disappeared. I went with Harry after moonrise to the Gotami Vihara near Borella, belonging to the Pieris family, which George Keyt, commissioned by Harold Pieris, has frescoed with the Life of Buddha.

It is a small temple in a coco-palm grove, a very retired and lovely spot. The moon was already high behind the pagoda. The curtain in front of the Buddha's image and the solid figures of disciples all round the temple, as well as the outer wall decorations, are ugly in the extreme. But Keyt's frescoes—which are rather too near for one to appreciate fully—are very effective and often beautiful. The design is fine, and many of the groupings, but the effect is rather overwhelming owing to a certain fussiness in the background motifs which should take second place. And the figures are perhaps in general too big. The treatment is traditional, and the old priest in charge does not find the frescoes too worldly.

Harry invited me to Kurunegala, to my joy. He had never heard of the Rock Dance of which Parker writes. . . . I fear it is no longer performed.

14th January. Hindu holiday: a loud banging of crackers next door.

I had been promised a lift to Kandy by a Minister, but though I rang up at the hour appointed, he had already left, leaving no message. I settled down rather sadly to read Davy and Parker, and found that the hill Hantana where the first *Kohomba Kankaria* was performed (so they say) is exactly opposite the de Silva bungalow. Kurugalle, where the wild boar was wounded and changed into a rock, is a few miles to the north. It still bears the mark of the spear which wounded him.

Ignatia suddenly came and announced to my joy that they will drive me to Kandy this afternoon. I appreciate this all the more after this morning's disappointment.

We set off about 12.30 and had a delicious drive; elephants in streams, markets, shadows of palm-trees lying across the ground between the upright trunks. Leston pointed out a place on the road where a huge landslide caused by torrential rains had engulfed a whole line of cars and buried them irretrievably—driving them down a steep cliff into the ravine and covering them with an avalanche of rocks and earth. Leston had providentially been held up by a similar flood many feet deep at a higher point of the road, and had to wait many hours for its subsidence, which saved him from a like fate.

Found St. George's in a calmer mood, so that I suppose things are financially better. The moon rose enormous and still seemingly quite full, in a sky dappled with fine—but not obscuring—clouds. We drove down to the temple and up a long hill to Trinity College, where an aunt's husband is schoolmaster. Its chapel was built ten years ago, but save for one special chapel, has never been roofed in—except by corrugated iron. It has innumerable pillars and a colonnade; and gives the impression of a temple. The pews are unfortunate, for it is superbly built, and the sculptured stone pillars and carved wooden roof and fittings of the chapel are very fine, in the best Kandyan tradition.

We drove higher and higher through the trees, winding up to a semi-circular house, above which I climbed still further to a terrace with a magnificent view of the whole of Kandy and the lake, and a very wonderful panorama in moonlight of the Dumballa range. Then down to the Dalada Maligawa, which was full of worshippers sitting on the ground or strolling about, waiting for the coming of the preacher. A table stood ready for him, with pillows on it, presumably for his books. Unfortunately a bar of electric light gave an unsympathetic all-overish illumination, but the moon shining down on the open court was very lovely—though with a sinister mask-like expression. (I have never before seen the moon's face with two round little eyes, mouth and nose.) Then we heard sounds of drumming coming

Dancing figure: medieval ivory

Ivories from Nevill Bequest

Ivories from Nevill Bequest

Delgoda's dance-school

from the dressing-room, and soon the monk appeared under a canopy in an orange robe, accompanied by the drums of temple guardians with their flat, round hats of red and gold. The crowd greeted him with a kind of murmuring cry, and punctuated his sermon with the same sort of applausive sound. Cold night. This time the 'boy' who had previously hung my hot water bottle on a nail near the window, where I did not find it until some time afterwards, put it *under* the bed, instead of in it! There must be some method in this madness.

The Hindu festival now in progress is called the Festival of the Cow—when rice boiled in milk is offered to the sun. It is really the beginning of harvest. (Yesterday I noticed how yellow the rice is getting in the plain. It is ripening, although still emerald green towards the high country.) The Festival of Makara Sankavanti marks the entrance of the sun into the Zodiac sign of Makara. The passing of evil influences and coming of the sun are celebrated with the festival offering of rice boiled in milk. The Hindu house is swept clean of evil spirits and a sheaf of corn hung over the threshold. Flowers are placed symbolically while the milk-rice bubbles on the fire. Owners of cattle bathe their animals and decorate them with flowers, rubbing them with sandalwood and holy ash. When men prayed to Brahma for sustaining food, the god drank up oceans of nectar, and trans-muting it into an easily-assimilated liquid, appeared in the form of a cow, and caused life-giving food to flow as milk.

The chapel we saw belonging to Trinity College is an exact copy of the old wooden Audience Hall where the Supreme Court still sits. The training college at Peradeniya is on the same plan.

15th January. Minnette and I set off in Rajapaksa's car for Embekke with Malagamana as guide. It was a glorious day. As we rose from the main road we passed an *ambalan*: one of those pavilions with steep tiled roof which the kings placed every few miles along the road to shelter travellers. It was on a hillock between two wayside boutiques, and in it sat an old man who was the guardian of the Embekke temple.

He said he would go with us, but must first go home to change his cotton cloth for a better one. He lives along an enchanting path, winding above paddy-fields, below a tea plantation, with a marvel-lous view of the mountains. His house is charming, verandaed, with

117

an old Sinhalese door, and painted tables, and a painted fourposter bed, unmade.

The country off the main road is enchanting, and reminds one of Bali; the same dazzling foliage, emerald paddy-fields, background of mountains, beauty of people standing about in sculpturesque attitudes. I saw today also the minarets of a mosque on a hill. These are the bald red hillsides of new tea plantations. An ancestor of Keppitipola, the curator, joined in the insurrection against the English in 1848 and was executed by them.

We wound up and up through enchanting landscapes, and halted finally at a village from which only a footpath led to the temple of Embekke—down rocks, across paddy-fields, skirting palm-groves. A great grey rock, which had at a distance the appearance of a smooth, round surface, was called *dawul-gale*—drum-rock. In the middle of the fields was a very ancient *ambalan,* based on a great grey flat rock—a drying-ground for washermen. It had a steep roof with the characteristic lozenge pattern of tiles: many pillars supported the roof, which contains square patterns of carving. Some were abstract designs, and some of dancers, much worn by age but very fine. The same panels are on the entrance pavilion of the temple, to which we climbed, crossing a narrow stream and passing along a village street with charming houses—pillared and carved. These wood carvings I had seen badly reproduced in casts in the museum. They are very various: double-headed eagles, lions, etc., devouring elephants or vice versa; wrestlers, seated kings, women suckling a child, abstract patterns of rope designs, rosettes and many others, and always again dancers. Unfortunately the light was bad and the pillars almost completely overshadowed by the wide eaves. The sculptured bands are repeated higher on the pillars, and there are some splendid carved lotus-flowers, resembling tassels, crowding below the rafters. The main pavilion has been restored, that is to say, the rotten wood has been replaced. Unfortunately the splendid carvings have been creosoted, which gives a very unpleasant surface and makes them still more difficult to photograph. The temple is extremely picturesque, with a beautiful harmony of steep roofs and a delightful square painted chamber, like a bell or clock tower, surmounted by a finial with a brass figure of Lakshmi on four sides, and a brass ball on top. It is an enchanting spot, with a great bo-tree in an enclosure overhanging it all. Returning, we saw a young elephant with grave reflective eyes, just arrived back in the village from its day's work, and crunching playfully the kitul-palm leaves which it had just dumped on the ground for its evening meal.

Sederaman came, and Rajapaksa, who runs a shop for arts and crafts, interpreted brilliantly for me his account of the origins of Kandyan dancing and mumming, and versions of the *Kohomba Kankaria* story.

16th January. Sederaman appeared faithfully at nine with his fiddle, and we began on the Rabbit *Wannam*, which is really rather horrible with the fiddle. He calls it 'doing it with music'—as if drumming were not! I got the shape and rhythm and plan of the dance, but when Rajapaksa arrived with a car we abandoned the *wannam* to go off to Gadaladeniya and Lankatillaka, turning off the Colombo road, till we came to the foot of a great rock, up which led a stone staircase— steps lightly cut out of the rock. On the top is the temple—small but very elegant, with a 'digge' (room for women) who used to dance as well as the men; now drums are kept there. Between the dagoba and the temple one walks over the well-swept sand to a school where boys and girls are taught together (English optional). It is a large pillared building with open sides, very simple and attractive, and clean. The temple looks out over wonderful landscaped palms and paddy-fields to the mountains—always Kurugalle and Hantana in the back- ground. The path down which the *perahera* moves—ten elephants— was shown us by Sederaman. Each temple has its own *perahera*: it must be very moving in these remote temples. Everything had great charm. It is quite a complex of building—*dagoba*—priest's house— village school and the various *ambalans*. We wound on through the same enchanting avenue of slender palms—areca, coco- and cabbage- palms—towards Lankatillaka, visiting on the way an influential Sinhalese gentleman who had recently moved from a charming old country house in Sinhalese traditional style to a neighbouring new house, quite ugly and without atmosphere. They were sitting in the loggia filled with photos of the Royal family at all stages of its genera- tions. He talked English quite well. The *Kohomba Kankaria* is a yearly occurrence there, to give the household a 'nice feeling' and please the village. There are many new tea plantat ons, which undoubtedly scar the landscape of Ceylon badly. But round here the estates are more generally owned by the inhabitants, and the workers on them are local —not imported Tamil labour, so there are none of the unpleasant coolie 'lines'. We saw Lankatillaka towering above the trees on its great grey rock, and climbed to it over a broken paved road, which must once have led the whole way from the bottom.

A double staircase—the old gently-graded one, and a newer one with deeply-cut regular steps—climbed the bulging, elephant-grey rock to the courtyard of the temple. We saw the single priest depart-ing on a begging mission, so could not get inside the temple. It has been very much spoilt by a dreadful whitewash which entirely obscures the texture of the stone and drips like bird-droppings on to the guardian elephants, that have not been whitened. The architec-ture is lovely, with its intricate pattern of columns and roofs and ele-phants. The closed temple door showed the old painting. The courtyard had many bo-trees. Though Lankatillaka is actually much higher than Gadaladeniya, the view is less wide.

On the way back, visited Dolapihille, and was led by him to a point from which one looked over the site of the new university, and Hantana and Kurugalle, from this point much foreshortened—one in front of the other; Hantana's wood-crowned slopes and all the range very clearly marked.

Rajapaksa took us to see the school built by missionaries, which was the model of Trinity College. It stands on a hill, and is a really splendid example of modern traditional Sinhalese architecture, every-thing being in perfect taste—the ebony carved reading desk—carved pillars and inverted lotus capitals—great brass-bound chest, etc.—all the fittings are superb. Visited in his tiny workshop the old man who is the master craftsman of these carvings and saw his designs and delicate fretwork drawings; he is a very fine artist.

After lunch we set off for Matale, a wonderful drive by winding streams, rich and shining vegetation, looking out to the Dambulla hills. Then we dropped to cocoa plantations and picked fruits of rich colours, varying according to their ripeness, beautifully modelled. The single street of Matale is low-lying, and a mile or two beyond is Aluvihara. This is tremendously impressive. Many pilgrims were climbing up between the huge piles of fantastically-shaped, leaning rocks, among which trees, beautifully growing, reach right up to the topmost terrace, whence one looks down through the windows of the rocks to a vast landscape of hill and fertile plain. It is a stupendous view. The paintings are pretty horrible and new, but the rock-hewn Buddha is fine. Minnette took, with the priest's permission (who sat watching us from his loggia), a root of a lovely plant with cactus-like long pointed leaves; they were soft, green above and warm red under-neath, with little bunches of pink flowers of the transparent texture of bougainvillea, hiding between the leaves. The mixture of huge rugged rocks, sandy floors, architecture and various levels of spreading trees is particularly harmonious and inspiring.

We returned by a different road in order to visit Degaldoruwa, which we found on a very bad road just before sunset. An invisible bird with a sweet, lingering, solemn and beautifully-phrased note—rather like a nightingale and conveying a very special emotion—was singing as we climbed the path to the temple. We walked on first beyond it and climbed a rounded hill of elephant-grey rock, streaked with white, which led up to a grassy plateau with an immense view of the mountains and valleys. There was a dagoba and a grand bo-tree on a stone base, high above the ground—perhaps the level has been changed. The sunset was sensational—flaming and lucid, with silvery snowy cumulus and fleets of delicate clouds. This plateau was once the site of a *devale*. Down a steep path to the temple, of which a young priest with a huge bunch of keys unlocked the carved door, and we entered a dark outer hall, of which we could only dimly discern the painting. In the inner chamber candles were lit by the priest, and we examined as best we could the lovely painting on ceiling and walls: a frieze of the Buddha's life, scenes of hell, demons and abstract designs, but all exquisitely coloured and very harmonious. The Buddha, a figure of great nobility, on which one can meditate in absence, is lying behind an old glass window, because the oil dropped on him by pilgrims was spoiling his paint. It is one of the most moving and devotional statues I have ever seen. Behind his mitred head is a small door for snakes to enter by, but when I climbed up to see, the priest said it was not suitable for women, and I hastily retreated, to his amusement.

We saw what we could of the paintings in the outer hall—interiors —storeyed houses—processions—scenes of Buddha's life—painted in strips; very lovely in colour and design. The damp is injuring the paintings in places, but they are astonishingly well preserved. The moonstone is particularly fine, and of a somewhat original shape. This hour and this temple were the climax of the day. The moon tonight rose above long silver feathers of cloud, like finely ribbed sand. Now, later, it is seemingly as full as ever—with the same malignant white mask I saw last night.

17th January. Walked to the Dalada Maligawa. The drumming was just ending, although it was only 10.15. No sign of Dolapihille, who, it afterwards turned out, had waited for me from 9. 45 to 10.15, having said he would not be there before 10.30. I visited the small temple— originally sacred to Natha, of whose origin nothing is known—met Dolapihille, and visited with him the excavations of the King's Palace, which the English ruthlessly covered up and partly destroyed. The stone sculptures inside are as crazily whitewashed as at Lanka-tillaka and Aluvihara.

This afternoon I set off by bus in blazing sun to a village some miles off, where Malagamana was waiting for me at the post office. We walked about one and a half miles by paths between the paddy-fields —fortunately fairly dry—to the *maduwa* where the dancing was to be held, i.e. his dance school. A delicious walk, skirting groves and hills above the high green rice, somewhat beaten by the rain. Charming little houses perched here and there on eminences. There are really a great many tucked away—far more than one imagines.

Uneasy, stuttering conversation with Malagamana about the places he had visited abroad. I find it difficult to make my English 'basic' enough to be understood. The *maduwa* was already half-full of chil-dren and women, many hanging round the open walls: a table at the end with an armchair in the middle for the headman of the village. He and the clerk talked fair English. Splendid display of drumming by a young man and two old—one Malagamana's uncle, who is really a terrific old chap. They all produced medals and certificates, and all were the finest performers in Ceylon! *Pantherus* by three little boys—one of whom was excellent; an immensely spirited *nayyadi* by the same boys.

122

The tall drummer did somersaults and walked backwards on his hands, without breaking the rhythm. He also performed a strange feat which must have a name. While still drumming, he removed five or six small glass beads from a cotton thread and kept them in his mouth. Then he inserted the thread, and with his tongue worked the beads on to it, so that they emerged one by one from his lips and fell down the thread. The drumming was very soft during this extra-ordinary operation.

Drumming here seems to me at least as important as dancing. It is an eloquent language, which was formerly used in war to convey messages—a kind of shorthand code, or Morse—very exact. The old man enacted a battle on the drum—very exciting, and made extra-ordinary sounds, threateningly loud, which he then proceeded to reproduce on the drum—advancing upon me. There was also a wonderful altercation of conversation between two drums, and a series of repetitions, by one of the rhythm stated by the other—never quite exact. A famous *Kohomba Kankaria* dancer was brought forward. All the famous dancers and drummers who have not been abroad have strange, fascinating faces. Malagamana is obsessed with his *Kohomba Kankaria,* and now introduces another *devol yakum,* which only he can arrange! But I am also obsessed by the *Kohomba Kankaria* and deter-mined it shall come off. Walked with the headman and Malagamana and the clerk over more footpaths and a bridle-path to a point of the road much nearer to Peradeniya. It was now dark. A car—belonging to someone who had left it to visit some friends—consented to take me home.

I forgot to mention that on our way to Degaldoruwa we passed a house where some drummers were performing—there were three. They were not costumed. The man—the other two were boys—did a comical kind of dance. This was said to be *Sokari.* Yesterday Dola-pihille showed me the Bhairavakande, rising opposite this hill—pos-sibly part of it—where the last human sacrifice was held under the last Kandyan King. The propitiatory offering was a young girl, who was carried in procession to the hill, bound to a stake, to be devoured by wild beasts. When the people went away, her lover came and rescued her. The King had slept badly, worrying over the sacrifice, and when she was found to be alive he offered her anything she liked to choose—land, jewels, etc. She chose her lover, who had been imprisoned for setting her free. And this was the last human sacrifice! *18th January.* Went out early to the Maligawa—but not early enough. The drumming was from 5.30 to 6.30, so had just finished. It is exhausting walking, as one tends to go too fast, because someone's clock is always wrong. Read *Exorzismus* all the morning, and set off by bus to Dolapihille in the afternoon. Minnette, who never goes by bus and never walks, is reckless in her statements about distance and short cuts. Spent two hours with Dolapihille, being violently bitten by midges, listening to stories of drums and Ravana—and discussing dancing. Tried to catch a bus which did not stop, but happily was given a lift by an elderly architect from Gampola whom I 'thumbed', a procedure he was certainly unused to, but took very well.

As it was not quite time for the temple drumming I started up the steep Garrison Cemetery road, and climbed through the dense luminous, glorious foliage to the very top of the woods, where we had gone by full moon. This is the finest view of Kandy by far. The sun was setting, and a sharp shadow fell across the silver lake. Superb sunset behind the mountains. The temple was still empty, but drummers were collecting, and more and more people—women, children, young men, girls, fathers with babies in their arms—came streaming up with flower-offerings on betel-leaf trays. The flowers are exquisite—jasmine, frangipani, stephanotis, asters, champak—and fill the temple with wafts of delicious perfume as the offerings pass. The drumming began, two older men beating the *dawula,* keeping the measure; two younger ones performing wonderful fanfares with trills on the *tom-tom.* It is a glorious form of service. Before it begins, the children run noisily about, playing among the pillars; now there was silence except for the marvellous drums. The people began collecting up the steps before the shrine and, when several priests arrived, the great doors were unbolted and unlocked, and a few were allowed in. This part of the service ended with a performance on the *bera* (big drum) in front of the shrine by one boy. It was extraordinary how warm the tone of the *tom-tom* appeared, after the harsh insistence of the big drum. There were a great many youths among the worshippers. The flower-offerings are bought from boys who sit at little

Ritual screen used in *thovil*

Moment of trance in *thovil*

Punawa (Ritual vase)

Flame-throwing during *thovil*

tables outside the temple. They are always deliciously fresh and taste-fully arranged. The beggars in the outer court, who sit eternally crouched on the ground in a circle, are temple pensioners. Rice is distributed to them daily out of the immense quantity cooked daily in the temple, none of which is used by the priests. As I arrived at the temple from my walk Sederaman stepped forward. He had come from Colombo with Malala and Mr. Roderigo. I heard that a *Kohomba Kankaria* is to form part of the Arts Festival!

19th January. At 2 a.m. this morning a car arrived, and there was much shouting of 'Boy' and great bustle. I thought it was my hired driver arriving with the car, but it turned out to be some people from Colombo to see George de Silva, who had to be given food in the middle of the night. Presently it drove away, pursued by weaker cries of 'Boy' and 'Driver'. My car never turned up, so I went to the station with the unfortunate Boy, who complained of his lot, and seemed to prefer service with an English family, where all was well ordered and the food was delicious!

In Colombo this afternoon I visited Godakumbura of the Archaeo-logical Museum, who sent me his third article on *Kohomba Kankaria*. He is an enthusiast, has been used to seeing it all his life, and remem-bers it being performed by eighty to a hundred dancers. He is a burly person, very open and sympathetic. The workmen engaged on a skeleton building of bamboo were chanting a rhythm as they hoisted a great iron rafter, on which a man was poised. Their naked brown bodies, moving in rhythm, were very beautiful. I hope to go to Kurunegala with Harry Pieris on Saturday. At the moment his car is out of order, just when most needed.

20th January. Early by rickshaw to see Malalasekara, who was just starting off with a car-full of children to be deposited at various schools. I discussed with him the possibility of *Kohomba Kankaria* for the Arts Festival. He took kindly to the idea.

I then went to see Hulugalle at the Office of Information. He was a little vague about the possibility of assisting me to see *Kohomba Kankaria*.

Next to Fogl who limped and looked ghastly, with a yellow com-plexion, red eyes and minus two toe-nails owing to his terrible adventure down the Mahaveliganga. He said the Tourist Bureau was voting me 500 rupees, and rang up Hulugalle to confirm this. It appeared to be true and I was elated; but began with time to feel some doubts.

Called on Nugewala, lay head of the Temple of the Tooth; two other ministers were present. He gave me a lecture on *Kohomba Kankaria*, as being a great religious festival which required three months' preparation, enormous offerings, including pigs and chickens. He said he was putting one on in July.

Visited Dr. Spittel, who is a delightful person, very intelligent and informative about the Veddahs. He said the Seligmans' work contained descriptions of everything relating to them, though presented in note form and needed sifting. He said it is true that the pure Veddahs have almost vanished. They have mixed with Sinhalese and borrowed from their customs. They tend to be show figures. In his latest book he treats them as quite vanished, but a few do actually remain—they are all hunters. He thinks them a mixture of negroid and Australian, at the period when one continent united all the people of these countries. The negroid type in Ceylon is of course not confined to the Veddahs. They are not hairy in their original state, and have only slight beards. The very hirsute ones of which he has some photos are mixed. Their lack of hair relates them to the Malays, Chinese, Burmese, etc.

Malalasekara came in after nine. News of *Kohomba Kankaria*. He had seen Malagamana and Sederaman. If they produced *Kohomba Kankaria* here it would cost 1,000 rupees. I did not mention the promised grant by the Tourist Bureau, which I now regard as highly problematic.

Ignatia, I discover, must not travel by bus—it is *infra dig*: no doubt also for Toni. A rickshaw is just permissible. For me, fortunately, who have no social standards to keep up, all is permissible!

I forgot to mention the extraordinary chorus of crickets which filled the air, like millions of tiny whirring wheels, directly after sunset, as I came down the hill of the Eastern Redoubt.

21st January. Today I visited Will Pereira in his little house in Wellewatte. I find his gentleness more and more sympathetic. In his own small room his voice is less harsh, and his smile extraordinarily pleasant. I find he has a great love of music. He is unused to general conversation, and it was this which made his voice appear so harsh when I first met him. We talked as usual about the Kandyan kings and the resistance of the Kandyan nobles to the invaders. He is of opinion that they were far more patriotic than the southerners. He showed me portraits of kings, and a tracing of the skull of Keppiti-pola's ancestor, which had been sent to London after his execution, as he had so much interested, when alive, the English doctor who knew and admired him. I am happy to say that it has now been returned to Ceylon.

Thence by bus to the Secretariat and interviewed Jayaratne, head of the Tourist Bureau, about the *Kohomba Kankaria* grant, which was by no means so sure as Fogl thought. But it was soon agreed on and he made part payment, though evidently a little sceptical as to whether I should send the article I have to do for them in return for the 500 rupees.[1] In the afternoon I visited Edriwira, head of 'Ceylon Tours', who will give me special terms for a car to Ratnapura. Letter from Molamure, who has fixed up a Pantheru for the 28th, and from Harry Pieris announcing that we start tomorrow at 2.30 for Kurunegala.

22nd January. At five the Mendez set off for the Eastern Provinces where the Americans are building a huge dam, with which Leston is in some way connected.

I left with Harry Pieris for Kurunegala in his friendly but rather wheezy little car, to visit the family coco-palm estate under a jungle-covered rock—a very lovely place. His father, who ran it in the interests of the peasants, divided up his estate among his ten children. Harry, being the eighth child, gets only a small portion, but adminis-ters for his mother. Though he belongs to a rich family Harry is not interested in making money. He is a rather academic artist, though anxious to encourage originality in others; but he is an excellent portrait-painter, as Martin Russell pointed out in an article in *Marg*. Fashionable Sinhalese ladies are not inspiring material, but I have seen some drawings of peasants which are altogether delightful. Harry Pieris is too indolent to work hard, but he cares very much for beauty, in a family which as a whole does not think in those terms.

The estate is really most lovely, though the monkeys I was promised as gambolling everywhere among the rocks between us and the great

---

[1] This article was never used by the Tourist Bureau but has been twice reprinted and will appear in a forthcoming book of essays.

jungle have not shown themselves. The house is very large and somewhat neglected. It was despoiled of most of its furniture on rumours of
a sale. When bombs frightened Colombo everyone piled their goods
and themselves here, and the swallows who had their nests in the
eaves were driven away, because of the snakes which might hurt the
children. It was almost dark when we got here, and we inspected
my bedroom by candle-light and as we had arrived unexpectedly
found the mattress covered with bee-cocoons, which came crisply off,
and spent that night on the floor. The bathroom adjoining is however quite grand, with coloured tiles and a deep, tiled bath—too dusty
now to bathe in. The closet has three seats of various sizes, like the old
family affairs one sees in ancient houses in Europe.

A young man from Kurunegala—Dodanwatawana—came to
dinner. He is delicate and reminded me vaguely of the Greek poet
Demetrios Capetanakis. He reads the English periodicals and has
read a surprising number of English books. He had just ordered my
translation of Svevo's *Zeno*. Perhaps I can induce him to write something about himself and his discovery of English literature. There are
few books he has not heard of, and most of them he has read. The
fireflies were quite extraordinary. The sky was blazing with stars,
which seemed to loose themselves and be flying through the air—
then swarming in indescribable brilliance in certain of the trees,
which they turned into living Christmas trees.

23rd January. I slept extremely well, with no disturbance from
cocoons. Walked out early, and tried in vain to find a path up the
rock. Golden orioles, gorgeous pheasants, but no monkeys.

We drove to Yapahuwa, past the three great rocks: Athagala (elephant rock), Ibbagala (tortoise) and Andagala (eel rock). There is a
huge spreading tree whose name I do not know, which sheds a
wonderful shade upon the road. The great staircase—which is all
that remains of Yapahuwa (one of the old Sinhalese capitals)—is
immensely impressive. They are excavating below where the city lay;
it was enclosed by two moats, which joined with the impregnable
rock to form a firm defence. A dagoba and the priest's house (he is
an astrologer) lie below, and then one mounts up steeply to the first
stage. An iron staircase leads perpendicularly up a rock to where the
stone sculptured flight of steps begins. The fragmentary friezes of

Staircase at Polunaruwa

Ananda at the Gal Vihara

dancers and the great animals—elephant and lion—are very fine indeed, and the lovely staircase with its great gateway and windows stands superbly against the immense rock wall. Here was once another Maligawa—perhaps also a palace. The view over a vast panorama of paddy-fields, palm-groves and mountains, is glorious.

We lunched at the rest-house of Maho and arrived back in time to pick up Dodan and climb the Ibbagala, on the summit of which is a *vihara* and enchanting little settlement in which lives a very wise-looking ancient priest with two or three little boys. He has a small museum, crammed with gifts—some valuable—many images of Buddha and all kinds of other objects, secular and religious, given him by grateful patients. For he is a healer, and has a remarkable cure for tonsillitis. We talked to him in his little room, also full of furniture, books, etc. The dagoba on a higher rock, surrounded by garden and trees, is enchanting, immediately backed by the jungle, in which we visited the two elephants which go on the jungle track in the *perahera*. The sunset was sublime over lake and mountains as we descended the faintly-indicated rock staircase over the great granite surface of the rock. The fireflies tonight were more astounding still. They had concentrated in a temple tree—covered with flowers—just outside my window, and every moment their celestial dance was joined by stars which came sailing down from their stations in the sky. Early this morning while it was still dark, these starry beings had changed to wide temple flowers.

24th January. Harry announced his intention of driving direct from here to Ratnapura, his car having recovered. He went off on estate work, and I to the town, picked up Dodan, did various errands, and now am writing before we set off. Two hours late in leaving, which means that we shall only arrive at Ratnapura after dark, instead of at Kahawatte in daylight. The drive was glorious, through very strange country, where screen behind screen of yellowing rubber-trees stood out on the heights like stage scenes. Deep valleys, high hills, glimpse of mountains, many lovely human beings in sculptural poses on the road, in a kind of dream. We crossed many rivers with golden sands silted down by the rains. Harry talked about Paris, where he spent six years, and about the colour-bar, to which he strangely takes no exception. Impossible to see anything of Ratnapura, except that its

I 129

position is obviously very lovely, and that bungalows are placed all over the heights surrounding it. At dinner we were offered the gems for which Ratnapura, city of gems, is famous. Harry insisted that Delgoda was a proctor, I can't imagine why, and that therefore he must live in Ratnapura! This was certainly wishful thinking, as he lives even beyond Kahawatte, which is sixteen miles from here. The rest-house is on a high hill, looking over to the mountains.

25th January. I got up at five and saw the dawn behind what I took for Adam's Peak—a high, pointed mountain facing us. A huge rolling landscape of mountains and wooded hills, very Japanese in the early mists, the peak piercing the clear sky, and two stars just below the last sickle of the moon. I was in a fret to be off, but that did not make us leave any earlier!

We arrived at Delgoda's just before ten, dropping Harry's bag first at the rest-house of Kahawatte, where I had hoped to spend last night; and turned up a steeply rising red lane above paddy-fields.

Mr. Delgoda was standing at the top of the steps awaiting us. The landscape is enchanting, with wonderful foliage. We sat awhile in the loggia of his house, and then walked by footpaths, passing on the way a charming thatched village, to his school, consisting of a number of *maduwas,* in which the school teaching and the various crafts are carried on—weaving, mat-making, carpentry, ivory-carving, gold-work and lacquer work. It seems sad that with such lovely designs and old Kandyan work as still exists for a model, so few of the really beautiful designs should be used. The government trade department, says Mr. Delgoda, prefers an ugly messy treatment of the lacquer, but perhaps with a little humouring could be persuaded to like something better. It would surely be worth trying.

After lunch the dancers came up, and we had an enchanting display of *pantheru* and *udekki* (hour-glass drums), the small boys doing *pantheru* (tambourines without a parchment and hung round with small cymbals) and the bigger ones *udekki.* One of the small boys was extraordinarily good, a real leader and full of invention. He belongs to the *goi-gama* caste, as does also a big boy who leads the elders. But caste matters nothing to Delgoda who, if the boy is gifted, gives him a free education.

The drummer, Henrick, was first seen by him in a dance troupe at

Kegalle and as he was an orphan Delgoda adopted him, and only later discovered his great gifts as a goldsmith, to which caste he belongs. There is nothing Henrick cannot do. He now teaches ivory-carving and dancing, as well as working in the garden. He was given by Delgoda a complete literary education. He is very handsome as well as having a most beautiful voice. He sat on the floor and warbled with the utmost modesty.

Then came three dancers from Kegalle, and sat in a row against the wall.

Mrs. Delgoda did not appear, indeed no female member of the family, but a son-in-law and two small boys were there.

Harry left about 6.30, and then we settled down to work. I took notes while Delgoda talked. After dark we had music. Henrick, the drummer, sat on the floor and drummed. Delgoda in a chair began to sing, and then old Henrick sat and sang too, and played with the *pantheru*, its metal rings gleaming in the lamplight. The men from Kegalle sang too. Then came folk-songs by Delgoda and Henrick. It was a wonderful experience.

After supper, to which came a Water and Irrigation officer, and two young friends of the son-in-law, I wrote again.

Delgoda inspects over a hundred schools but receives nothing for it, except twenty-five cents a mile towards rail expenses.

There are apparently still some fine old masks five miles up in the mountains which I must try and see some day.

26th January. I slept very well under a rayon counterpane. Went for an early walk with Delgoda and saw the whole range of Adam's Peak spread out in the early morning light.

Harry, bored by being alone at the rest-house, came at eight—for once too early to please me.

We looked in on the way back at Horana, where there is a school on the model of Santineketan, which was opened by Tagore. There is no one there now and the workshops are empty. A very lovely creeper, like a milk-white jasmine, but unscented, overhung a tree by the house. This whole region is rubber-plantations, and has the colouring of English woods in autumn—very lovely, and somehow odd in contrast to the palms. The trees stood out in sharp relief, like theatre scenery, rank behind rank.

It is a very lovely region, hardly any houses to be seen, and continual change of scene.

27th January. I went with Ignatia to a sale-room, and discovered with her help the missing postcards of masks from the museum collection. She made many good bargains, especially a bundle of resplendent clothes, oriental coats, etc. I profited by a pair of most elegant silk pyjama legs, which I still wear. Ignatia enjoys bargaining, at which I am so bad.

A visit later from Cedric Seneratne, my friend in the Tourist Bureau, and a friend of Molamure. We went together to visit Thornley, head of the photographic society; a young but important business man, who was a great friend of Lionel Wendt, and told me how all the estate left by Lionel Wendt and already realized in cash, was to be devoted to building the new art centre. I hear that this has now been completed.

Thornley talked a great deal, and gave an account of a water diviner, a certain Miss Penrose, whom he had met on the boat coming from England, who revealed extraordinary powers of divination. Like the Abbé Mermet she divined from maps, never having herself visited the spot. She had not been to Ceylon, but laid her finger on a spot where she said there was much gold. Thornley denied that any gold was found in Ceylon, but she insisted, and said that if it were touched one would certainly be killed. Though still sceptical Thornley checked up and found she was actually laying her finger on a dagoba crammed with treasures, the recipient of endless previous gifts from Buddhists. Certainly anyone who attempted to touch it would be lynched.

28th January. I should much have liked to go to Polonnaruwa with Harry; but he was difficult to get moving. Suddenly at dinner-time Ignatia, who had often talked of taking me in her car, announced that we would start next morning very early. All arrangements had to be made very hastily and a permit to take photographs obtained, which can only be from the head of the archaeological department, Mr. Paranavitane. Mrs. Ratnasuriya most kindly came with us at that untimely hour, and the permit was obtained.

29th January. We started at 5.15. It had only just stopped raining, but as we neared Kurunegala the sun was coming out, and by the time we reached Dambulla (8.45) it was gloriously fine. Sigiriya loomed very large, but seemed very far away, though only eleven miles. The fantastic shapes of these huge rocks and the underlying grey rockiness give the Ceylon landscape a quite peculiar character.

How wonderful the Dambulla caves are, especially the cave which contains the powerful statue of Vishnu. This is a work of amazing beauty and power—wide shoulders, and very narrow waist—a great athlete Yogi. The irregularity of the rock roof gives great life to the decorations, which seem to hang like real stuff. Many of the great figures of Buddha are hewn directly out of the rock. The decorative bands are very fine, and the architectural details fascinating. There are various depths in the cave layers and avenues formed by the disposition of the figures: bands of light fall across the shadowed spaces. I came here in 1935 with Malala, but had quite forgotten how impressive the great cave is, and how varied the figures, which are seldom stereotyped but do not look inexpressive. The Buddha-To-Be is there, and one hidden behind a curtain is particularly holy, I forget why. The only disturbing things are the wooden posts which hold up the lights—which were not lit, by the way. On the cords between these hang bits of cloth, coloured or white, which are presumably offerings. There are two or three more caves, all with magnificent engraved keys and locks, and there is a sublime Buddha, marvellous in impression of power, though certainly not declared by any outside sign. This Buddha was made, they say, by Divine agency, though all the others were by human hands. The beauty of the path up the rock I had also forgotten: the great horizon of mountains—the highest had not emerged from cloud.

We arrived at Sigiriya about 9.45. Visited first a small vihara in the jungle, about a mile away, over a track only recently covered with water. A delightfully irregular staircase leads up to it, but it is not particularly striking, except in its rocky situation. It is called Raja maha vihara, and is of the same date as Sigiriya. The work on the top of the rock has advanced enormously. I climbed there at midday, blowing at the top like an old cab-horse. It is very wonderful—two tanks—innumerable traces of stone paths—the foundations of the palace are already laid bare. It is many acres in extent, though the rock looked as if its top surface would be small. The view is superb, but the climb—in part over narrow footsteps on the rock face, and partly by a perpendicular iron ladder—is certainly tiresome. The hornets which used to haunt the rock have been destroyed by D.D.T. —is this impious? The lower level of the fortress has been considerably cleared, and looks like a park or garden. We explored the throne and royal tank. Everywhere the rocks are covered with grooves, which are no doubt the foundations of buildings. It is a formidable business, but absolutely fascinating, and the upper rock is extraordinarily beautiful in colouring. The moat has now been largely excavated.

We had lunch beside the water—covered with tall white lotus. Two young women were having a delicious bath and washing their clothes. They never stopped pouring pails of water over their heads with graceful movements of their slim bodies. At midday the workmen on the rock came prancing down at a great rate, making me feel very clumsy.

The drive to Polonnaruwa is not very interesting, and the road is badly camouflaged as a proper one by sand and a sprinkling of tar. We began exploring after tea. The light was extremely favourable to the frieze of dancers.

30th January. We visited the exquisite lotus pond, shaped in a perfect flower of stone petals, round which flitted countless butterflies, and hosts of monkeys disported themselves. There are apparently numbers of wild elephants, so that certain *vihares* are closed towards evening. We saw traces of one this morning, who had broken a path up to a lonely stupa standing on a plateau, dominating the whole jungle and looking out to the mountains. Last night a huge elephant had climbed to it, and broken away the brickwork in places, leaving vast heaps of dung behind. The pilgrims had tied branches to a tree where the path forked and gave us one too. The stupa is a circular one of brick, with only a few storeys left. There are also two very ruined Siva and Vishnu temples, with frescoes which must have been exquisite, but have been preserved too late, and are horribly destroyed by damp; there are traces of exquisite figures and faces, resembling Ajanta. I paid several visits to the Gal Vihara, equally beautiful and solemn and still in full sunlight. There were many worshippers who had come through jungle paths to make offerings. It seemed to me that those figures must impose silence on everyone; I could not understand the pilgrims chattering. I had forgotten how superbly they are composed, and how majestic they are; I had remembered them as rather casually grouped. The veining of the stone is remarkable, particularly on the face of the standing Buddha, and the recumbent Buddha's stone has the veining of wood. All these figures, divided by a shrine (which unfortunately has to be wired off on account of the mess people would otherwise make of it) must be one of the grandest ensembles in the world. The silence that emanates from these prodigious figures—one sitting in meditation, the other standing, with knees slightly relaxed, and the third reclining on his side (one foot slightly shorter than the other)—is altogether inspiring. The expression of each face, though the eyes of all are closed, is very different, enigmatic and tremendously impressive. After our visit to the stupa and the northern temples with their ruined frescoes, I asked Ignatia to wait for me while I approached the Gal Vihara from above. Perhaps this was the finest view of all.

We drove along the Bund and sat looking out over the strange spectral forest of skeleton trees rising from the silvery water. Great birds perched on the branches—I saw a pelican, vulture, snake-bird, and many others. By the lotus-pond there were many birds, as well as monkeys, and an exquisitely moving song. After lunch drove to Minneriya Tank, where the foliage has not left the submerged trees.

Wonderful drive back towards Kurunegala, and turned aside to visit the Ridi Vihara (silver temple). It stands beneath a great rock, about a quarter of a mile above a little village, up many flights of steep, roughly-hewn steps. Deliciously shady, glittering foliage and glimpses of the mountains. It is one of the oldest *viharas*, 1,600 years old, and has on its small terraces several notable things: the wooden carved pillars of the priest's house in the style of Embekke—a wonderful little densely-pillared stone temple, very perfect, with lotus capitals and carved pillars, all with dance figures but very much rubbed, and in the topmost temple a wonderful door of ivory and silver, which has been sadly despoiled of its lovely carved ivory frame, but still has two exquisite dancing figures at the bottom on each side, one exactly in the attitude of the museum ivory comb—with decorative tassels flying upwards in the movement of the dance; the other preparatory to this movement, with the tassels hanging between widely spread knees over the accordion-pleated skirt. Above is an ivory plaque of five women twined in beauty. There was a painting, not beautiful, of about twelve rather Lesbian-looking ladies. We were also shown some painted in dance attitudes under the offering-table in one shrine which had a fine carved stone doorway and some Portuguese tiles inlaid in two rows before the Buddha image, said to be the life of Christ. There was a charming Chinese lamp with painted glass sides, illuminated by the candle inside. The old priest was most sympathetic—so was the whole of this enchanting temple.

2nd February. Read Upham at the museum this morning in quarto edition with coloured illustrations of *bali* figures. Dr. Nell who lives now at the Dutch Burgher Union in a room full of treasures, told me of this book, which I have since acquired at a great price in London. He had bought in London an *ola* about caste from the widow of an official. He told me how at a ceremony he once attended the same *pingo* (weight) of rice went to potter and king.

In speaking of the community of gods in Ceylon he told how when the bus reached a point of the road after Koslanda, from which Kataragama was visible, all the inmates got out and offered towards the temple. The Buddhists break coconuts, the Hindus light candles. No doubt the Christians also make some sign, since St. Anthony is the acknowledged patron of all religions, and Buddhists pay ten rupees to advertise a cure in their favour.

3rd February. Went to see Harry at 9.30, but we did not leave till 10.30 to go to the temple of Sapugaskanda, beyond Kelaniya. From the rock on which it is built, a wonderful view over the ocean of palms to pale mountain horizon. A pseudo bo-tree on the rock was full of small green woodpeckers whose voice is delicious in chorus—rather like pigeons, but more varied. They were so like the leaves that one could only see them when they flew from bough to bough. A boy belonging to the temple drummed the call to prayer, playing with great dexterity the *tom-tom* and *dawula* at once. Building work is going on at the temple, a dagoba is being put up, and I saw the treasure-chamber inside—the only part left hollow till the end, awaiting the Treasure. The old paintings in the temple are quite charming; birds and flowers, reminding me a little of Bauchant. The ceiling panels are also excellent, with ingenious symmetrical twining of figures, like the curious designs of wrestlers. Bands of naïve Buddhas, and Jataka episodes, charmingly coloured. But in one shrine where the moderns have got to work there are absolute horrors—as bad as the worst Catholic Passions. Figures hideously sculptured and coloured in every kind of theatrical attitude—no doubt they are done on plaster. These are what the people seem to love.

We visited on the way back a pottery shop on the road, which had innumerable red pots, charming in design and decoration, done in white outline—flowers, fruits, formal patterns. A little boy was working there with the most engaging smile.

CHAPTER VII

Magic Ceremonies—My First 'Kohomba Kankaria'—Clairvoyants —Temples at Ambalangoda—A Bad Omen

3rd February. Reception at Arts Gallery for opening of the Arts Festival. Swarms of people, but the only ones worth attention were the 300 Kandyan dancers, some very small boys indeed, with *udekkis, pantherus,* drums. They lined the path across the grass, on which green powder had been sprinkled to give the illusion of verdure, leading from the Gallery to the colossal statue of Visvakarman, made of brick and mortar and plastered over, holding in its ten hands the various symbols of the cultural trades practised in Lanka. This stood on a platform high above the ground, and on it, between great brass lamps, Malalasekara made a very long speech, followed by a shorter one by the Prime Minister. The path was covered with white sheets— no doubt hired out by laundrymen from the week's washing! After the speeches the dancers hurried off to the *Perahera,* which started in the road outside the Gallery. We managed to get in the front row by following the dancers, only a few of whom I recognized. Elephants already loomed large in the twilight lit by torches. The crescent moon was still high through the boughs of the flamboyant. An old man, very venerable, with white beard and dress and ceremonial square hat, sat motionless on the first elephant, whose strangely small eyes gleamed with ambiguous meaning. Behind him came dancers, drums and the huge tusker from the Maligawa—his tusks sheathed in gold, like Siamese dancers' nails. On his back was a lighted casket. Two small elephants, each bestridden by three men in red, accompanied him.

There was sometimes a frenzied outburst of drumming and dancing in front of the elephants and the car which incongruously heralded the Hindu part of the procession. The elephants looming through the night produce an extraordinary impression.

We sidled our way back to the buildings and began to look for the Batticaloa Theatre—at last discovered it, and saw the dancers ready dressed on the stage, though no tickets had yet been sold and there was hardly anyone in the theatre. Our suggestion that the audience should be let in first was thought good, and the money collected afterwards. The dancers produced an alarming impression. One, a man of seventyfive, was made up as a dancinggirl, and looked the embodiment of aged depravity. I heard he was a good dancer. Another manwoman—presumably an attendant, whom I at first mistook for a princess—was minus a left eye. They were all most ingeniously and even splendidly dressed in tinsel and paper or thin cotton stuffs studded with gold. They are Tamil fishermen, and the dramas are from the *Mahabharata* and *Ramayana*. One has the impression that the performance is a relic of some really imposing Court drama, for their costumes, and particularly headdresses, are magnificent in design, though only made of oiled paper and mica. The swinging skirt of the king, like a lampshade in shape, was really very striking. Krishna was also there. The manner of their acting reminded me somewhat of the old English mummer's plays, with the dancing thrown in. At Batticaloa they dance out in the open on a round stage, and show off their paces individually. Here they gave the impression of being completely disorientated by the stage. The old man—the dancinggirl—almost fell off backwards. The dancers, as I have said, are fishermen: they dance all night, supported and invigorated by frequent potations, and no doubt towards morning acquire some life: in fact, in their own surroundings they may be quite good. On this occasion, faced by an auditorium and on an unaccustomed stage, they were not at all interesting, though the fight between Krishna and the King Balarama had some animation, and might be exciting. They are perhaps influenced by puppetshow technique; in fact they reminded me of puppets. Their stepping was neat and certainly rhythmical, and the movements of the arms reminded me somewhat of Kandyan dancing. The claim made for them on the programme of combining the vigorous bodily movements and the War Dance and the artistic grace and rhythm associated with Greek drama seems to me excessive and even ridiculous. The weapons are interesting, and Arjuna's bow beautiful, also the headdresses, which are rather like Chinese gold and filigree headdresses.

These are undoubtedly the relics of the drama described at great length by Hugh Nevill in *Taprobanian* about eighty years ago when he was stationed for two years at Batticaloa. One hopes that, even though Tamil is not to be an 'official language', these fishermen will be encouraged to continue their dramatic efforts in Tamil.

Independence Day. I went rather crossly in the afternoon to Torring-ton Square to see the 'Marathon runners' arrive from the four quarters of Ceylon. The big *maduwa* in the middle of the ground, built as usual of banana stems and decorated with palm leaves, was charming. The *magulbera* drumming was unfortunately obscured by a dreadful loud-speaker which kept promising to stop but never did. The flight of pigeons was charming as such flights always are. It began to rain, but I felt I must sit out the Prime Minister's speech and its translation. for someone had kindly given me his seat.

The next few days were taken up chiefly by visits to the Arts Festival, where I saw a variety of wonderful things, scarcely spoilt by being 'got up' for the occasion. It was also during the Festival that I went with Harry Pieris to a most extraordinary ceremony, for which he had by chance seen the preparations, on his way back from the estate. I have recorded all these things in my diary in some detail, and hope to publish them in due course.

8th February. I went this afternoon to a lecture by Austin de Silva, chief librarian of the Museum Library, on charms and magic in Ceylon. His lecture was fascinating—about demons, devas, sorcerers and *kapurales* (devil-priests), with lovely line illustrations.

I conversed with him next day about all these charms and magic. He believes in them absolutely; so must I, though understanding is a different matter. I cannot at all understand how a charm can work on an indifferent person. Perhaps it cannot. The person injured is per-haps already in a state when injury by the will of another is an easy matter. But then we must believe in astrological dispositions and horo-scopes—as everyone does over here.

De Silva told me some stories which seem fantastic, but which he says are authentic, sitting gravely in his office in the Museum Library. A young man wished to elope with a girl whom he was not allowed to marry. He procured a love-charm which was to draw her irresistibly. He remained at the gate while a messenger took in the betel leaf which had been charmed. The girl was preparing vegetables and throwing away the skins, in a heap for the cow, who was in the yard. The betel leaf was laid on the table and somehow got swept away among the refuse and was eaten by the cow—which immediately became rampant and rushed after the lover, raging and tearing; he fled and desperately climbed a tree. It was only after a counter-charm had been procured that the cow gave up tearing at the bark and rearing against the trunk, and returned to normal.

Another story was about the mayor of Hikkaduwa, who is a great maker of charms and has many masks. He would never allow drums to beat outside his house. One day a wedding procession, ignorant of his prejudice, drummed loudly in passing his gate. He made a charm which sent the bride mad and the bridegroom into a frenzy of dance. It was only when they sent to beg mercy with many apologies that he allowed them to return to normal.

Story of a house near the sea—haunted by a spirit which crashed about among the furniture and seemed to be breaking all the glasses—though nothing was actually broken. I think it was in this house that Mr. de Silva actually saw food lifted off the ground and float to the ceiling, without any apparent agency.

There is no end to these stories. He believes in the human sacrifice story of Bhairavakande. He says everyone in Kandy believes that once a queen could not conceive, and it transpired that she was possessed of the demon Bhairava. He consented to leave her and retire to this hill, on condition that the sacrifice of a pure maiden was made to him every year. It seems this virgin was carried in procession—no doubt with dancing—to the top of the hill, where she was exposed, tied to a stake, and left alone. In the morning fear, cold, and above all I suppose, suggestion had done Bhairava's work for him. The girl was dead. The rescue of the girl by her lover took place, they say, in the last King of Kandy's reign.

A dawdly town visit with Ignatia, who buys the oddest mixtures of good and bad, like all collectors, and generally emerges with some treasure. She has been pursuing the subject of *punawas,* those pots which hold the torches in a *bali* ceremony, and are said to be broken on a bull's head, before being thrown away by the *kapurale.* Ignatia says it is not so; they are only carried on a bull's back, and then broken in a stream by the *kapurale.*

11th February. Harry called for me at 5.30. Sri Pada at last, towering above the mist, which sometimes rose densely in front of us on the road. Very lovely effect of pure blue sky above green enamelled hill/ tops, around which the mist swirled.

We had some difficulty in discovering Tiverton Estate where my *Kohomba Kankaria* is to be held. We went on the way to George Keyt's house across the paddy/fields. A beautiful girl, whom we had seen dance the other day, was transformed directly she held a pot under her arm, the *Kalagedi,* or water/pot, about which I have read a charming ballad in Nevill's transcripts. We saw also two men saw/ ing wood with lovely movements.

We drove on to Harry's old home, a most lovely spot in the jungle. From a kind of plateau above it there is a view of all the hills sur/ rounding Kandy. An old man with a great net was catching butter/ flies of brilliant colours—a sad but beautiful sight.

Later we discovered the Tiverton Estate. It had no name up on the two dirty grey gates. We wound up the red road above a wide valley to the *maduwa,* where labourers were busy making offering/boxes of green banana stems which look very fresh and charming—rather like three beehives with widely plaited walls. The owner of the estate, Jayawardana, a heavy oldish/looking man, expanded slightly when talking Sinhalese. He took us over the house which he bought to/ gether with the estate several years ago from an Englishman. It is spacious, but only furnished with bits of things left over by the former owner—a few chairs, even a telephone. It has evidently been long unused and in its ugliness it is now fast decaying.

We hear there is to be a monster *Perahera* at Anuradhapura, which has taken off many elephants and dancers. I should mention that I had at last collected my cheque from the Tourist Bureau, after many official formalities.

We visited Minnette. George de Silva had already dismissed three servants that morning, and taken them all on again by midday. The whole family, however, were in good spirits, owing to his chief political opponent having lost his seat and civic rights at Kandy.

12th February. I woke at 4.30 and went to the Maligawa before 5.30. Many were ahead of me waiting with their offerings for the doors to open, and sounds of drumming came from inside—tuning up the drums. Then there was a sound of bolts being withdrawn, and finally the doors creaked open and the crowd flowed in, the stream dividing, and little rivulets of people spread into the various shadowy corners of the temple. All went to the well to bathe themselves, and then a great crowd waited on the steps of the shrine, holding up flower-offerings and sleeping babies till the doors opened to let them in. The great drum beat perpetually, and above this the *tom-tom* spread its torrent of notes, with the *horenewa* flute shrilling above.

I followed up the narrow staircase to the room of the relic, but only looked through two brass-framed arches, through which they all passed. Day had come. By six the drumming was over.

A hot bath and slept. This hot bath is an enchanting luxury. The Conservator of Forests, from whom one gets permission to visit the Game Sanctuary at Yala, told me there was dancing last night by the boys of Trinity College. If only he had told us in advance!

We arrived at 7 p.m. at the Tiverton Estate, where, as I have said, the *Kohomba Kankaria* was to take place.

At the right hour the weapons of the god were brought up in a small procession and laid on a table; afterwards they were set upon a screen facing the altar. I have in my notebooks a detailed description of this extraordinary ceremony, which began, as it were, with the climax; for the drumming which opened it and the dancing which followed were certainly the most exciting I have seen in Ceylon. I do not propose to give it here, as I have a more picturesque ceremony to describe elsewhere. The whole of the long, all-night performance was not very well knit together, but that is natural, for it was rather hastily improvised. One day no doubt I shall see a perfect *Kohomba Kankaria,* but I am certainly grateful for the opportunity of seeing this one, and for the co-operation of Malagamana, who had shown a great deal of energy in getting together the dancers and musicians. His pink and green voile dress was certainly odd, and his manner rather overbearing, but it was not an easy task to keep the dancers within bounds, each team being anxious to show off its virtuosity to the utmost. The verbal eloquence of the Sinhalese is most striking. Their technique in declamation seems on a par with their dance technique, and the rhythm of a long speech by the proprietor seemed to me very fine, even though I could not understand it. His style was not declamatory, but the music of his speech was unmistakable. Malagamana's was harsh and hammered out, which made it rather unpleasant to listen to.

Most wonderful of all the dancers was an old man who danced throughout with endless energy and knew every detail of the ceremonial by heart. There always seems to be one of these wonderful old men, who acquire a new lease of life in these recitations and the action which accompanies them, and never tire of reciting *mantras* (spells) which to those who do not understand them get a trifle boring, and who does understand? Molamure, an expert in the dance and of course proficient in Sinhalese, could not attempt to understand the spells, which must often have been altogether unintelligible even to the speaker. The comic passages are sometimes tedious, but delight the audience, as do the comic passages the audiences in the island of Bali. I remember one occasion which began funnily owing to the brilliant miming of the old man who was reciting, but in the end became an insufferable bore to any but the initiate.

The audience is a perpetual delight on these occasions, rising up in a wall of black and white to the night sky, lit by the full moon. They also served as a shelter from the night air which was very chilly, and as they gradually moved off became considerably cooler.

My exposure-meter was stolen during the night, a real calamity; it will I fear be irrecoverable, except perhaps by a diviner.

Harry left halfway through, from sheer cold, though these occasions in any case do not particularly delight him. Molamure insisted on seeing it out and so did Ignatia, who was taking me home in her car. I admit I was half-frozen towards the end.

I tumbled into bed after a delicious hot bath, and went to breakfast at 9.30 feeling fairly fresh. Wrote up my notes till lunch, and another half-hour's sleep completely restored me.

Went with Harry to visit Douglas Amarasekara, in a lovely house

Reliefs from
Embekke temple

Relief from Embekke temple

Masked dancers, Yapahuwa

above the river where he and his mother live together. He is a curious and interesting creature, and talked with the semblance of a Cambridge accent. He has very large luminous eyes set in a round face which, judging from his photographs by McBean, was oval and really beautiful once. He showed us many photos taken by himself at Chelsea—extremely good: postmen, builders, women, etc., but chiefly of young men who were friends of his. He speaks rather ponderously, even pontifically, but is really a modest gentle creature, and his manner is due no doubt to his living always alone, and conversing only with his mother whom he adores, as she does him. He has written a book called the Language Book, which might be interesting: not because he is learned in languages, but because he is certainly an interesting and original person. He showed me some of his poems, of which I liked one definitely. I gather he was some years in England, but his private world impinged so little on the bigger world of letters that he had not even heard of Stephen Spender. I am certain that he would understand and love Edith Sitwell. His father is the famous academic painter of celebrities, Amarasekara, who was Harry's first master. One understands how it is that mother and son prefer to live together above a really wonderful bend of the Mahaveliganga, looking out to the mountains. Below the garden are groves of slender rubber-trees, now in their autumn, exquisite in colouring. I felt at home in that lovely place, which alas I never re-visited.

We went to Jayawardana's to the deserted *maduwa* of the *Kohomba Kankaria,* but could get no news of my exposure-meter.

Sunset on the road and a misty full moon.

Harry took me to visit his cousin Lakdasa, the bishop, who has just been appointed to the See of Kurunegala and hopes to be inaugurated with a *hevisse* (drumming ceremony). He is a little affected in manner, but very sympathetic, and anxious, almost more than anyone I have met, to foster native arts. I discussed with him and Harold and Peggy Peiris the best means of helping the dancers. He has given them the ground for the school which is being built at Hurenagama, and proposes to buy them a paddy-field, so that they may be installed with self-respect on the land. He spoke of their 'pigging it' at Caldecott, but I doubt if this is Guneya's view of the matter; they are preparing for a tour in which he is glad to be taking part, and the stay in Caldecott is a temporary stage. We all agreed of course that the thing to do was to develop self-supporting schools all over the island, rather on the model of Mr. Delgoda's at Kahawatte. Certainly the government should subsidize them, but only if it waived the right to dictate their procedure.

We spent much time telephoning, by Harry's special wish, to discover the whereabouts of Sir Kenneth Clark, who was announced as a passenger on the *Orcades,* returning from Australia, and finally succeeded in getting passes to visit the boat. The harbour was very lovely as we approached the *Orcades,* which seemed to me a nightmare of exposure, all glittering efficiency and publicity—a kind of floating Butlin's Camp.

Kenneth received us kindly, and talked about the aboriginal art of Australia, for which he has a great admiration. The paintings are done on bark and beautifully coloured. They have since then become more familiar, through photographs, etc.; no doubt Sir Kenneth's admiration has had something to do with it. The artistic convention is curious: the inside organs of the animal are portrayed in singular design on the outside of its body. He also admired the ingenious and clearly designed road-signs to indicate the way in a trackless bush, and the white and pale red earth, which he compared with Piero della Francesca's landscapes.

15th February. Harry called towards evening and took me to see a young painter, Gabriel, who teaches at St. Joseph's College. He is a devout Catholic, and the majority of his paintings are of the Crucifixion, Descent from the Cross, Resurrection, etc. A scholarship would be invaluable, but the Selection Committee prefers something more flashy. Harry has succeeded in getting him some teaching, and helped him in various ways.

I spoke to the girls of the convent where Ignatia was educated about the dance and music of Bali and its relation to the life of the people. I emphasized also the relation between bodily structure and technique; and tried to infuse into them a little of my enthusiasm for the arts and crafts of Ceylon. The Mother Superior is a charming, humane and cultured woman, with a great sense of humour. Mrs. Abraham, the geography and arts teacher, was most enthusiastic. She is not allowed to take the girls into Buddhist temples! What a pity.

She showed me some of the children's drawings, which I liked immensely. A few go on painting well into their teens—a hopeful sign.

16th February. Ignatia and I fetched Harry early, and we went to Kotte to consult two clairvoyants about my exposure-meter. We bought *en route* some betel leaves on which to make our offerings. The first clairvoyant read by an arrangement of letters on a slate. She was a nice-looking woman, living in a charming house in a country lane among coco-palms and hedgerows. We were the only clients. When I had placed my offering of two rupees on betel leaves in front of her, she told me to touch one of the letters—arranged in a kind of wheel on the slate. She then immediately began a long discourse, the gist of which was that I had lost something through my own carelessness. She said it was stolen by someone belonging to the place, who had hidden it at a little distance from the house—between south and east. There was a chance of my recovering it, if tactfully handled, as the thief was feeling rather uneasy about the theft. She said it was stolen in the very early morning. All this streamed out without hesitation, and without a single question being put by the clairvoyant. It was distinctly impressive. The only sounds were occasional 'Oh's' from Harry and Ignatia, on various notes of understanding. Her description of the thief's appearance seemed to correspond to people who had been present, but I may so easily have imagined a resemblance, that I would not name my suspicions. I did, as she asked, put my finger on three letters corresponding to the initials of the persons in question. She eliminated two, leaving the most probable, according to her description.

It was now Ignatia's turn. She consulted the clairvoyant about her father, and it appeared that his illness, the chaos in his home, and his probable life duration were all exact.

The second woman we visited lived in a much humbler house. She had one eye, and had two clients with her when we arrived. Her method was to sit in a sort of box holding up a wick floating in coconut oil, supported by a betel leaf, to a saucer with a smear of candle-grease in the middle. She immediately began her recital—without looking at me or paying any attention to me. She said the object was gone for good and all and I should not get it back. The thief sold it in a town eleven miles off to a man who dealt in jewellery and silver objects. I interpreted this as meaning a general shop. I have written on this subject to Malagamana, enclosing extra money for the old man who danced through the night. Perhaps he will feel he should keep it; but he may be moved to help to find the exposure-meter.

(It was actually brought later to Rajapaksa's jewellery shop for sale. Of course I wish he had bought it; but I was then in India, and he was uncertain whether I would want to pay the sum asked.)

19th February. Visited Malalasekera in a rickshaw. The children were charming—especially little Vijaya—immensely gay, not quite four, who is the soul of mischief, as he should be. Malala is lending us his car to go next day to Ambalangoda.

I had some talk with Chitra Sena who made me feel still more the extreme difficulty and profundity of Kandyan dancing. He told me that his guru, Lapeya, is coming and bringing an *ola* (text) containing the procedure of the *Kohomba Kankaria*, and he invited me for the evening. This was most kind, but I was already pledged to a competition at Wellewatte, at which Sederaman, Malagamana and T. D. Pereira are judging. It was indeed something out of the common. The famous Prematilleke with his revolving discs is more in the nature of acrobacy, but it is an astounding feat of grace and rhythm. Only two groups competed: Rajapaksa, the dancer belonging to Keyt's school, and a group from Kegalle, for which old Henrick beat cymbals and sang.

The leader of this group was the truly magnificent Kiriganitha. His *Wawawannam*, sung in mixed times (he gave to each a different rhythm to play), is astounding, and quite new to me. He is certainly far subtler than Rajapaksa, who seemed to me all for solo display, and he got only second prize. The costumes were splendid—all the metal polished and brilliant like a very grand prize harness; all the voluminous flounced or pleated clothes, sashes and frills dazzlingly white.

There seems no end to the invention of these Kandyan dancers. Their musical and above all their rhythmical sense is fantastically developed. I am just beginning to feel I might try to write something about Kandyan dance, just because of my conviction of its great difficulty. It certainly takes years of study before one could hope to grasp its extraordinary richness. Lapeya, Chitra Sena's master, has promised to give a detailed demonstration of *Kohomba Kankaria* next week (and he did). He is a very fine looking man. He has thirty pupils, but no official school, preferring to till his land and teach on his own.

20th February. Got up at five. Malala's car came at 6.15. The nest of Harry's darling sunbirds is hanging in tatters, destroyed during the night by a cruel bigger bird.

We drove through the delicious morning to Ambalangoda in one and a half hours. Spent some wonderful hours in the viharas. The position of all is enchanting, and the children so beautiful who gathered round. Two men and a boy were bathing at a well, stroking their almost black bodies with a kind of *volupté*. Harry made sketches of a very pretty little girl who carried a baby. She did not come out very pretty in his drawing, but his sketch-book is full of lovely figure drawings. The Totagamuwa vihara is in an exquisite position on a hill above a great lagoon. On an island in this lagoon is a Buddhist monastery of German monks.[1] The frescoes are particularly lovely, as regards costume, design of material, musical instruments, dancing, conventional flower decoration, perhaps jasmine in black and white. The two great doors into the shrine are of unequal height, so that the lunettes are also each at a different height. This is an added beauty. The old frescoes of all these temples are in great danger, and what re-places them is horrid beyond description. In Sailbrinbaramya boards and décors and even iron bars are stood against the remains of fresco, and they will soon all be rubbed out. All these frescoes ought to be copied. They are so wonderful—such priceless documents. For weaving designs they would be invaluable. Someone ought to exer-cise control over the destroying vandals. There are some curious figures of Europeans introduced, with ridiculous effect. The Jataka stories are exquisitely illustrated, with a delightful sense of spacing and of decorative values.

The view from the last-named *vihara* is quite lovely. It has the effect of an already painted picture—too much perhaps—the earth rising red and rocky, palms, and two distances of sea and further land. Beautiful rest-house at Hikkaduwa, on a green lawn by the glorious sea, red sand and rocks—continually changing colour of the sea. We saw many beautiful people in lovely attitudes: little boys with their

[1] See Wirz, *Einsiedler auf Taproban.*

lashes casting a shadow on their cheeks. Continual boom of the sea heard from the vihara. Lovely red path, rayed with tree-shadows, between the coco-palms.

Went this evening to see Chitra Sena, and he did some basic rhythms of *wannams* for me, and characteristic bridge-movements with quicker tempo. His teacher is a splendid drummer, as well as dancer. This dancing becomes more and more enigmatic. Best to search for no meaning, but regard it as among the most magnificent movement ever achieved. The whole Kandyan dance seems to be underlaid by the *gaja-ga* rhythm—the elephant's head. But what he did tonight was purely ecstatic—every body movement imaginable. I suppose it has its limitations, though at the moment it seems to me to satisfy every requirement of the dancing spirit; and just because of its limitations to be more great as pure movement. 'Tourbillon, mon tourbillon, je suis en toi, o mouvement, en dehors de toutes les choses.' (I shall have to wait and see if I contradict this after seeing *Bharata Natya, Katha-kali, Kathak, Manipuri*.) Certainly the dancers and drummers are the aristocracy of Ceylon.

21st February. We visited Major Weinman at the zoo, to try and get some information about Hagenbeck and the Kandyan dancers he took to Europe. Weinman is a colossus whose enormous tummy had positively to be tucked away when he sat down. His pale little boy David found no knee to sit on, and had to perch on the chair arm. Major Weinman could throw no light on the dancers being engaged by Hagenbeck, who was, it seems, a business man in Ceylon, as well as collector of wild animals. Exquisite exotic birds and fishes, crested, striped, brilliantly coloured; a great and beautiful elephant drawing, as if it were a feather, a huge water-tank.

I visited the sailors' church of St. Anthony, to register a vow if he returns my exposure-meter. It is a great church, empty of pews and seats, but full of devotion—a church inspiring to faith. Almost all present were men, who behaved exactly as in a Buddhist or Hindu temple, with an entire absorption in their prayer and worship almost unknown in any churches in Western Europe, except occasionally in Catholic countries and always among negroes, Protestant or Catholic. I walked home along the shore at sunset, which the railway quite spoils unless one is in it!

22nd February. In the Matara express which runs all along the shore. The first stop was Moratuwa. The coastline is very lovely. There are many palm-roofed encampments on the beach, mostly very poor. In my carriage was a honeymoon couple. He, delicately handsome. She will be plain in a few years, but is charming now. Inland, densely-populated coconut groves; nets drying; fishermen hauling nets. After Moratuwa the shore encampments became less poor. Beautiful out-riggers, golden sand—covered sometimes with silver-green tufts of grasses, like the foliage of sea-pinks. Egoda Uyana: cows lying just above the waves, wonderful long crystal breakers, a few goats stroll-ing among the palm groves, cactus, prickly pears, the first lagoon. The bridegroom has a lyrical face—not the bride.

Paradura, second stop. Coir rope under shelter of palm roof. Now the red houses begin, of baked earth. A river flows almost to the shore, and is lost in the sand; carpet of convolvulus. Now a wide expanse between us and the sea; enchanting shadows of the coco-palm cover the ground; an ambitious bungalow set alone near the sea; mango groves; bright brown bodies gleaming under the eaves of houses. Almost all the palms are sheathed in palm leaves a short way up the trunk—is this to climb by? The fronds are knotted together. Flowers of vivid colours.

This was the end of the pleasant journey. At Kalutara South I got out and walked up to the town, and there forgot that Sederaman's school was called Government Training College, and asked for Central School. I went by a boneshaker bus in the opposite direction, and found only a village school. Back by bus and on to Katukurunda, where I had to get out and walk up a hot road towards an abandoned aerodrome. Halfway a most improbable-looking tonga drawn by a bullock led me, by dint of gentle prods to the animal's back, to the still unfinished Training College. Scarcely more than a bungalow or two are ready for habitation: only 50 are there of a planned 400. They have a large property, with coconut palms, gum-trees, paddy-fields, and unfortunately an unhealthy-looking swamp, whose mosquitoes devoured me, while I sat with Sederaman taking down the themes and sequences of the *Kohomba Kankaria*. The director was a very nice man, who sent me in some lunch. The visit, though most difficult to bring off, was worth it. I collected valuable material, in fact *almost* the last word; although of course the missing songs and music make it a very big 'almost'. The dancers keep these mysteries to themselves. Sederaman, it seems, had a lawsuit with Hagenbeck because of the latter speaking of the Sinhalese as 'wild men', which was how he presented them to Europe. Apparently the first batch who went were better cared for. Afterwards they suffered dreadfully from cold, and were only paid fifty rupees a month.

23rd February. I can only remember the evening, which began at five, when I went to fetch Harry for a *devapurana* at a remote spot across the ferry. We got slowly under way, fetching the Buddhist priest Rahula from the Ludowyks, who was to guide us. Slowly we got going again, and picked up Weerawardena at Lake House. He had almost given us up. Set off on the twenty-six-mile drive in Mrs. Pieris's big open car; crossed the ferry at Hanwella; the river was so low that we had difficulty in moving at all. On the opposite side we met our guide, who directed us to the remote house about seven miles further on. The road got worse and worse, till we had to get out to examine the ominously cracking bridges we had to cross. Finally landed up in a coco-palm grove, and we saw the lights of the dance floor, in front of a large loggiaed house. It was an enchanting scene. At the far end was a beautiful *torana,* of plantain, decorated in various designs of red, gold and silver paper, which sounds rather tawdry, but is really deliciously fanciful. It consisted of five triangular leaves, linked by vertical and horizontal bands, above large squares of woven plantain, with a space for the gateway. I think the design must be taken from some Indian gateway of stone or wood, and it is no doubt constructed on exact mathematical principles related to the eight angles. A white cloth was nailed over the front, which hid the recess in which Pattini's jewels were kept, and below this the offerings and cloths of the *kapurale.* The *torana* was under a palm-leaf roof, and at the other end of the ground were a variety of altars and shrines for offerings to various gods or demons. One contained food for Pattini, another her jewellery, which was fetched later to be deposited in the *torana.* Offerings were made at all these shrines during the night, and obeisance was continually made to them by the dancers. A coconut wick was kept burning in them. One recess, of plantain woven in a kind of lattice, contained the *Punawa* (pot), which we were later taken to see. It was very brightly coloured, the base covered with those splashes of different colours so beloved by Delgoda's craftsmen. There was a fine tiger-head for lid, which though it is 'statutory', I had not seen before. A thin torch was lit for us in each of the twelve orifices. This would not be destroyed till four in the afternoon. The ceremony, by the way, had been going on since the previous night.

Opposite the *torana* a wide ladder with rungs very far apart led up to a platform high up in a palm-tree, which was hidden by strips of palm leaf. A torch was kept burning all night at the top. This was the central scene of the visiting *Kapurale's* trance, but this came much later. The crowds of people and children were beautifully grouped all through the night, and from time to time an exquisite flower-like face would open beside me into a smile, and I would touch a tiny, shy hand. The *Kapurale* and his son, who proved a splendid dancer, in spite of his heavy build, had powerful noses as well as physique. His profile reminded me of some medieval India sculpture. He improved enormously during the night, and did for about an hour a magnificent series of dances, supported by the old drummer, his teacher, who rapturously followed his invention. For this dance he put on a splendid dress. I put two rupees on some betel leaves for the divination of the *Kapurale,* but he did not reveal anything about my exposure-meter. Harry went to sleep in the car, which fortunately could not be moved an account of another behind it. The dancing, which had not been very good, suddenly became particularly fine. The *Kapurale's* son, light as well as powerful, did a magnificent dance with the old thin drummer accompanying him. It was of a rather difficult design, inclining to a very quick motion round the ground, with his feet very close together, and a continual half-turn on his axis, which made the short *tutu* into which he changed (being now got up very splendidly) twist and vibrate continually. It was a very proud dance, like a turkey-cock. Weerawardena took some superb photos during the whole performance, which I have described in detail in my notebook. We left about 6.30 a.m. after the *Kapurale's* trance, which I found rather painful to watch. He wore a short many-flounced skirt, and a high white headdress bound with blue. His son, whenever he seemed to be getting out of control, rushed forward and seized him, holding him up above his own head like Hercules lifting Antaeus. The *punawa* (pot) would not be broken till four in the afternoon. The crowd, which had rather melted away, gathered again for the *Kapurale's* trance. Harry woke in time for the extraordinary episode of the visiting *Kapurale's* long trance, in which he dashed with his torch into every corner of the grounds and through the house, and climbed the high-runged ladder, just visible writhing on the platform behind the palm-leaf curtain, supported by attendants. Rahula did not quite believe in his trance, but to me it seemed genuine.

We had a delicious drive through the dawn and early mists, and saw Sri Pada rising pink and clear against the sky. For the third time I saw the last crescent of the waning moon—rising at dawn—with the old moon in its arms.

24th February. Revived after a short rest, and went into town to fetch ticket and food control permit. Prince Peter of Greece's lecture on cultural anthropology, which I thought a little crude, was crammed, and everyone was obsequious to a degree. Autograph hunters thronged. Prince and princess brought a familiar Claridge whiff into the atmosphere. Polyandry was his principal theme, and Freud was dragged in. The girls' crocodile from St. Bridget's was of course there.

25th February. With Ignatia to visit two temples—off the Kandy road —which she had been reading up—the Attanagala vihara, 1,000 years old: a king gave his head to a poor man, who was hoping to win a reward by killing him. In the atrocious modern representation of the episode he was shown as bloodily beheaded—like a Catholic martyr—though of course he must have removed it magically. The octagonal vihara—which is much spoilt by its wooden-roofed enclosure—has some extremely interesting headdresses of fantastic and very varied design: each kneeling figure having a different one. This was the only beauty that remained, apart from the layout of the temple court and the leaf-shaped lotus-pool beside a curious little cave containing two footprints in the rock—one large, one small.

We drove thence to the Warana Raja Maha Vihara, which is on top of an enormous rock. The group of great grey rocks is very lovely —their fantastic shapes always stir me. Under the shadow of one huge rock, as we approached over the paddy-fields, oxen were threshing—a very beautiful scene, which I really preferred to the entirely spoilt vihara. The slow rhythm of the turning oxen, small boys, old men standing motionless. A series of cement staircases lead up to the vihara on the rock. On each flight the name of the donor (our next-door neighbour) is blazoned, and their generosity for electricity and water-power praised. The view from above, across an ocean of palm-trees, is most lovely, and the disposition of the terraces among the rocks.

26th February. A bad start for Ambalangoda, where Leston was to take photos of the murals. I was ready before anyone, but failed to interpret a faint knock at the door as a summons, to indicate that they had been waiting for me fifteen minutes in the car. After I had joined them I suddenly remembered that I had forgotten my fan, and jumped out again to fetch it. This was disastrous, a bad omen! Superstitious though I am, this particular omen was unknown to me, though I have since discovered that it is very common. Even the usually so smiling Leston was nervous and shaken, and Ignatia sat silent, too upset to speak at all. Toni, who was driving, was the only person untroubled by the bad omen, and by the reactions of his parents, and when suddenly ordered to turn back, did so without comment.

It was not till we were home again that I discovered *I* was the cause of all the trouble. Naturally other offences came out then in a flood, and at last I drove off alone in a rickshaw to calm myself, but after a while returned and made peace with Ignatia, sealed by tears. I was more shattered by the discovery of my alienness, and of all the susceptibilities I must have hurt in return for so much kindness, than by the loss of the photos which Leston was to have taken of the murals at Ambalangoda.

In the late afternoon Ignatia went with me to Chitra Sena's house to take down the version of Vijaya's former birth from Lapeya, who had most kindly brought his precious text. She translated this amazingly well, on the spot.

CHAPTER VIII

Return to Ceylon—Kandy 'Perahera' — Another 'Kohomba Kankaria' — Anuradhapura and Mihintale

At last after my Indian excursion I have a standard of comparison with the great Kandyan dancers, having seen many of the best teachers of *Kathakali, Kathak* and *Bharata Natya,* and many great dancers of various schools.

This time my vision of Ceylon on arriving was quite different from the first; no longer flooded as after the great tornado at Bombay, and the retarded monsoon, when all was watery; this time the north was a cold grey and white, salt lands bordered by flaming red, and then, in and out of the sea, mottled islands, like crocodile, tortoise or lizard skins, with roads across them that seemed to end in water. The land is now outstretched like a great brown skin, with dark pools of shadow cast by slatey cotton-wool clouds, and fawn or emerald fields near the coast. A fleet of glittering emerald cloud sails above the earth far below the blue sky, and through it one sees exquisite iridescencies of land and water. It seems inexorably flat. Scrub, with a scarlet ribbon of road winding through it, and strange to see, ending in a grey flat. Scrub is everywhere, perhaps really high jungle too, with curious blue lakes and grey crater-like eruptions. Now we are over the mushroom-brown coastline, broken by many small creeks. It seems entirely deserted, but there are some emerald squares which mean cultivated fields. The sea is strangely grey under a pellucid sapphire sky. I am glad to sit in the sun. Clouds cover the sky and partly hide the mountains. A rust-coloured river serpentines through the jungle—very bright apple-green fields are interspersed. Huge cumulus clouds rear towards a brighter sky. The intention of the weather seems a little indeterminate, and the plane too is a little wobbly. Now the land has a rather waterlogged appearance, with irregular patterns of opalescent paddy-fields. Only the sectional lines show clearly that they are fields, and not streams or lakes. An occasional flare of red earth breaks the green and grey monotony, or a flourish of red roofs. Now the stream is yellow, and the flooded fields blue, purple, slate grey . . . Colombo.

This time it was Harry Pieris who met me, in an elegant new car. All imaginable festivals are on at once—Jaffna, Dondra, Kataragama and Kandy. I am staying this time with Harry's brother, Dick, a grave business man of meticulous habits, and Sheila, a daughter of Rajapaksa the famous portrait-painter, who did many portraits of Ignatia. They live in Rosmead Place, quite near to Harry's house, and are both endlessly kind and hospitable. I have a flat to myself, a perfect bed and private bath: what luxury! Sheila is very ingratiating and anxious to talk French, in which language she and her father always converse. I am delighted to oblige.

I forgot to note the man in Madras who sat on the pavement in Mount Road and continually bent forward crying: Amen! Amen! A small naked child sat beside him all day. What a strange beginning to life!

27th July. End of Ramadan—another public holiday! The library shut in consequence. With Harry to Kelaniya towards evening. The many prostrated people and the general movement were charming. We walked along the river bank above many swirling currents, and returned to the temple for the drumming, which was exciting, though not of the quality of the Maligawa.

28th July. With Harry to Kurunegala. A magnificent flaming sunset through the trees lit the strange rocky hillside which skirts the road at one point. A lovely drive along a narrow road through dense forest, lit only by our car lamps. The fireflies, which had not appeared since my last visit, again abounded in the trees—an exquisite febrile dance. Unfortunately the rain drove them in. Downpour during the night.

29th July. Rain. Went on a search for Lapeya, Kandyan teacher of Chitra Sena. Set out with Dodan, who was held up by various transactions in the town. Finally we reached—on Dambulla Road— a village school, and were directed to the new government school;

157

down a very muddy, unmade road to a magnificent lake surrounded by strange shapes of distant mountains. The school is still half-built, and there is a good deal of mud round it. But it is an excellent place. The headmaster has realized—he said—the dream of years. He chose the site, and in face of the opposition of the parents he has a co-educational school—500 pupils and 150 girls. I saw the boys' dormitory. All the schoolrooms are open, with a low divisional wall from the passage. We saw a specimen of a lesson in Kandyan dancing given to boys, and one girl doing Kandyan dancing very nicely. It was the day before they set off on their yearly archaeological expedition, so they were given yellow rice and ice-cream. The boys were sitting before their yellow rice—they had already eaten the ice-cream, being unable to wait any longer. The dance-teacher, Sanaliya, who is Guneya's cousin and is somewhat like him, said he was Lapeya's master. It appears, however, that they both learned from Sanaliya's uncle, who might, I suppose, be Guneya's father. The boys did a song from the *Vessantara Jataka*; the scene where the Buddha in a previous incarnation gave away his children. Walked in the sodden paths of the coco-palm groves at dusk—there was an effort at sunset glow.

30th July. A few fireflies about last night, and rain held off. This morning brilliant intervals and heavy showers—less and less frequent. I went again with Dodanwatamana in search of the dance-teacher Lapeya to a temple, near Potuhera, where lives an old priest known to Dodan. We had to go along a precarious track above the paddy-fields, which the car just managed to negotiate. Rain fell again in floods—an elephant was grazing in a field. The old priest revealed that Lapeya, or Guliya, lived on the other side of the main road at Bebilagomuwa. We left the car by some booths, and a man led us across the paddy-fields by a path much broken by the rains, through sodden coconut groves to a charming little group of houses of sunbaked earth, with three elegant granaries, or rice-houses. They are shaped like eggs—the narrow end at the bottom and the wide end at the top, covered by a strong circular roof of straw, thickly lined. The well is bound in with rattan covered over with clay. A fine new one was Lapeya's. A wide road divided the two groups of houses. It all looked very clean and prosperous. His old father—who had been a drummer—came out and talked to us; they were charming people. Lapeya had gone to Colombo for a wedding with a group of dancers—no doubt the string of lamps preparing at Chitra Sena's was for this. He told us of a *Kohomba Kankaria* at Tiragama—to take place on 11th August—so we went off there, turning off the main road at the level-crossing off Tiragama. We drove along a delightful hilly road for two or three miles, picking up on the way a very beautiful boy with great liquid eyes and a noble intelligent expression. We arrived at last by twisting lanes at a particularly muddy corner (the mud being entirely wet sand), and found a large *maduwa* being constructed in front of a house, in readiness for the various celebrations—*Thovil, Kohomba Kankaria,* etc., which seem to extend from the 4th to the 11th. The occasion is a vow taken against the recovery of a small son from chickenpox, and also the first rice feeding of a baby. The doctor and his family came out to greet us and gave us a drink. I sat down by mistake on a bench outside the veranda, but was shooed inside to a chair, with a horrfiied gesture by our host—the benches were only for people of low birth. The veranda was crowded with chairs, and we saw into a dark room similarly crowded, which seemed to be full of women and bedsteads. We were warmly invited to their celebration. Unfortunately the *Kohomba Kankaria* is on the last day of the Kandy *Perahera*. I gather that plenty of toddy will be flowing.

To the Ridi Vihara in the afternoon, rather a disappointment. The only lovely thing left is the fragmentary ivory door, which looked more ruined than before, especially the panels (entwined dancing figures) over the lintel. The best are the two lovely square dancing insets at the foot. This evening great families of monkeys—a whole tribe—disported themselves on the perpendicular face of the great rocks facing the veranda, and swung among the branches, perilously plunging from bough to bough. Later—the moon, and a wonderful array of fireflies.

31st July. Set off early to Kabelalewa, where the frescoes are of which Weerawardena took photos. Very lovely drive through an alley of rain-trees on the Yapahuwa road, which passes the Yak Desa Gala—a huge rock from which Kuveni is said to have thrown himself down in grief at Vijaya's betrayal. The ground at the foot of the temple rock is wide and wild, partly cultivated, and beautiful with flowers. There is a wonderful view of the mountains, today veiled by rain clouds. A steep flight of steps leads up the rock—not those delightful shallow steps one finds on the rock face of some of the Buddhist temples. An ugly roof has been built in front of the long gate, and some nasty repainting has been done of the Buddha in corners of the cave. The frescoes are less interesting than the later ones at Ambalangoda, consisting chiefly of the Buddha and monsters, semi-human, rather resembling the figures of Hieronymus Bosch. But there is a splendid group of deities on either side of a seated Buddha on the lower floor of a four-storeyed palace which spreads out all over the roof of one corner of the cave. The painted railings and elaborate border designs, and all the decorations of the palace are very fine. There is also much fine patterning on the rocky roof. The Bodhisatvas are a little dull. There is a lotus-pool under the perpendicular rock and a superb view of the green country and distant mountains.

We drove further along the road to visit an older temple, Nura-kande, to reach which we had to walk several miles along a sandy bridle-path, between plantain gardens and coco-palm and jungle. A great purple rock appeared and disappeared elusively, and finally we arrived by detours at the real temple rock, which is exceedingly re-mote. There are traces of earlier ruins, then shallow steps up a rock and one passes through a labyrinth of precariously poised huge rocks to a kind of little plateau, where a champak-tree overhangs a rock and a long passage opens on the rock temple. The decoration of the roof is beautiful, following the irregular surface of the rock, and the Buddha—who lies in a slightly curving position—is very fine. His profile exceedingly noble and the deep shadow of his brow falling on his finely-modelled cheek. This temple has not been spoilt. A few steps further up is another rock recess containing two Buddhas—one reclining and one seated. Both are unfinished or have been partially destroyed. The reclining one is surprisingly African in the stylization of the face, like the Benin copper masks. I have never seen anything like it in Ceylon. Besides Yakdesa Gala (the rock of the Yakka's curse) are Tonigala (the rock of lamentation) and Vilakatupota (the vale of tears)—associated with the sorrows of Kuveni.

Kuveni (Asua) thus relates her story: 'When shipwrecked and forlorn I found you, and gave your men food and home. I helped

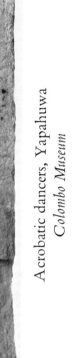

Acrobatic dancers, Yapahuwa
Colombo Museum

Nude dancer, Yapahuwa

you to rout the Yakkas and raised you to be king. Pledging me your troth you made me your spouse. Did you not know then that I was of the Yakka's race? Loving you with unquenchable love, and living in such love, I bore you children. How can you leave me and love another? The gentle rays of the rising full moon are now to me the blaze of a red-hot ball of iron; the cool spicy breezes of the sandal groves are hot and unwelcome; the cuckoo's sweet song pierces my ears as with a spear. Alas! how can I soothe my aching heart?'

In A.D. 113 Gaja Bahu rolled back the Tamil tide of invasion, and brought back many captives taken by the Tamil king. He settled a large number of Tamil captives in the Alutkuru Korale of Colombo district, Harrispattu and Tumpane (Kandy), and parts of Kurune-gala district. The Kandy *Perahera* commemorates Gaja Bahu's triumph, which has become more and more a religious festival since the eighteenth century. Goddess Pattini holds a high place in this festival. Her worship was introduced by Gaja Bahu. He brought from India her golden Salamba (anklet)—copies of which are symbols of her worship; oaths are taken by them in courts of justice—an oath dreaded by Sinhalese peasants.

1st August. By bus to Kandy. The caretaker—who probably never goes by bus—said it left every half-hour, and of course this we be-lieved. In fact, it left about every two hours. It was exceedingly un-comfortable and slow, continually rising through wonderful woods, but no mountain views. I was picked up by the de Silvas' car at the Queen's and brought up here, St. George's. The house is in a more than usual state of disorder, as Minnette is architecturally pulling it to pieces and reconstructing it at the same time. This is inevitable; but I have a much nicer room in consequence, though doorless. The dining-room wall is being loudly demolished in the interests of a lotus-pool. Cold rain adds to the discomfort, but Mr. de Silva seems happier now that the legal business is settled, and is certainly calmer, though occasional murmurs arise from Mrs. de Silva. For whatever he thinks of he must do immediately, no matter whom he wakes up in the process. He never tells where he is going with the car, nor how long he will be away. Everyone is subordinate to him and must adjust themselves. His voice is high, almost a squeal when exas-perated, but yet how lovable he is, devoted to children and natural beauty! I cannot forget seeing him sitting for hours in the garden of his son's tea-estate, holding Mrs. de Silva's hand and gazing out over the sublime landscape for hours in complete silence.

The garden is full of flowers, though much beaten by the rains. Apparently this is an unusually early *perahera*. The rains are as abnormal during this moon as the great heat-wave in Europe which, alas, I am not there to enjoy.

2nd August. This evening I went down to Kandy to see the *Perahera*. It was dusk. The *Perahera* was not due to come out till 8.30. There were very few people, it being actually the first day, though since the 28th things had been going on in the temple, rites of various kinds. Six or seven elephants were lined up, busily munching huge plantains strewn for them and unwieldy boughs of kitool palm, tearing off the pith with careful feet and trying to cram in the woody stalk. They were all hooded, though their ears flapped free and undecorated. They wore various coloured hoods. Four more were aligned along the wall of the *devale*, also busily munching. They are certainly very untidy eaters and leave almost more on their plates than they take off them.

I went into the temple, drawn by the insistent drumming. The special 'casket' elephant—also busily feeding—was being dressed in his howdah and canopy. His hood is far the most magnificent, red and studded with brass knobs (perhaps gold) and his ears are also clothed in close-fitting hoods of the same stuff and pattern. There are jewels on his forehead: perhaps the red stone is a ruby. He took up all the space at the foot of the steps, so I had to go up by the longer way into the temple. Drummers hard at it in the temple, and I was beckoned to come and see the dancers dressing. They were dressing in every corner. Several recognized me and smiled a welcome. I saw people on the wall of the *devale* and went in over a very muddy enclosure to inspect their 'grandstand'. Meanwhile the elephant with Hindu relics in a casket on his back came slowly down the steps, and was taken up the road to the other *devale*, no doubt to fetch more elephants. Torches were being lit, and men were climbing the backs of the elephants, with bronze umbrellas or old-fashioned weapons. I peeped at the temple elephant's toilet. Nugawela had come to the top of the steps, dressed all in white like an old Sinhalese nobleman, looking very portly in his crisp white skirts, with a white biretta-like hat and black shoes studded with brass nails. Other temple officials collected in red pancake hats. The gun went off: a tinkling of anklets filled with small seeds announced the dancers, who came trooping down from the temple and took their places along the road space between the elephants—who began to move off and take their station along the lake road. There were *udekki* groups and *pantheru*, and some drummer groups.

Many torches now rent the night, and the great relic-bearing elephant came slowly and majestically down the temple steps between the stone elephants, always bringing up one foot to join the other before venturing on a fresh step. Torches and dim figures of elephants were now seen filling the dark road from the further *devale*. Nugawela, under a white umbrella, took his place in the procession, and walked during the whole of it. A group of *Pantheru* dancers, chanting a slow song—perhaps of praise—danced with very slow motions before him, after making each a deferential obeisance.

The *perahera* got under way, with forty elephants, many groups of dancers—by no means the best—drums and pipes. It looked exceedingly beautiful as the torches moved slowly forward with the elephants, occasionally stopping, while an elephant did pipi, or a group of dancers performed. Some of the *pantheru* and *udekki* dancers were tiny little boys, and some had no instrument to dance with. The tempo of the dancing got quicker as the *Perahera* proceeded, and was quite vertiginous for a moment. I discovered from a policeman where it would be passing, and went back to the temple and along the *décombres* of the old palace, to where I could see the torches and elephants and dancers coming down King Street past the further *devale* —and the casket elephant and dancers and drummers trooped again into the temple, while the slow tinkling of the elephants' bells moved away in various directions, going home. Then I too went home, by cloudy moonlight.

3rd August. Recriminations of grown-ups and yells of infants began the day. The yeller made friends with me, and I then silenced her by yoga exercises and took her for a walk.

Tonight went with Minnette to the *Perahera.* Many more people sitting along the edge of the pavement, but I could not raise the number of elephants to forty. We saw the *Diyawadana Nilame* (lay chief)

—Nugawela—being dressed for the procession. He was at the stage of a white frilled shirt with gold buttons and a vast amount of scarlet stuff being wound and bound and flounced round him. This again was covered with many yards of voluminous white, very scientifically arranged by an old expert, and again bound tightly round with a wide belt. All this was to 'make his stomach', an essential attribute of dignity of the Kandyan nobles. He showed us some magnificent printed South Indian saris—very lovely colours, which are absolutely fast, and chose a particularly beautiful old one of infinite richness and subtlety of design and blend of colours to be draped in above all his other trappings. It was very tastefully arranged and drawn up between his legs, a tail falling behind as background. This is one of the loveliest 'cloths' I have seen—cotton worked with gold threads. The variety of patterns is extraordinary and the harmony of colours. It is, like the Javanese batiks, as soft as silk, and has an almost velvety surface. We left him to complete his toilet, and at his suggestion fetched our shoes from the temple threshold and put them in his office. This was a very fatal step, as we had great difficulty in procuring them afterwards.

We went with Nugawela's permission to the Octagon, which contains the temple library, and from which the view over the lake and all the converging roads is superb. The *Perahera* was getting under way. We saw the elephant from the *Natha devale* moving out with torches through the trees to fetch the elephants of the *Maha devale*, and soon the road below the old palace was blazing with torches, and one saw the dim forms of swaying elephants and groups of dancers in their shining white skirts and glittering headdresses. Soon the temple drums uttered a tremendous volley, as also did the old temple gun, and the drummers and officials in their circular red hats came hurrying down the steps below us, and soon the dignified form of Nugawela bearing the golden casket—under a canopy of what looked like a transparent patchwork of lace. The casket was bound on the elephant's back, and soon he lurched down the steps, passed through the great gateway, its gold canopy glistening under the arch, and the *Diyawadana Nilame* (lay chief) followed over flower petals. A great burst of drumming greeted his arrival under a white umbrella in the middle of the road, then the low bows of the dancers and a chanted dance, ending in a stylized walk. The same procedure as last night, but a variation caused by our failure to find our shoes—which left us stranded in the temple. I was much surprised and even shocked by seeing a young man in trousers, but apparently connected with the temple, walk calmly through it in his outdoor shoes—not even sandals. Finally the key was produced and we got our shoes, and went along to the old palace, treading delicately among the ruins to see the *Perahera* returning from the *devales*.

4th August. Dolapihille has many stories. He belongs, it seems, to the old Kandyan aristocracy. He was arrested in 1915, aged eighteen, when riots broke out all over Ceylon, in consequence of a *perahera* having passed a mosque, in defiance of Muslim feeling, or possibly of police orders. The British official before whom Dolapihille appeared had been told his crime was incitement to revolt, because he had prophesied in a letter that there would be trouble in Kandy. The police appear to have been thoroughly told off, and many English to have lost their posts through their bad handling of the matter. Dolapihille certainly came out with flying colours. It was almost dark when I left him, full of stories.

Dolapihille supposes the *Kohomba Kankaria* to be a type of dance which has come down from the Demon King Ravana, and is not in origin Indian at all. That it is indigenous is very probable. He called my attention to the extreme virility of Kandyan dancing and the exact laws which govern it: the line of the body and neck. Curves are not tolerated—or were not—for now the curving of the elephants' trunk is shown, and the sinuous windings of the snake. Really, I see no reason why in the *Wannams* the technique of the *Ves* should not be modified.

Randoli, which appear on the sixth day of the *perahera,* are the empty litters of the chief Queens, meaning originally the Queens themselves, or principal spouses—'the golden spouses'. The *Perahera* is a festival of the aboriginal gods, and really only secondarily of the Tooth, or anything to do with Buddhism.

The litters or conveyances of the Queens are now carried symbolically.

The *Perahera* that existed in Kotte—now a suburb of Colombo—was a parade of chieftains of the Kotte King. In the hill country the

Perahera is the festival of Natha, one of the devas at Kandy; but his origin is unknown, and his attributes.

The festival of Alutnuwara is at the temple of Dandimuda (or Dedimuda), one of the devas at Kandy, a god not to be trifled with.

There is also the *Perahera* of Gadaladeniya and that of Gampola, the attempt to stop which caused the huge upheaval of 1915. The police—according to Dolapihille—received bribes from Muslims, and ordered the drums to be stopped when passing the mosque. The rioters—or those who had cognisance of them all over the island— were suspected of siding with the Kaiser! The English seem to have lost their heads.

When I returned from Dolapihille, by bus, it was quite dark. The dinner was gloomy, at the table in the window, sufficiently far from the light to make eating most uncomfortable. Minnette's structural alterations always seem to cast their shadow too far ahead; so the standard lamps she has in mind, essential to the new position of the table, were not forthcoming, and no one seems to have considered the possibility of candles. The doltish boy from the estate filled my hot-water bottle and hung it on a nail in the bathroom, thus showing that he anyway remembered his former mistakes. Never by any chance does he put it in the bed.

The house has in small ways changed its shape considerably since I came. Holes appear in floor or ceiling and are filled in or enlarged as the case may be. A floor that looks as if all the waters of the ocean would not wash it clean suddenly appears possible to walk on, and an attached lavatory seat which has been floating about for days now is seen anchored to the floor, though other essential attachments are lacking. There are no effective doors, only doorways, but even when they are put in I doubt if they will make much difference. But Min-nette issues always radiant from her dressing-room, like one prepared to scale an upper sphere, and always with the same confident hope of a million rupee contract in Colombo or Bogota.

I walked to the Savoy Hotel, where Raven Hart is living. It is a charming house above a terraced garden looking over the lake. The food is said to be particularly good, and the washing arrangements less so. We talked about his Torres Straits book, and he told me of a village not far off in which Kandyan dancing—up to a short while ago—formed part of the service of the Mass at the Catholic church.

The weather had been superb, but now a few clouds—which I did not think dangerous—formed a magnificent shield to the sun. Elephants were passing along Lake Road on their way to the *Perahera*— big and small. Very lovely coco-palm trunks aligned along the curving road. I visited the Vishnu *devale,* where there are some fine old painted cloths hanging on the walls; also the *Natha devale.* By the time I had had coffee at the Queen's Hotel it was pouring with rain. I took refuge in the Maligawa, but could not get permission from Nugawela to watch from the Octagon, unless the chief monk there would give permission, in spite of my having no permit. He would not, without a permit from the Government Agent, who lived in a bungalow near the Old Palace. So I trailed off in the dark rain with a policeman to find the unlighted path to the bungalow, which led past the Old Palace and the gaping ruins—I had no torch. The Government Agent was not there, and back we went. By this time the dancers and various emblem-bearers were beginning to come out. It still rained hopelessly. Natha's elephant—his scarlet cloth lit by the torches— came cautiously down the steps of the *devale,* and moved off up the road to meet the Vishnu elephants. I had seen great heaps of torch-holders earlier in the Vishnu temple. In the Maligawa some boys were dressing, in paper crowns and with whitened faces, and a parody of the *Ves* dancers' dresses. I watched one man being dressed— tightly bound round with wide scarlet sash, and arranging his yards and yards of creased white cloth so as to fall in loops above and under his sash.

The rain was hopeless. I waited some time on the wooden stand in Ward Street, and then retired to the Queen's Hotel, where the atmosphere was gloomy and cold. They knew, of course (which I did not), that the *Perahera* would not be allowed to pass the hotel.

It was nine before the gun went off and the *Perahera* got under way. It was a long time before it came lurching down Ward Street, carefully turning off so as to isolate completely the Queen's streets on all sides. The reasons for this boycott were never quite clear to me. I heard vague rumours of differences of opinion; but what the truth is, who knows? The *Perahera* when it did come was very exciting, in spite of the umbrellas. Even some of the elephants were ridden under umbrellas. There were seventy-two elephants, great and small, and a lot of vigorous dancing and drumming. Three functionaries walked under umbrellas—the lay chief and two others: one in white embroidery—very dazzling; and one with a crimson velvet, gold-studded jacket. They all wore black patent shoes, studded with brass nails or silver. The *Randoli*—litters of the Golden Spouses —came last of all. It was immediately in front of them that the official walked in a crimson velvet jacket. Directly it was over there was a rush from the stand, and everyone streamed past the Queen's. But we were not allowed to go down Ward Street towards the street by which the *Perahera* would pass, but had to make a big diversion round by the fair. I walked damply home. A watery moon was breaking through the clouds. The hills were clear, and a star shone.

7th August. I walked up Bhairavakande, where the last human sacrifice is supposed to have taken place. A long winding path and flights of steps lead up to it, fringed by cottages. Past one of these I had to climb by a tiny path, overgrown with long, coarse grass, to the grassy plateau which is the summit. The view is superb over Hantana and the symmetrical streets of Kandy—and to the varied range of the Dambulla mountains. A brilliant day, all the storm passed. I found my way back by winding paths among plantations to Maria Estate, Wattegama, down the steps of which two boys were coming who talked English well. They led me by a short cut to the bottom of the hill by which one climbs up here. They told me I had arrived at the right moment to learn about Eastern dancing, because Ram Gopal and Kay Ambrose were here. The splendid sky clouded and the thunder began much earlier this afternoon, with heavy rain and clouds low on Hantana.

Visit from the police, who had been told there were things stolen last night from the house. This was a very Russian interview; they had to keep drawing our attention back to the matter in hand. It was continually straying to the route of the *Perahera*. Meanwhile the dining-room was being painted in three colours, and all the furniture lay heaped up at one end. A discussion started between Mr. de Silva and his son about the morality of raising a sum to pay

200 dancers for the reception of Lord Soulbury. It seems to me a harmless and positively beneficial extravagance, as some of the money is to go into the dancers' pockets; but it passed into an argument on motives being the only criteria of actions, and here the principles of Freddy seemed to me preferable to those expounded by Mr. de Silva.

We went to Mr. de Silva's office and saw the much-diminished *Perahera*—only Nugawela walked in it: the two other temple dignitaries were ostentatiously absent. There were about eighty elephants, but according to the habitués they were drably dressed. Personally, I thought a few of them had very lovely coverings, but there were a number of rather Puritan ones in dark blue or black with white frills. I found the sea of people surging to see the *Perahera* almost as interesting as the procession itself. There are at present no acrobats or stilt-walkers, and not a great number of dancers.

8th August. The situation has changed. We saw the *Perahera* from the Octagon. The night was fine, though not bright moonlight as it should have been. The contending temple chiefs had made up their differences, and three walked in the procession, which meant that more dancers also came.

The *Perahera* was truly superb. The face-cloths and heads of three elephants were illuminated and also the canopies over the relics, and a white cloth was laid continually in front of the elephant of the Maligawa, and rolled up when he had passed over—to be spread again in front. The lay chief was more splendid than ever in a golden hat, which must have sat heavily on his brow—a magnificent gold-embroidered jacket and sumptuous skirt. Both the others were equally grand. Ladders stood against the wall of the Natha temple, up and down which white figures climbed continually. The wall was covered with spectators, who must have been waiting for hours. We had to show a pass to the Octagon in order to be admitted past a police cordon on the main road. The drumming and dancing was most superb, and make Anura's statement that the average Kandyan dancer is not 'presentable' more ridiculous still. Nothing can be more wonderful and elegant than the Kandyan dancer's dress. It is not his 'inferiority complex' which prevents his 'talking and explaining and demonstrating' his art: it is his native good sense. It is quite a new thing for dancers to explain their dance in words. Their dancing is sufficient demonstration.

Did the seemingly clown-dancers in last night's *Perahera,* wearing tinsel crowns and devil-dance costumes, merely dance as a parody, or were they authentic devil-dancers? There were very few. Perhaps to-night will show.

The rhythm of the drummers while stationary and while dancing is naturally different. A very lovely movement in the dance is the opening obeisance to the lay chief, in very slow tempo, which gradually increases in speed till it becomes almost—but not quite—a frenzy: certainly ecstatic.

The dance of the drummers is quite wonderful. Their movements are limited by the drum they hold in front of them, but their energy and agility is extraordinary, and I have seen a dancer do a somersault while holding the drum. The long passage of the *Perahera* down the lake and round the square was very beautiful, with flaming torches and glittering canopies of the slow-moving elephants. We sat in the garden of the Old Palace to watch the return of the procession, and saw and heard the lovely cascade of bells as the dancers ran up the steps of the Maligawa. We seem to have missed a dance contest at the *Maha devale.*

The Queen's has quite changed, and is now a hive of activity. Guests arriving. Every corner full, in anticipation of the *Perahera* resuming its old course. Arthur Molamure is here and promised to take us with Ratwatte to the *Maha devale* after the *Perahera.* The crowds were enormous—also in the afternoon for the reception of the Governor-General. The street he passed down was lined with bam-boo arches fringed with plaited palm leaves, and Mr. de Silva had got quite a number of flags hung out. Two hundred dancers and drum-mers, led by Ukuwa, were lined up in front of the Governor-General's car. A garland was hung round his neck inside the car by Mrs. de Silva. The dancers preceded him all the way down Trin-comalee Street till the turning to the Town Hall, and later ushered him into the King's Pavilion. Two elephants led them. The eye-glassed, rubicund Lord Soulbury was highly delighted.

Octagon again, more wonderful than ever. A number of bald, yellow-robed Buddhist monks covered the crenellated wall at the top of the steps below which the elephants were being caparisoned. They were in lovely sculpturesque attitudes, and reminded me for a moment of Michelangelo figures. Their strange, intent faces added to the beauty of the group. Great animation inside the temple, which Harry and I explored pretty thoroughly. We saw where the casket lives which is carried round on the temple elephant. This room—where the relics are—has most lovely ivory carved doors, still perfectly preserved. These are double doors, which make a lovely perspective looked at from afar, into the golden shrine. These doors are really magnificent. There is a further one—much more like the door of the Ridi *Vihara* in that its ivory framework is badly broken up, bits having obviously been removed—according to the priests—by the Dutch. We saw the torches piled up in the courtyard ready to be lit, when the gun signal should go off. Lovely scene from the Octagon, like a series of miniatures—elephants, crowds, and the beautiful expanse of empty green grass of the temple square, with occasional white flecks of seated people. The elephants began moving out along the lake road while it was still dark, i.e. before torches were lit. Later, when the flares were lit, they were seen to stretch almost as far as the Queen's. When the gun was fired, the lay chief made his usual gorgeous appearance—but even more resplendent in silver and gold. The dancers and drummers were already in great numbers in the road opposite the temple gateway, squatting on the ground. At last—an hour after the announced start—the gun went off, and immediately an insistent drumming and piping began inside the temple—dancers and drummers jingled along the gallery, and there was a great rush down the steps. A carpet was laid for the lay chief, his canopy was spread above him—torches flared all along the route—and down the whole road, up to the *Maha devale,* was an endless vista of flaring torches—slowmoving elephants—glittering canopies, lit with tiny bulbs. The elephants' tusks were covered with gold sheaths and a tiny bulb lit the points. Far away beside the lake one saw a dancer twirling flaming torches, and below us was a dancer balancing many brass bowls on as many poles, holding one also in his mouth. The dancing was exceptionally fine: *pantherus* with their white kerchief and long streamers, tight red sash with triangle of colour over white skirts. It was the *Maha devale* which had the best troupe of dancers,

171

some from Kegalle. This is the Vishnu temple. I forgot to count the elephants, so captivating was the show. The reflection in the lake as background very lovely.

Later we went to the *Maha devale* with Arthur Molamure, who is a friend of the nephew of Ratwatte—the lay chief. This was the best part of all. Elephants belonging to the temple came slowly up the slope and grouped themselves. Dancers performed below in the open space before the temple. A group of *Wannam* dancers and *pantherus* from Kegalle. The hawk-*wannam* done by five, wheeling together with sloping arms, was very effective. Their gyrations and leaps were very splendid, their singing harsh and discordant. The *pantheru* dancers were rather ineffective, as they did not change from hand to hand with the quick wrist turn which is so lovely, so that the mixed circle had not much point. It was wonderful to see behind the dancers slow-moving elephants passing. On the way to the hotel we saw the *Perahera* of the four *devales* doing its last turn. Arthur Molamure said this is the most important part—the lustration of the town by the gods, no doubt pre-Hindu gods, though with Hindu names. The litters which I thought were empty contain—according to Molamure—weapons, symbols of the gods. There was something very solemn about this late small procession.

10th August. Dined with Harry and saw the *Perahera* from the Queen's. What a come-down! It became an ordinary procession, with elephants, dancers and drummers—seen among tourists—no perspectives of swaying canopies among smoking torches. I had no pleasure from it. The crowds rose in tiers on either side; tourists clamoured within the hotel. The situation was retrieved by our going up to the *Maha devale* and seeing the return of the *Perahera* from there. This was wonderful, altogether amongst the people, and the gradual falling-out of the elephants at their respective *devales* was very lovely. Then came all the lances and dancers, and Ratwatte—who in all his purple splendour found time to greet me. I regretted not having gone to the water-cutting ceremony at the Mahaveliganga, when I heard the drums and elephant bells in the dawn moving along the road. Even then I *could* have gone, but imagined they were returning, when they were only going out.

11th August. Lunched with Harry and we set off for Kurunegala, but got fascinated by seeing bits of the *Perahera* setting out to their starting-place and finally drove up behind the King's Pavilion and saw the whole *Perahera* from above the *Maha devale,* facing my lovely Hantana Gala. Reached the estate at five, and found Harry's niece and cousin, who had come for the *Kohomba Kankaria* near Tiragama.

We arrived there as night fell. The large pavilion we saw building ten days ago was already fairly full of people, and the drummers were in part of the plantain screen inlaid with squares of fresh palm leaves, depicting Buddha, etc. A fine plume of plantain framed its canopy and a long plantain bud hung down over it. Below it was a heap of coconuts and a plantain effigy of the wild boar, with cunningly cut bristles on his back, and the bow and arrow which killed him. The drummers were making beautiful obeisance to their *guru,* the altar and each other. There were fifteen of them, one a small boy, and their performance was magnificent. They came to ask for a present after each individual *tour de force,* and we made a very bad show, because we had brought hardly any money. The beginning was so splendid that we were not prepared for the subsequent falling-off.

First of all there was a loud-speaker from which announcements were made in strident tones, and unbearable music issued. This gradually poisoned one's enjoyment, as did the persistent punctuation of the dancing by whistles. Twenty dancers presently emerged, the smaller ones not yet invested with the *Ves* headdress. Lapeya was there. They were magnificent dancers. I was particularly struck by the dancing of an old man with a ravaged face, which gave the impression of being half eaten away. He was superb. I have never seen better dancers technically. They indulged in acrobatics, back somersaults, back bends on the ground, etc., which have nothing to do with *Kohomba Kankaria*—unless it is held to be a receptacle for all the sensational elements of Kandyan dancing. Anyway, it was most magnificent. The whirling leaps, high in the air, were in the style of devil-dancing. Some of the dancers were said to belong to Fred Fogl's group. Perhaps these were the dancers he said he had arranged for us to see. We heard that the variety entertainment would last till 1.30, and then the *Kohomba Kankaria* would properly begin, lasting until midday. But the noise of the loud-speaker and the whistling and the general atmosphere—rather antagonistic, I gathered, to the host—decided us to leave at midnight. If I had felt well, I should probably have stayed, but could not face the vulgarity of the loud-speaker. It was certainly a most startling display of Kandyan technique. The few first movements of the *Kohomba Kankaria* during which they called on all the gods to bless the house and its owner, were the same as I remembered for the Peradeniya *Kohomba*—the initial very exciting dance with lit coconuts, the pursuit of one man with a flaming torch, the lining-up of drummers and dancers and a sort of contest between them, were wonderful numbers. Perhaps the whole drama of the *Kohomba Kankaria* is felt to be too boring—perhaps they do not know it. I see how exemplary the performance was, got up for me by Sederaman and Malagamana. The drumming contest was wildly exciting, and the opening numbers of the exhibition dances. Now I almost regret having left (it is still going on at eleven o'clock next day) but the noise was unbearable. The loud-speaker exhorted them—I believe—to get on with the play, but they would not, and were continually interrupting. They paid special attention to me, hoping, I believe, to be taken to America!

I forgot to mention that the day *perahera*, as we saw it, was very lovely. The colours of the elephants' trappings give a quite new sensation of splendour; the headdresses of the dancers glittered superbly in the sun. The snakelike thongs of the whipcrackers were exciting to watch—the enamelled bowls of the plate twirler—the enamelled staves of the spears—all the details of form and colour which one cannot see at night.

12th August. Quiet morning, reading the guide book to Anuradhapura. Lovely drive there after lunch, making a detour by a small red road to pick up a companion for Robert, a former servant of Harry's, Jakdasa, whom we found at a shop in his village by a charming canal which ran for miles along the side of the road. This canal—like a winding river—was somehow very European in feeling. We turned off to the village at a point when the landscape was becoming very romantic, rising to a stone parapet which perhaps skirted a tank. Jakdasa's mother was a handsome old woman with far more character, it seemed to me, than the average bourgeoise of Colombo. We visited Godakumbura, who had been busy since dawn paying people, and was off early next day to Mihintale. He gave us a young man to show us round

13th August. We picked up the young man and visited first a *vihara* where there are several lovely sculptures—the lovers—two naked figures side by side, but only very modestly embracing; a Buddha among attendants; the seated horseman with his horse's head beside him, looking as it were over his shoulder. Below, round the water pool on the naked rock, a delightful relief of elephants bathing. View over Mihintale and the tank from the top, reached by an acutely painful stone ladder. Drove along the great tank, exceedingly lovely, bordered with spreading rain-trees. Visited two bathing pools in the King's Park, with sculptured bathing elephants, reminding one of Mahabalipuram. Some of them in very low relief, with raised trunk, trumpeting, or sporting among lotus flowers in a tank. The pools are very artfully made, and must have been enchanting—with several passages enclosed by a somewhat higher outer wall. This restoration work is in an early stage still. Unfortunately a lot of trees are being cut down, and the ground is being replanted—it may be that the trees were rotten. When we climbed the bank again the tank had completely changed from a smooth lake to a violently agitated choppy sea—very beautiful against the dense background of forest trees.

We drove to the Western Monasteries, in the first of which I saw the finest revels imaginable. A great number of monkeys were climb-ing one particular tree, many with little ones clasped in their arms or on their backs. Suddenly the whole party began to leap from this tree to another, across a wide intervening space. This cascade was really marvellous—a positive stream of monkeys—some hesitant before the wide leap, probably the old monkeys. The mothers with their young leaped blithely into space, and one saw the boughs bend and sway beneath their weight as they disappeared immediately among the dense foliage. At every spot where we halted we saw the same wonderful array of monkeys—they were very tall monkeys, grey and black, probably langurs, singularly graceful and gibbon-like. We saw several admirably sculptured urinals, one in the shape of a house, another with a finely ornamented framework; also one obviously intended for No. 2. The hole seemed very small, but no doubt they were actually well provided with a flush in such admirably constructed buildings.

Presently we came to a fine seated Buddha, surrounded by a green stone railing, and, further on, another on a raised platform, similarly enclosed. This last is really magnificent, but its nose has been badly lengthened in restoration, which distorts the facial expression. Also a superb moonstone, surrounded by a grey wooden fence, not offensive, but rather a tiresome intrusion. It is supposed to keep the cattle off. The reliefs are of elephant, horse, lion and bull, also swans with lotus buds or grapes in their beaks and magnificent garland designs. The innumerable pillars which cover great regions of the forest are most moving, indicative of the glorious city this must have been. Also the levels vary, making beautiful perspectives among the trees. There are many tanks. We passed on the way the famous Twin Tanks —two side by side, with the stone steps down to them wavy and tumbling, every stone out of the straight. This may have been caused by floods. We saw Abhayagiri with its ruined top. Near it an ugly new dagoba is being built.

We drove along the road to Vijayagama—a place I much want to visit. Our stupid guide represented it as impossibly far, and Harry is as nervous as a Nanna about his pet car, which seems very tender indeed, and only intended for town or the highest of high roads. So we turned back, and may go later on foot. But I fear not! At Srimahabodhi, a dreadful restoration. Whitened elephants, a very badly shaped dagoba, poor little guardstones half buried in the earth.

In the afternoon to the biggest tank, which is a great inland sea, with sandy beach, with waves breaking very convincingly on the shore, exceedingly beautiful. Mihintale and its dagoba very clear, but I am afraid I shall only see it from the distance. On the way down from the bund we saw the charming layout of a moated monastery, with octagonal foundations. Robert's eagerness to visit monuments is very touching. He is apparently always hoping to find some unknown image of Buddha. He keeps a diary. Vessagiriya—a series of rock-cells—is all that remains of an enormous monastery, which must have been very lovely. The immense rocks are precariously balanced in a tumultuous mass, from the outside not so very impressive, but directly one has begun to penetrate and climb them, extraordinarily fascinat-

176

Deer in animal sanctuary, Yapahuwa

Bronze figure of Tara
British Museum

ing. Many stone beds of monks, as on the great cliff above Sitinna-
vasar,[1] and cunningly hewn channels above them to draw off the
rainwater. A few fragments of fresco are all that remain—a woman
seated, with one arm raised and left leg drawn up. The toppling
rocks are bound together by huge ropes of tree roots, which perhaps at
first helped the destruction of the buildings, but now form majestic
rope-ladders. Very wonderful, as at Angkor; only here there is no
masonry for them to embrace. There are narrow steps hewn in the
rock at many points, by which one can climb quite to the top and
wander about from rock to rock, looking down on the layout of the
monastery—a few pillars—steps—foundations—guardstones, and
beyond over an ocean of palms to Mihintale and distant mountains.

Climbed the bund at sunset, which was not sensational, and
dropped down to visit a moated pavilion, which continues the
elephant-carved baths, but is rather too much like a Royal Horti-
cultural Society's competition of rock gardens.

Godakumbara to dinner. He only confirms Harry's resolution not
to visit Vijayagama, which is apparently much more distant than
represented in the guide book, but certainly one of the most interesting, because of its situation in the jungle, its sculptures, and complete-
ness of its plan.

13th August. I found Harry reading on the veranda—a handbook to
Mihintale. He announced we were going there, when I had quite
given up hope, and decided not to mention it again. It was one of the
most delightful expeditions. One plunges suddenly into this moun-
tainous region, which we had seen from Vessagiriya, and the long
wide shallow staircase mounts *à perte de vue* up the parklike mountain-
side. Each flight leads one to a splendid terraced woodland, with
widespread massive ruins, mysterious huge troughs, which must have
been used for cooking food—for this was probably the dining-hall.
From this first terrace also a steep flight of steps—or rather two at different angles—lead up to the *Kantaka Cetiya*, which when I came
with Malala in 1935 was in the earliest stages of restoration. The staircases are flanked on both sides by champak trees, which are now in
full flower and very lovely. Small tanks and lovely woodland,
devious paths leading away into the recesses of the mountain—it is an

---

[1] See *The Other Mind,* plate 8.

enchanting place. We climbed first to the topmost dagoba which is still very ruined. The bricks it was built of are shallow but unusually wide, like bricks we use for tiling. Marvellous view over the plain and distant mountains. The three tanks of Anuradhapura visible, and the viharas seem enormously distant from each other, seen from above and afar. The Naga Pool—where a hooded cobra seems to rise from the water—is a deep narrow pool under an overhanging rock—meant to be pure water but now very dirty. We dropped on to the Lion bath rather unexpectedly. A small lion head actually pours water to feed the bath—the great rampant lion is below, under the water.

Climbed between the champaks to the *Kantaka Cetiya*, which has some of the best pillar sculpture of Anuradhapura. Very fine atten-dant deities occupied in all sorts of amusing ways, and with quite a variety of animal disguises, making offerings, dancing, teasing each other. Very finely-worked pillars, and some splendid examples of the characteristic *panchula*—or flower vase, with plants wreathing from it. There were two small Nandis, horses, and a lovely female figure—in fact two, but one much destroyed. Splendid foliage designs and lovely colour of the stone. It is an enchanting monument. Explored the monks' cells under the massive fantastic rocks. A stone path bordered by a low wall led round one massive rock, with a great promise of discovery. I longed to follow it, but Robert went alone and reported there was nothing. These wooded hills certainly hold many other monastic dwellings and shrines. It is a very romantic, lovely spot.

Relations of Harry's were already camped on the terrace where we had slept at the Grand Hotel. A long, rather wearisome drive to Puttalam, where we lunched by the lagoon. Then to Munnesaram to see the Hindu temple, of which Pattini is the chief goddess. A curious temple at the end of the village, rather like a Catholic church —the images were all clothed. I had hoped to find my Abyssinian boy,[1] but had no luck. At Negombo more relations of Harry's, and a charming garden, romantically planned.

16th August. Visited Dr. Nell in the Dutch Burgher Union. He has *mudras* for me, and notes, and a seemingly authentic story of the last human sacrifice on Bhairavakande. His father and grandfather and someone else knew the girl—then an old woman—at Kandy, who

---

[1] Reference to a ceremony not yet told.

had been tied up and rescued by a noble in disgrace, who had been banished to the other side of the river. He only returned on the death of the king in 1815, and the romance of his marriage with the rescued girl is a fiction. Nell thinks dancers probably accompanied the procession of the victim. She alleged that Bhairava had appeared to her and told her he no longer desired human sacrifices.

To tea at Queen's House—Lord Soulbury, Joan Ramsbotham, Colonel Rose, Lord Semphill, and a very young, jaunty aide-de-camp. The garden is glorified by the most beautiful banyan-tree I have ever seen, a forest of pillars, very straight and of great beauty. It is a complete temple. The branches spread very wide over the lawn and over the tea-table, so that it provided—beside grateful shade—a generous scattering of bird-droppings, which fell mostly on me.

CHAPTER IX

Some Journeys in Ceylon with Harry Pieris—My Best 'Kohomba Kankaria' — The Magic Boar of Hantana — A Village 'Perahera'

18th August. Lecture by Austin de Silva on the harvest ceremonies. Either at the paddy-sowing or the harvest, I forget which, a man in a demon mask, dressed in black and with a girdle of rice straw, dances all night to dispel evil influences.

20th August. This afternoon Harry and Ralph Pieris took me to Pasyala, the country home of Sir Paul Pieris, the historian. About two miles of winding road lead up to this indescribably lovely place, between coco-palm plantations and iron-wood trees. The great house, beautifully designed in a kind of crescent, with wide corridors and a circular pillared loggia, looks out over a deep ravine to a jungle-covered hill and down a wide green lawn to an immense vista of mountains. Splendid trees throw just sufficient shade. Lady Pieris designed this house entirely, and planted the trees. Wild animals, cobras and dappled deer come up round the house. I was speechless from delight. Then Lady Pieris, seeing my joy in so much beauty, said: 'You must come and stay here.' Ought I to have shown less pleasure than I felt? I cannot tell; I still hope to pay this visit one day. Lady Pieris, who is very intelligent and very beautiful, talked incessantly; so did Justin Deraniyagala, her son, who kept pouring out a torrent of unintelligible names and implying a thousand mysteries which one must fathom, if one wants to understand any-thing about *Kohomba Kankaria*. Huge tomes were brought, said to contain the whole text, which lasts a week, but which he said no one now understands. I think he resents that an outsider should dare to occupy herself with such a private thing as the dances of Ceylon. He reeled off the names of the different *Thovils* which he said took place constantly within a radius of five miles, and told me of devastating things which happened to Europeans so rash as to attempt a photograph.

On the way we went afterwards to Justin's studio, a white-pillared pavilion which I had noticed on the way up. We saw his pictures at sunset, inspirational pictures which can be judged by no standard but their own. They are more poetic than George Keyt's, and beautiful in colour; especially his use of green delighted me. There were endless drawings by Justin of female nudes; he is certainly a fine draughtsman.

I would gladly have stayed on and on in that divine place—but alone, silently, and walked down to the river and among the rocks. Yes, I should like to spend weeks in that paradise.

We drove back in darkness—the trees lit by the car lamps.

I visited Caldecott in the hope of discovering what the chances are of a car for tomorrow; but Fogl was giving a lesson in ballroom dancing, and I did not see him.

21st August. After waiting four hours, I set off at last with Noel Pieris and the kind owner of the car whose name I never discovered. We were supposed to start at 6 a.m.; but it was after midday when we got off.

We went first to Nittevala, Guneya's village, which is, I find, under Ratwatte's jurisdiction. It looks much more neglected than last time, owing to Guneya's absence in India. His son, Sanadasa, who received the investiture at Buddhagaya, was there, and his charming little daughters. I questioned him about the first dancing of the *Ves* dancers in the *Perahera*. He said it was thirty-five years ago under Nugawela's uncle, who persuaded the dancers that the *Perahera* was a religious procession, and that therefore they could dance in it.

Guneya, dressed cleanly in a white jacket and dhoti, came with us to find Heenbaba, his nephew. Suramba, the very old man of ninety-five, whom I vividly remember coming up the path when we went down to look for Ukuwa, is Guneya's uncle and Heenbaba's grandfather, also Guneya's master. We drove along a narrow upper road towards Matale, with a dramatic view of the stormy mountains—exceedingly lovely. Below we looked through trees on to gold and emerald paddy-fields—the emerald lay in a brilliant crescent in the middle of the gold. We alighted and dropped steeply past several charming whitewashed thatched cottages to a stream, and by narrow paths crossed the paddy-fields and climbed the opposite hill by a path which is obviously generally a torrent. There on a longish terrace was Heenbaba's house. We sat in the loggia, while the family one by one came to do obeisance, the lowness of the bow being in proportion to the old-fashionedness of the people. Some quite prostrated themselves and took the dust of our feet, but there was nothing servile about it. An enchanting baby of five months was there, very dimpled and curly and laughing. But the gem was Heenbaba's father, a most beautiful old man with brilliant eyes set in a fleshless face, beautifully modelled, and a very subtle smile. His glance was swift as a bird's, but never furtive. He looked as if he could not have an ignoble thought—I felt him like a benediction. After we had drunk the compulsory 'crush', we carried off Heenbaba.

To Gampola, where the car-owner had business, almost in darkness, rain falling heavily; of the return I remember little; I was chiefly asleep. Home at twelve. I had only had a bun and a half all day, for I was too sleepy to eat when the others had their supper.

22nd August. Exhausted, but gradually revived, and spent the afternoon with Heenbaba taking down the *wannams, talas* and *adaus*. He sang the *wannams* beautifully, and I made him dance the original and new versions of the Hare, the Frog and the Conch. The Horse and Hawk have only one version. It was Guneya who made the new versions since being in Colombo, and for stage purposes. The Frog was copied from a real frog. The mimicry and acrobatics to which it gives rise is remarkable, and it would be pedantic to quarrel with such masterly interpretations even if one might somewhat prefer the old stylized form. The Horse is sufficiently representative, even in the old version, and needs no reform. Heenbaba's voice and rhythm are excellent. Mrs. Ratnasuriya came to interpret.

23rd August. Slept from 9 p.m., and went to Caldecott at seven to work with Heenbaba. He told me yesterday that his grandfather objected to the innovations introduced into the *wannams*, in the direction of more miming. Noel Pieris said these innovations had been introduced in order to make the dance understood by an audience which cannot follow the text of the *wannams*. I cannot feel strongly about it. In fact, I have almost come to the conclusion that it is a pity not to let their great gift for miming and acrobacy and their charming fancy have free scope, quite apart from the stage. Why should they be confined to the old versions—if there really were old versions? It is very difficult to discover how they used to be done, for there is sure to be someone to raise the cry of 'Unauthentic'. I got Heenbaba to do the twelve basic steps. But they do not cover the technique of the *wannams* as now performed, and certainly not the technique of the *Ves* dancers, any more than the five positions and their variations and the other technical details of classical ballet cover the actual performance of a Massine ballet, into which so much that is new has been introduced. When do they date from, I wonder?

There was talk of the *Kohomba Kankaria*. Fred Fogl is a visionary; he pictures a marvellous performance, visited by the Governor-General and his suite, and all the Kandyan grandees. But I suppose he will come up against many prejudices. Noel Pieris—more realistic says the performance turns on the presence of the Governor-General. They count on me to ensure this, which of course I cannot do. I have already written to him, but can only invite and urge. I expect the great *Raja Kankaria* will melt into thin air.

24th August. Just before 4.30 a.m. I heard Robert's small voice outside the window: 'Are you ready, Madam?' I was surprised to find Harry already finishing his coffee. We set out soon after through the dark, empty streets, and picked up Moses, Harry's photographer, outside the People's Park at Dehiwala, with his photographic apparatus. He had been waiting half an hour. The roads were slippery from rain. When day came it was cloudy, with a fine space of blue and cumulus cloud over the sea. Sunrise very watery, and the mountains in cloud. Gradually lights went out, and one after another people came out on to the roads, bullock carts, bicycles—day had come. We reached Wellewatte at eight, and had breakfast by the lovely clean, golden beach—where I paddled, fourteen and a half years ago. It seemed cleaner now, than then. We went on to Matara—very showery. Entered the fort by the single arch, and walked on the beach by the rest-house. There are some nice old Dutch buildings, and the yellow Star Fort outside with Dutch coat of arms. Exquisite coast-road to Dondra, where we visited the methodically destroyed *devale,* of which only a few stone pillars—a fine sculptured gateway and a few guardstones—remain. There was a long avenue leading to the temple from the sea, where now is the lighthouse. A fine old *Kapurale,* with a witty face and some English—if he had some teeth he would not look more than middle aged. We visited Galge, where there is a small stone shrine with flat stone ceiling, on a hill. Here I lost my sun-glasses, a great loss. Some miles further to Tangalle, which is the most exquisite rest-house on the coast. It is in a deep wide bay, and is so built that it looks to sunrise and sunset. I longed to stay in this delicious place and explore the villages which must nestle in palm-trees around the great crescent of the bay. Sun and showers. We turned inland as far as Beliatta. Between Galle and Matara we passed the great statue supposed to be of a king, hewn in a rock, so that it is inset and framed by the stone. It is very fine, and when we first saw it the sun lit it very strikingly.

From Beliatta we branched up to Mulgirigala, continually rising till the huge rock towered above us. The landscape is broken in many places by rocky hills, which rise superbly above the ocean of green palms and paddy-fields. We had to take our shoes off at the foot of the steps and climb up rather jaggedly to the first rocky chambers, where there are enchanting murals, of which Moses took many photos. There are four belts of fresco on a red ground—green trees—blue and yellow—white-skinned people among the brown and black and white.

The upper band consists of domestic scenes—royal and popular—boutiques and wonderfully-designed stuffs. It is a treasure house of old Ceylonese dresses, *Ves* headdresses, crowns. These are particularly remarkable—royal crowns with golden spikes, quite different from any others I have seen. There are many kings with crowns, and many kinds of trees with lovely foliage—iron-tree in blossom was the only one I recognized, besides areca and coconut palm. There is a love-scene—of a woman lying somewhat awkwardly on a bed fondling a man who stands over her. Behind the curtain a waiting-woman seems to be commanding silence with her finger to her lips to a fair young woman—a very Italian Renaissance scene, though they look more like primitives. The women dancers are striking—one little dancing figure is remarkably like a Balinese *Legong* and is wound tightly round in just the same way. One has a fan in her right hand, increasing the illusion. There are lovely glass lamps of the Dutch pattern in festive scenes—carved chair backs—many musical instruments—drum, *horenewa,* cymbals, trumpets, etc. There are flights of birds in a fine huddle above the trees.

The second band is chiefly *Perahera* with many elephants, some white, with decorated face-masks as now—and round hats, sur-mounted by a spike. They are ridden by grandees. There are many lovely flags and weapons—banners, umbrellas of state. The walls and lintels and every architectural space are charmingly decorated with paintings. There are toilet articles and food and ships, with big baskets and bowls, painted and lacquered pillars. So many characters to study—aged men, etc.

In the upper storey—up more steps—the frescoed rock is entirely hidden by a huge wardrobe far too heavy to move. The colouring here is lighter, and there is a good deal of white. I managed to squeeze myself between the *almirah* and the wall—but my nose was practically touching the wall! I could, however, just distinguish the dancers Harry spoke of, all in white. The women were rather amply covered. There is a beautiful green parrot, almost alone of the murals follow-ing the curves of the rock. The uncovered frescoes are much damaged. There are beautiful carved pillars, horses—rather skittish; a pair of elephants and, I think, a dancer. The frescoes show banners, *dawulas, udekki, horenewa,* with attendants in short jackets; *pantheru* and cym-bals; a lady in her kitchen; pots of grain; there were magnificent pots —one of copper—what did they hold? The view from the upper platform is most lovely and very extensive. A great rain cloud over-hung the clear blue, liquid sky. The shapes and colours of clouds were wonderful throughout the day. When the rain stopped I took a photo of little boys against the landscape on the edge of the rock. It is a magnificent prospect. The immense sky reminded one of de Koninck.

We returned to lunch at Tangalle, which it was hard to leave. A lovely row of boats with masts canted along the steep shore. We seemed to see a fish's head rise from time to time out of the water. The waves break into the bay from several directions, making a lovely counterpoint of rhythms.

26th August. I went with Noel Pieris to the *Kohomba Kankaria* at Medawala, given by the brother of the schoolmaster—just in order to make the house and its inmates 'feel nice'. The walk from the point where we left the car was fascinating. It is here always that my chief pleasure begins. The red path climbed for some distance, with wide, cloudy mountain horizons, then dropped suddenly by slippery, rough steps and paths to a large house and a few cottages—till we came sud-denly on the *maduwa* (pavilion) which was more like a market. There was no room for the dancers to dress in, apart from this *maduwa,* and it was full of tables and benches laden with baskets from which peeped a profusion of ornaments and stuffs; the dancers and drummers in various stages of undress were sitting or lying about. The benches already had a sprinkling of children.

The family is a delightful one. It was a great surprise to see the host —a simple, retiring man—suddenly installed on a seat covered with a white cloth, dressed in full regalia of a *basnayaka*, with a flat gold crown with a small topknot, a ruby-red short bodice studded with gold, a splendid belt and cloth of gold thread, receiving the homage of the dancers, who sang before him, each waving a thick white twisted rope with tasselled ends, which was the white cloth he would soon be dressed in. This cloth is never starched, but takes fine crimped folds from its tight wrapping, and makes a fine show when it hangs over the string which binds it round at different levels on the dancer's body, so stiff in appearance that it seems to be folded over cardboard. Twenty yards go to each dancer's dress, which should be pure white. But they are provided by the host and the *dhobi*, and when the white runs out other colours have to be substituted for some of the sashes and final frills. It was most interesting to watch the whole pro-cess of the dressing and putting-on of the headdress. I had never seen it in such perfection before, and cannot admire enough the amazing patience and skill with which the dancer builds up his costume—on the hips and in front, leaving the tight trouser legs free behind. The frills and flounces flow like milk or fruit over the borders of the wide, magnificently-worked belts, when the last touches to the costume have been made, and every foot of the twenty-two yards is so skilfully bound that it never comes to pieces during the violent dancing of the long night. I should like to know how this dress was invented, or from what it gradually evolved. The harness of beads used to be of cowrie shells, I believe. It is now very varied in design, and so are the richly coloured collars which surmount it. The little boys who were roped in to complete the contingent of dancers wore the bead harness above white cloths with red frilled waistbelts; the drummers the usual circular crownless hat bound with white cloth, leaving a becoming tail to hang down.

What struck me about it—as indeed about all *Kohombas*—is its curious disjointed character. I realize on looking back how well and sternly mine was pruned by Malagamana. It really was a great feat. There are long intervals of inaction. But in any case, last night's performance was a little haphazard, owing to the small number of dancers—of whom however some were excellent, especially in their own improvisations.

The incursion of Ram Gopal and his party towards midnight broke up the line of the performance for a while. It was during the episode where an old man with a torch leads the dancers round, moving backwards before them in a circle round the drummers, and sometimes overtaken by their onslaught and driven out of his course, which he recovers as best he can, dodging among the drummers— and often losing the flame of his torch *en route*. Each was anxious to display his prowess to the utmost. Toni took flashlight photos, then slept over the back of the bench in front of him.

The rain was appalling all the time Ram's party was there, beat- ing down with utmost violence on the palm-leaf roof, which stood up to it very well. The end of the ground by the *ayele* was flooded, and gradually the dancing drew up towards the *yahana*. Lightning poured through the openings of the *maduwa*. At about 2.30 a.m. I went to sleep in the house below the *maduwa*. I woke after just an hour, inevitably attracted by the drums and chanting, and returned to the half-empty *maduwa*.

They had just begun again, after their meal and a rest, and some were still sleeping at the foot of the *yahana*. The ikons looked very lovely on a glowing red ground upon the *yahana*, and the lighted windows of the *maduwa* very welcoming. I left at 7.30 a.m. before the killing of the wild boar.

The game of imitation was, I heard, meant to ridicule the Veddahs, typical boors. It is curious how they keep cropping up during the performance—as well as before it. The wild boar was brought out of its place under the *yahana*—a very nice one with fine pig ears standing up through its bristles, which were made of a grey flowering grass and looked extremely realistic; indeed the realism of the wild boar in its plantain effigy is always striking.

The walk to the road where the de Silvas' car was waiting, through the clear, washed morning air was delicious, but it rained again long before I reached the bungalow where Mr. de Silva had passed the night—a remote estate which is his special delight. The house seemed very derelict, or at least very sketchily furnished. Water indeed flowed through every room, but not alas through pipes! But Mr. de Silva was perfectly happy on his veranda, though he burst into uncontrollable rage at some incompetent workers on the road. The road was made entirely by Mr. de Silva. It is still rather sketchy. After the torrents which have descended all day with only ten minutes intermission it must be almost washed away. The wildness of the deep valleys was very lovely, but so full of mist and rain that I could hardly see them. Got back at ten; bath, breakfast and bed.

28th August. A glorious day, with a few violent showers. Why was I not content to see Hantana Kande from here in all its beauty and clarity, instead of trying to get into such close proximity to so much magic? The drive up was glorious, though the tea gardens have made ugly scars on the hills. Dambulla mountains in cloud, but when I started to climb from the point where the metalled road ended, it was perfectly fine. I made the mistake of refusing a guide, and of starting straight up the side of the hill above the tea plantations. The fearful grasses, taller than me, which hid huge rocks and slippery holes, seemed as if they would never end, and indeed did never end. The top of Hantana, seen from the de Silvas' bungalow, looks a beautiful smooth down-like summit, though razor-edged. How different the reality! Climbing was a nightmare, but once I got into the tangle I could only insinuate myself out, or beat down the endless creepers and prickly bushes which disputed the territory of this haunted hill with the spiky grasses. There were lovely flowers, too; tall flowering bushes with mauve spikes. I emerged at last, but only to find the grasses on the hill almost as long. I got occasional glimpses of the mountains, but found the Hantana Kande as prickly as the bristles of the wild boar. Did he suffer too, as he galloped up Hantana, pursued by the Male Raja? No doubt he found the protection of the tall grasses grateful. I never thought of meeting a wild boar, but I did think of meeting a snake or a leech. Fortunately I didn't—and all my scars were from scratches of the prickly plants. I left nearly all the skin of my legs there and half my skirt! The descent was more woeful still; I fell continually, and was quite buried in the undergrowth. I thought I should never emerge alive (and how should I otherwise emerge?). One ray of hope was when I found—deep buried in grasses, but just visible—a tiny path which perhaps wound up to the summit. I must evidently try again, but this defeat was sad. A great cloud of rain covered the mountain and the valleys as I drove down. An antiseptic bath prevented worse, but has not obscured my scratches. This journey—all the same—cleared my mind and put me out of reach of the spiritual arrows which have so plentifully rained upon me.

29th August. Mrs. de Silva received without blenching the news that five were coming to lunch, instead of two. She is convincingly Bohemian. She likes to talk to me about her early successes, and she must have been very pretty and desirable. Her father did not want her to marry at all and she seems to have grown up in the wilds. Clearly she wanted to be domineered over, as I ventured to suggest while I was washing in her bathroom, mine being temporarily out of use; as the wall had been broken down and the door removed in the course of Minnette's architectural operations. I heard a hen cackling at very close quarters, and imagined it to be in the garden. Again it cackled, closer still. It seemed to come from the clothes-basket. I called out to Mrs. de Silva, and she imperturbably replied that it was *in* the clothes-basket. It had been put there, I forget for what reason. It made the same egg-laying, self-satisfied cackle several times during the day, but someone always got in first and there was never an egg for Mrs. de Silva, who bore everything with unexampled placidity!

I went to Kegalle in the dancers' bus; I had wired to Arthur

Molamure to expect me. Talked on the way down to Narayan Maharaj, a shaggy, burly, sympathetic creature who taught *Kathak* to Kumadini.

The rest-house at Kegalle is above the road—one of a small colony of administrative offices, police, etc. I found a small boy to carry my bag. A note from Arthur Molamure asked me to go up to his house. He imagined I should be in a car, and was still resting. I trudged on up the winding road, accompanied by a bevy of little boys. It was very quiet and beautiful climbing above the paddy-fields. At last we saw the house above us—a long, low bungalow on a terrace, from which there is a marvellous view of Bible Rock and the mountains. A steep flight of steps leads up to it. A strange old bearded man came out very leisurely, but without smiling or attempting to communicate. I gathered from his gestures that Arthur Molamure was there, but the house was completely silent, and the rooms pleasantly empty, washed with very pale blue, many books, fine wooden ceiling, and a great carved door-frame. The house was built by an Englishman or Government Agent who certainly loved beautiful things and places. For it is lovely and in an exquisite situation. He had made four apartments, one at each corner of the long bungalow. Inside is a large sitting-room, like a wide corridor, reaching the whole length of the building. I had a short talk with Molamure before some Bandanarayake cousins arrived for tea, who kindly invited me to return with them to Colombo. A wonderful brilliance of flooded paddy-fields reflected the sunset, framed by coconut palms.

30th August. Everything tends to get very mouldy from the damp. The day was an alternation of rain and sunshine. Lyn Ludowyk came to fetch me, and we dined in the only good Chinese restaurant I have sampled here, and called afterwards on Mr. Nicholas, an excise commissioner,[1] and very learned in everything Ceylonese. His knowledge of the jungle, rock temples, murals, statues hidden in remote parts, is encyclopaedic. He has also written several volumes on Anuradhapura which he feels will never be published, for who, he asks, is interested in so much detail? He told me that the real name of Mulgirigalle is Muhundgirigalle, i.e. 'overhanging rock'. Another bit of information is that the *Kapurale* is the successor of the Puro-

---

[1] He was warden of the Department of Wild Life, till forced by ill-health to retire.

hita, or Brahmin priest, who was the king's chaplain, and presided over the secular ceremonies.

Mr. Nicholas promised to take me to see some jungle beasts in their true habitat before I left Ceylon.

I went by appointment with Fogl to catch the 7.20 train to Amba-langoda. Dick took me to the station, but Fogl never turned up, nor did he send the promised *Kolan* information. The train was very late, but managed to pass a few stations without stopping, and the journey along the coast was exquisite, and in a Pullman car would have been delightful. Four or five middle-aged, humble-looking men met me at the station. The youngest, E. Vimaladasa, was there to interpret. We walked the three-quarter mile to Gunadasa's house in the clearing of a coconut-grove—a very modest house, although he is reported a rich man. There I found also his old father, Pallis de Silva—the *guru* and mask-maker—aged eighty. Most of the masks—which were all on the ground in the first room of the house—are about 250 years old, they say. They are extremely fine, and made me very interested in see-ing a *Kolan* performance where there is clearly a great variety of dances. The masks were all brought out in groups for me to photograph, and stood up on an estaffage. I was afraid the photos would not be suc-cessful, as my camera jammed; but actually they are some of the best I have. I took the characters, set by set—police, soldiers, headmen, king and queen, rakshasa (demons), Africans, Moorish traders, ani-mals (bullocks, lions and tigers), and also the old guru and the family group. The dancers all belong to the family—they are working at various contracts up-country. They are builders, masons, car-penters and mask makers. They belong to the Kuruvanse caste, a warrior tribe of North India, who were fetched down as mercenaries presumably about two thousand years ago to support a Ceylonese king. They regard themselves as Aryan. They live so very simply, and in so poor a house, that it is difficult to believe Gunadasa's family is rich; but he apparently was well off before the 'depression'. The old father—who put on his circular comb to be photographed, and whom of course I could not ask to take off his dirty coat and shirt —still teaches young *Kolan* dancers; they are not professionals, except the drummers. Two of them put on *rakshasa* masks and the red boleros and flounced skirts belonging to them to be photographed in.

They also put on their ankle-bells, though they were not going to dance. It seems that they will put on a *Kolan*—it needs about a fortnight's preparation. Fogl has already guaranteed 100 rupees. We can certainly make up the amount of 200 or more.

Vilmaladasa came with me to the rest-house, and would courteously have waited to take me to the station, but of course I sent him away. I rested, watching the sea and rocks and the fishing boats which so skilfully move in among the rocks and land just at the right point on the sand. Many were drawn up on the beach in a row. The journey back was tedious, though the sky at sunset over the sea was most dramatic and beautiful.

4th September. Sivaram[1] came to see me, very charming, but looking very thin, and with a bad cold after the awful crossing from Tuticorin. It is tantalizing to know that the great annual festival of Onam is on now in Malabar in his village of Parur: there will be *Kathakali* and all the *Tullals*. The origin of the Onam festival is this: when King Mahabali was ruling in Malabar, as the tenth incarnation of Vishnu and Krishna, an 'insignificant Brahmin' approached the king and asked him for three feet of land. In two steps he covered all Malabar, and still had a foot to spare. The king had to add his head to make up the full measure. He had to leave Malabar, but before he left he asked the Brahmin to let him visit his people once a year—from the 4th or 5th September is a ten-day festival, during which a man dressed in yellow clothes and holding a small drum takes a bull to every house. While he sings the bull will shake its head, which is hung with bells, and move about according to the rhythm. The bull's face is painted.

Sivaram told me that Kunju Kurup's school of *Kathakali*, now considered superior to Vallathol's, is near the Krishna Temple of Ambalapuzha, about ten miles from Aleppey.[2] It is entirely supported by three well-to-do brothers of Aleppey, professional players on the Nagaswaram (bamboo flute). The boy famous in female parts is Karunagaran Nair. There are twelve boys in the school. Kunju Kurup's famous parts are the poor Brahmin Kujela, Nala, disguised as Bahunga, the groom, with a black face; Hanuman, discovered by Rama's sons Kusa and Lava, as an old and decrepit monkey.

[1] A gifted young Kathakali dancer from South India.
[2] I afterwards visited this school and learned a great deal there.

Old masks
Nevill Bequest

Kolan masks

Drove to Kandy with Harry. The road had never looked so lovely. There was much activity in the paddy-fields—chiefly of women—planting out the paddy roots; also at one point, two batches of men with great hoes moving rapidly among the mud, covered from top to toe in the wet soil and hoeing the ground. They were singing passages of the *Vessantara*. Then they merged into one group—it was a lovely scene, as the blades of their hoes flashed in the sun to the rhythm of their singing. I got out and took some photos. Then they came crowding round the car and put out their muddy hands for money. Their almost-black bodies were coated with lighter mud, rather as if they had applied henna all over them.

Dr. Nell told me about the *Perahera* at Alutnuwara, near Kandy, where was formerly the image of Vishnu made of sandalwood, which was washed up on the shore at Dondra. It has now been removed to the *Maha devale*—Vishnu temple. All the elephants are brought to be blessed at this *Perahera*—without their trappings. It must be shortly before the Kandy *Perahera*. They do obeisance before the shrine—is it empty now?

Speculative conversation with Martin Russell about the Kandyan dancing. We agree that it is not exactly folk-dancing, indeed really very far from it. It is the heir of a great tradition which must have come from India. It has—in common with Balinese and Javanese dancing, and perhaps all Eastern classical dancing—a conception of nobility, of noble behaviour, which is unknown in the industrial world and the reign of Demos, under which kings and queens and gentlemen seek not to distinguish themselves from the people, but to ingratiate themselves by approaching more and more to the lower levels of behaviour. A noble conception is ingrained in these peasants —noble bearing and noble behaviour. It seems certain that the nobles used to practise dancing. No doubt, as in India and Java, dancing was part of a courtly training. How did the Kandyan dancers acquire their nobility of bearing? When they do an *adau* and beg for a present, they look equally noble, and if it is refused they do not lose their nobility of bearing. This conception of nobility is certainly implanted by their literature, with which they are familiar, though they may neither read nor write. Contact with the West did not drive it away —even in a menagerie the higher animals also have it!

Martin talks of introducing order and discipline into their dancing. But surely it is there already. It is different from ours, but the conception of auspicious days and hours and the observance of ceremonial certainly corresponds to a discipline. The question of presenting them on the stage is a quite different one; but Martin says that in Bombay the fragment of *Kohomba Kankaria* which was presented made a great impression. The audience dimly divined an ordeal, a consecration to some solemn rite. But which part did they show? He came away with the impression of a rite connected with human sacrifice: possibly this was the origin, for there is something obscure and mysterious about it. Why are their gods worshipped on the *yahana*? What is the significance of their weapons? Ratwatte says the *Kohomba Kankaria* is the synthesis of all devil-dancing. But how did the stories become attached to it? It becomes in fact increasingly mysterious.

5th September. Early to Amunugama for the opening of the new brick school. We met the *Perahera* coming with drums and *horenewa* (flute) and dancers to meet the Governor-General. The road was lined with frail arches hung with slivers of palm leaf, and an occasional elaborate solid bamboo or plantain punctuated the long passage. Women and children peered out of cottages. The school is built on an eminence above the road, where the old palm- or paddy-roofed school used to be. The white walls were decorated with curved strips of plantain leaf—marked like tortoiseshell—which held paper flowers and white strips of paper fluttered from the rafters. The hall has a low wall round it, so that everyone can look in, but the stage is enclosed. It is a charming building, but the space for outside dancing is not large enough. This seems a pity. The garlanded Governor-General advanced solemnly and listened to a murmured speech from Suramba, to which he replied. He then cut the cord and declared it open, burning his hand by the inevitable explosion of a match. A concoction of herbs looking like black mud was applied too long afterwards to help much. It takes some time to mix, and the secret was not given away. Elaborate sweetmeats which looked much nicer than they were filled the interval.

Guneya's dance of the Horse *Wannam* was far the best item. He is an exquisite artist. His technique is very remarkable, but his execution is so effortless that his amazing spins and whirls seem the most natural thing in the world. What a contrast the laboured contortions and expressionism of Rajapaksa. His face wears a perpetual grin, and he is always striving after something which I feel he never attains. He is a fine dancer, of course, but for me it is spoilt by his expressionistic methods. Suramba and the other three drummers were very fine. They were led by Suramba, and followed his changes of rhythm to perfection. A row of Buddhist priests chanted a hymn to the Governor-General, then came an invocation, from which the names of many gods emerge. The small boys' *pantheru* was quite nice, but the three dances done by six girls with cymbals, sticks and arm movements alone—the latter being an adaptation of a *Wannam* which I had hoped to see Guneya dance—were much better. They had greatly improved, and one little girl was very good. Their rhythm and co-ordination of movement were excellent. Jayana did a modified *Kathakali* hunter's dance in predominantly slow tempo, but very good. He has a beautiful face when dancing, though his effort to keep his mouth shut when talking gives him a curious pinched expression. George Keyt, with long hair, looking very prophetic and rather pompous, poured out a cascade of talk to the Governor-General.

Visited Martin Russell's house; enchanting above the paddy-fields. A huge Atlas moth emerged from its cocoon while we were there, trembling at this first exposure of its huge wings from the crumpled cocoon. It was most lovely, with a chessboard of gold and brown in cunningly adjusted squares and transparent triangles of mica on its exquisite wings. A fine border enclosed the wings. After a few minutes its trembling ceased, and it flew into a tree. It reminded me of Bali, where Walter Spies hatched out some magnificent Atlas moths, only to transfix them with a pin for sending to Germany.

6th September. Set off after lunch with Mrs. de Silva and Minnette for the hill-village of Hanguranketta, to which the road coils and twists with many hairpin bends above the Mahaveliganga. It is a glorious road. The wide river bed is strewn with enormous rocks, between and over which the torrent pours. It looks at times so like the Dart or a lake or Scottish stream that the coconut-palm plantations covering the hills seem very incongruous. Vista after vista of mountains open up—continually new and wonderful horizons as the road mounts and curls. Below—far below—the paddy terraces rise in crescents of emerald and gold from the river bed. The village is unique in Ceylon, I hear, certainly more like an English village with its green, on and around which the booths of the fair were pitched. It also reminded me faintly of Tenganan, in Bali, with its wide streets, except that Hanguranketta has only one main street and no ramps. At one end is the *Maha devale*, enclosed in walls, with a wide grassy space round, and beautiful *maduwa*, with a double row of pillars leading up to the shrine. A small shrine stands apart, up a flight of steps. These pillars and the whole temple are evidently newly whitewashed, very much obscuring the beautiful reliefs of dancing figures. We were not allowed to see the sculptured twining female dance figures, which Devendra had told me were exceptionally good. The roof of these and of the Maligawa—which is across the green—is very lovely, wide and spreading, with shallow tiles. In front of the Maligawa— Buddhist temple—is a tall and imposing building in Dutch style, which serves as a kind of entrance hall, rising steeply to the main temple, which has several lovely shrines and many murals, some of which are good, about 150 years old. There are no modern monstrosities here. A great many flights of steps unite the different levels. The white *cortège* of figures surrounding the Buddha are imposing. Some charming nuns or dedicated women—a bevy of them—surrounded us, and an amiable tusked Trustee took us round. A path across some paddy plots cuts across to the steep main street which rises to the *Pattini devale*. In all these the torches stood ready against the night's *Perahera*.

It is deliciously rural: paddy-fields rising in a wide semi-circle like a Greek theatre border this main street on one side, among coconut groves. The rest-house lies above the village, rising through many tea-estates into the hills. It is a peaceful charming spot. We sat on the loggia, just above a golden paddy-field, and women and children passed continually up the path with tea-baskets on their backs, cheerfully chattering. I walked up the same path, which wound continually through the aloe-grey Grevillea trees, in stone-bound terraces, reminding me a little of the old roads in Mallorca. Here there are none of the depressing coolie lines that are seen elsewhere in Ceylon. The view of the mountains as they opened up line after line, with many pale blue peaks and an occasional grand wall of rock, was most beautiful. I longed to reach the top of the boundary hill and look over into the Nuwara Eliya world of mountains. But the sun had set behind the hills and already little streams of people were trickling down from one path and another towards the *Pera-hera*.

Certainly a village *Perahera* has great charm, and none of the organized policing of Kandy. One could move everywhere freely. By now the full moon was high, and the soft milky light streamed over the hills and paddy-fields—not brilliant, but enchanting. The dancers were dressing, in the various *devales,* for *pantheru* and *udekki,* and the drums tuning up. Elephants were ruminating in the shadow of the temple walls, ten in all—one quite small, but three massive fellows with decorative masks and ear hoods. The chief excitement was in the Maligawa—where a small company of *udekki* and *pantheru* dancers performed with great energy and a good deal of mirth in the hall at the foot of the steps up to the shrines of Buddha. One of them —the leader, perhaps rather drunk—had lost his head-cloth. He was brought up to make his bow by the tusked Trustee, and indicated an *adau* which I feebly rewarded. The *udekki* dancers, planted solidly be-tween widespread feet, with straight backs and knees at a very wide angle, made some complicated patterns. One of these—where the four dancers formed a bunch of their drums in the middle, and then one by one made an arch with their arms as they moved over the heads of the others, without losing hold of the drum—reminded me of some of the figures in an English sword dance. There was also a skilful leap by which they sprang outwards from the scrum into an open circle. Their vigorous half-turns and repeated beatings with one foot were very exciting, and the drummers excellent.

I went up in the bright moonlight towards the *Pattini devale* just as—with a great noise of drum-beating and a flare of torches—the procession began to descend from the hill. The elephant shone in the moonlight, and his bright trappings. On his back were three men —one quite young, in white, with a flat angular white hat and carry-ing a long wand garlanded at each end with white flowers—a very lovely sight as the procession slowly descended the steep street. On it was also carried the covered litter of Pattini, beside which several young women walked on either side. I cut across the field of dry paddy squares to the Maligawa, where the dancers and drummers were all coming out, and the special elephant waited below the *pattiripuwa* (observation station), a place built for kings to watch games. The elephant was waiting to be loaded with the gold relic-dagoba we had been shown earlier under an embroidered cloth in the library, where, by the way, there are shelves of the most beautiful lacquered and ivory-bound olas. When the elephant had been loaded with its relic vessel behind a cloth which was held up by two men while loading (no one rode on this elephant), the procession started and took its place behind Pattini's. Meanwhile, the *Maha devale* was flaring with torches, and soon the drummers came out, and a rider—also in white, with the same garlanded bar—mounted the *pattiripuwa*. In this portion of the *Perahera* there was also a litter—possibly two—Vishnu's and perhaps Lakshmi's. There were the usual banners, carried by little boys, and the umbrellas and ensigns. Whip-crackers went in front of the procession like petard-throwers, and as the *Perahera*—now united—moved round the green, one saw the fire-dancers whirling their flames. They carry an iron bar with a flame at each end, and dancing cross it at great speed over and under their arms, making the impression of a swiftly-revolving wheel. After two circuits the *Perahera* broke up and returned to their respective temples. The drive back was exquisite—the hills mottled with trees; the pale paddy-fields; fantastic rocks in the river; shadows of the coco-palm. I fell asleep, preparing for a start before dawn today for Weragamtota.

7th September. I woke up suddenly at 3.45, got up and washed and walked out in the moonlit garden. It was deliciously warm and cool at once. But the car promised by Fogl never came. Till six I could not sleep, my heart and solar plexus beating violently at all the problems raised by this mishap. Has he the 1,000 rupees of which he spoke? Has he any hope at all of support from Ratwatte? It seems to me I had better go to Malabar immediately. The short passage in the train when one looks over the marvellous amphitheatre of paddy-fields to hills and high mountains is almost worth the tedium of the train journey. This time the *sawahs* were all glistening in sunlight—flooded—and the house or temple I like so much rose like the Ark out of the waters. Some were tender green, but most were flooded.

Kankaria'—The Magic Boar of Hantana—A Village 'Perahera'

8th September. All fixed up for Bangalore and Malabar. Called on Fred Fogl, who was quite unperturbed at not having fetched me for Weragamtota. He told me that a car crash had delayed him, and drew up a large list of things still to be seen. But shall I ever see them?

9th September. In the plane over Ceylon. Glorious clouds and very blue sky above. The eastern clouds are cumulus and brilliantly illu-minated—the western of cotton-wool variety, but built up splendidly into the exquisite blue sky. Now they are floating low down over the green earth and the blue sea: a wonderful contrast of colours—every shade of blue, and fleets of luminous white clouds moving among the drifting vapour. The earth looks like a green carpet covered by tightly curled mats. The contrasts of light are most sensational. To the right lie vast snowfields. Now all the vapours have assembled themselves into a delicate fleet, casting shadows as it sails over the earth, with an occasional galleon in full sail splendidly shining. The purple shadows animate the land. Here and there are circular lakes and curious dry round patches of sand. The cloud shadows are like frisky dragons, cavorting along. A solid roof of rumpled snow, with strangely moulded bosses, breaks off suddenly; and the mottled land-scape near the sea—yellow and mauve and grey—with a grey fringe along the sea, is of the utmost fantasy of colouring. Purple sands under transparent waters lie like shoals of fish. Then a sudden island lifts its head above the water, in shape like a starfish. Other islands emerge—green, brown and yellow, surrounded by a great semi-circle of sub-merged purple sand, and all along the sea-edge is a silver fringe of foam. The dark blue sea is now jade, but not one colour; its surface is broken by many currents, and the indigo shadows of the 'clouds' which lazily sail by. The young man opposite—who has a long, sensi-tive, thoughtful and rather suffering face—is also fascinated by the spectacle from his window.

Now there is a stylized frieze along the yellow coast, strange grey swordfish, and every imaginable shape of sandbank point their noses towards the irresolute land, which is continually breaking into water. Now it is mottled with red squares of cultivated fields—warm and sunny and solid under the lunar canopy of cloud. Ribbons of road curl among them. It is a quite amphibious landscape—or rather seascape. Suddenly the water solidifies into curves of mauve land, and then across the sea appears another coast—clothed in green trees and intersected by watercourses. Above this the clouds have massed themselves into a shining range of rugged mountains. A rainbow bridge has established itself across the sea—this is India.

CHAPTER X

Return Again—'Kolan' at Ambalan-goda — Yala — The Wounded Boar Flies Home

27th September. Dreamily, high up in the sky hang Olympian gold and blue cumulus clouds; a delicate shoal of small lamb-like clouds covers the silver-grey sea. Now a row of curiously shaped small islands lies flatly on the great expanse. The mackerel sea is blurred and illumined by a dazzling sun-path.

This time no one met me; the process of quarantine was long. I was alone in the bus. Dick's expected footballers are not coming, and I am warmly invited to stay on with Dick and Sheila.

28th September. Mr. Nicholas had kept last week for the jungle, and cannot again take leave, alas! It seems as if the *Kohomba Kankaria* is really coming off on the third of October! I cross my thumbs and wonder.

2nd October. A car which was to take us up to Kandy yesterday after-noon did not call, and I came up alone by train.

The journey seemed endless while I brooded on the disappoint-ment of so many hopes. As the taxi refused to face the St. George's Hill, I walked up by the steep short cut, and fell into a drain at the top of the steps. The pain was agonizing.

3rd October. Today my foot is immensely swollen, but apparently not sprained. Freddy de Silva said yesterday, shortly before my arrival, that he had seen the 'ferret'[1] hobbling about with a stick just as I actually am today.

4th October. Hantana Hill is more beautiful and clear-cut than ever,

---

[1] This nickname referred to my eager researches.

and looks so easily accessible. I shall never alas see the view from the top. There are so many things I shall never see!

Yesterday we made various attempts to get me a lift to Colombo by car, for the train journey was horrid to face, and I felt I must get down quickly to save what I could from the wreck of my hopes.

Last quarantine check; then to Paroles to get the prints of the *Perahera* which I had ordered. But the negatives, which were Fernando's, must have been taken by him when he left this firm for Lazarus, and at Lazarus they denied all knowledge of them or of my friend Fernando.[1]

A glorious afternoon on the small lawn of the de Silva's bungalow, where I had never sat before. Cumulus clouds of the utmost brilliance on the blue sky. Green parrots flitting about. Hantana through the boughs. Mr. Aberatne brought me down. He was glad of a companion, as he had beaten about for someone to go up with on Saturday—while I toiled by train! It was a wonderful moonlit drive. Exquisite phenomenon seen at Kandy at sunset. Through a canopy of semi-transparent copper cloud, the moon—pale blue, a real moonstone—mildly shining as if framed in all that effulgence.

7th October. I am in the train going to Ambalangoda. I did try to get hold of Fogl, in order to discover if he intended to go by car to Ambalangoda. But he was not accessible, so I must go without a photographer, as it is too late to get hold of Veerawardena. My ankle is none too good.

At lunch I heard from Mr. Murray, their planter friend, all about Fraser, the Scotch missionary who founded and built Trinity College, and is still adored by generations of Sinhalese. He got a bit 'rough' sometimes owing to shellshock in the first war, but always apologized and made amends. Every boy had to do clearing up and dispensing work in the slums of Kandy. His style of building—Kandyan—is admirable. He became afterwards head of Achimota College, in Nigeria.

I am seriously toying with the idea of going to Yala for three days. Instead of taking out travellers' cheques I will draw out cash, and have an expensive but delightfully solitary tour.

Rest-house at Ambalangoda. Glorious architecture of clouds over

---

[1] This was sad, and never explained: but I am convinced of Fernando's integrity.

the sea, behind which the sun is setting. Dove-grey and golden spires, with silver foam tipping the massive cumulus. Far away on the horizon liquid gold and shadowy shapes dimly outlined against sheets of molten gold. A suspicion of pale turquoise sky, never quite visible. Now the sun itself is dropping slowly out of the grey cloud mass. The coco-palms lean across the turbulent slate-green sea; heavily laden fisher-boats are struggling out. To the right is the great pale field of turquoise blue which I divined: overhead a flock of silver and mother-of-pearl clouds. Green lawns slope steeply to the rocks—bright green bushes of enamelled foliage. The bathing pool and white waves breaking and tossing uneasily among the rocks. It is very lovely. Now great flames are bursting over the firmament. The sky is molten fire—the horizon flaming, and pale fields of lemon sky lie among the flames. Fire bursts out among the lapis waves. To the right the whole sea is aflame, while to the south it is a cold grey. Gigantic mountains climb into the sky above the sunset.

A charming man, G. L. S. de Silva, bought me a programme of the evening. He had a very sensitive face, and seemed so much the host that I thought he was the rest-house manager. He fetched me in a car to the *Kolan,* which took place in the coco-palm grove attached to the house of a friend of Gunadasa. The dance ground was surrounded by ropes: a sagging roof of sailcloth covered part of the audience: in front of the dancers' dressing place was a tall erection of greenery, plantain, etc., which served as a screen, and was a very effective property when the high royal masks came out and were seen above it. Also the royal soldiers climbed it and peered from the branches, climbing about like monkeys. The crowd was enormous. This worried my friend Vimaladasa, who kept murmuring and clucking disparagingly. They had invited a certain number of guests, whom they hoped would contribute liberally. But these were swamped by the huge wall of villagers, and the repeated *adaus* of the dancers—who were not strikingly good—failed to produce a great deal. I can't help feeling that the show was not very costly, especially as most of the dancers were the boy pupils of the aged Pallis de Silva, who surely might dance for nothing. From the point of view of execution, the standard was not very high, and it must be admitted that the early part was rather boring—in which the various characters

203

were introduced. The sword dance of the four soldiers was excellent, and one would have liked a greater variety of exhibition dances.

The technique of the *Kolan* is curiously stilted, but I don't know if this is an essential part of it. The immensely heavy headdresses of the king and queen make dancing for them impossible, but the Jataka king was also not very mobile, though his crown was not cumbersome, and the queen was a dreadful stick who could neither act nor dance. The Veddahs were excellent, and their monkey antics extremely realistic and amusing. These were all little boys. I wish there had been more animal dances. I could not help feeling that the *Kolan* was once something very important. The fascinated attention of the crowd—which never melted away, and which certainly seemed to grow as the night wore on, till it burst into clapping at the Veddah's sermon to the wicked queen—showed how excellent a form of village drama this could be, and no doubt once was. A few drops of rain threatened once or twice, but the downpour coincided exactly with the end of the show, and then it cleared again, and I walked back in perfect moonlight; the moon only just past the full, hung very high in the sky, and lit ravishingly the delicate palm leaves, layer on layer, spreading out from tall, curiously leaning trunks. Rain shone in the moonlight on these leaves as we walked to the rest-house, making them glitter fantastically. I got to bed at 2.30, and was to be fetched at six in a car for Colombo. I woke at five and sprang up, mistaking it for six, so that I had an hour to lie in a chaise longue looking out to sea, while the golden moon faded in the sky and the water gradually glowed with sunrise. Sailing boats returning from the night's fishing came from far out towards the shore. Every time I counted them there was a fresh one, till they mounted to eleven. There is a strange and moving charm about these small lonely boats on the great sea, one by one aiming at the same shore.

I found that kind Mr. de Silva[1] had paid for my lodging. And later, since Fred Fogl had been unable to secure funds to pay for the *Kolan,* I ventured to remind the Bishop of Kurunegala, Lakdasa de Mel, of his kind offer of help, when I saw him at the opening of George Keyt's new dance school. He at once stepped into the breach. How grateful I was to him!

[1] Are not all de Silvas kind?

8th October. Drove with a police inspector and his wife, two amiable balls, to Colombo. I slept a good part of the way back, and also of the day. Towards evening Mr. M. D. Raghavan and Mr. Austin de Silva fetched me to go to a *Devol Maduwa* at Piliyandala, near the rest-house of Kesbewa. We picked up Wikramaratna (Pandit), and drove between paddy-fields and coco-palm groves to where the car had to be left for the *devol maduwa*.

Somewhere on the road we passed a small private *bali*. A woman was possessed by Kalu Kumara. She sat behind a cloth. Kalu Kumara presides over menstrual troubles, nightmares, etc., and is noted for his sexual appetites; he is a very lustful demon, but nevertheless it was he who brought the bo-tree to Ceylon, for he was a devout disciple of Buddha.[1] There were some very beautiful shrines of ivory plantain stems, and lovely crowns, with filigree arches of plantain. The dancing was very good. It seemed impossible that three should dance together in that small space, yet they never collided or even whirled. One drum was very effective as accompaniment. The floral altar at the end of the room was called *Mal Yahana*. This was a delightful scene. It reminded me of my first very small *bali* on the road to Matara, where the *Kapurale* lay outstretched in front of a woman, and took her ills upon him. She also was possessed by Kalu Kumara, judging from her description of the fearful black figure she met on the seashore in the middle of the night.

We arrived at last by small by-ways at the clearing in the groves where the *Devol Maduwa* was to be held. It is a place of historic interest, and the stone pillars which were dug out near by and have been set up on end—like a small stone grove—are supposed to have belonged to a former palace. There is a small *devale* with stone foundations, but the anklets and bracelets of Pattini are kept in a *devale* several miles away. This was not an exorcism ceremony, but a *Gam Maduwa* to bring blessings on all the village and strengthen good influences. There had, however, been dissension in the village owing —Pandit said—to political parties, and the beginning of the ceremony was held up, because sufficient cloth had not been contributed—they were twenty yards short. This made a great delay in beginning. The *Kapurale* was a fine-looking powerful man on whom the feminine

[1] It is possible that there is here a fusion of two different demons.

dress, necessitated by his being Pattini's representative, was particularly curious. He wore a woman's bodice and a white sari draped rather like Shanta's in *Bharata Natya*. The dresses of the dancers were not good—rather grimy and messy, and all wore vests. The village was perhaps poor. A table stood at the entrance to the *Maduwa,* a thing I have never seen before, on which contributions were to be made for the ceremony, to the village. The *torana* was a particularly fine one, seven-storeyed and five-leaved, and deserved the impassioned address later made to it by the chief dancer and conch player—who was a remarkable young man, always breaking into song and smiles. There is always some characteristic feature about each *devol Maduwa* distinguishing it from the others. In this case the chanted address, in Sanskrit and classical Sinhalese to Pattini and the *torana* were particularly beautiful. The dancing took place on various parts of the ground—sometimes at the far end from the *maduwa,* sometimes immediately in front of it. Sometimes—but this was later—down the whole length of the ground, formed into an aisle by the crowding people. There was one aged drummer who was throughout transported by musical fervour. He glistened with sweat, and followed the evolutions of the dancers with a kind of passion, as if he were drumming his soul into them. I find it rather difficult to decide from whom the inspiration proceeds—the drummer or the dancer. On this occasion I would say it was the drummer, though the small boy, who was a brilliant dancer, on one occasion set the *padam* (beat) himself, which the drummer delightedly absorbed. The repeated censing of the *Kapurale* seemed to send him into a kind of trance, but a very mild and contained one, compared with what I have sometimes seen. The old man, his mouth covered with a cloth, advanced under a canopy to bring offerings, and Pattini's emblems were also a feature of the *Kohomba Kankaria,* which I had not previously seen in *thovils.* The drummers belong, like astrologers, to the Nekati caste. This is a very interesting fact, which I had not heard before, and it seems very natural that both should be associated, for certainly the drummers are the most mysterious beings in Ceylon. Perhaps their rhythm has really something cosmic in it. I cannot otherwise account for the extraordinary effect it has on one—setting in motion far more than bodily movement. It is somehow metaphysical. I wish I could arrive at the meaning of this. The undercurrent of trilling vibration which goes on continuously is like the imperceptible movement of the sea on which breaks suddenly the vast rhythm of the waves. But of course the rhythm of the drums is very definite really, only intangible. I expect Dalcroze could have seized it, but it is always imperceptibly changing. Sometimes out of an oft-repeated, obvious pattern there breaks a new and subtle pattern. Incomprehensibly the relation between drummer and dancer is the most intimate imaginable. The orchestra in a European ballet does not *dance*. Here the musicians, singers and drummers are really part of the dance, not in the sense in which the music performed by the orchestra is part of the ballet, but rather as if the drummer were another limb of the dancer. To watch the drummer or singer is a very strange and terrific experience. It is almost frighteningly expressive. In vain one seeks for words to convey it. The drummer is dance mad. One sees that dance and music are absolutely inseparable, and in a sense the frustrated dance movement of the drummer increases his passion. I can't forget the ecstatic face of that old drummer, trying out steps with one of the dancers, who had a genial face even in the very early morning.

9th October. I have never seen so many smiling faces at a *thovil* as these dancers and drummers. I feel a great affection for them. The small boy, who was perhaps the *Kapurale's* son, was a wonderful little creature. I preferred his dancing to his somersaults, which one can see any day in an acrobatic turn. But his dancing was truly wonderful and his rhythms prodigious.

I foolishly left with Raghavan and de Silva, accepting too easily the statement that the show would go on until midday. But for my foot I would certainly have stayed. I am sure the two items I missed were the most important! I did not then know I could get a bus at Piliyandala straight back to Colombo. The rest-house at Kesbewa was fast asleep and looked so lovely in moonlight beside the great lake. No bed was to be had, but they let me sleep in a chaise longue (the 'boys' were occupying the comfortable camp beds), and I washed in the early morning from a pail on the veranda, looking on to the square lawn—enclosed by a hedge which looked very English. Then I returned by the first bus to Piliyandala and walked to the *devol maduwa*. The drums were still hard at it, but the scene had changed.

Many had left and the dancing was in the open at the far end opposite the *maduwa*. It moved down to the *maduwa* later, and the *Kapurale* showed me Pattini's beautiful anklets and silver bracelets, or perhaps this was a necklace made of silver shells. They live generally in a *devale* five miles away. A few *adaus* were danced, and as my old boys never turned up, I had to do the tipping. I felt dispirited at having missed two of the most exciting dances, though the flame-throwing and lighting of the lamps were very beautiful. The ethnologist and the librarian never took their eyes off their notebooks while the best dancing was going on. What people to go to a ceremony with! And this will be my last!

10th October. Fixed up everything for Yala, and Sheila is coming too. Lunch with Hubert Rajapaksa, her brother, who sang folk-songs with conventional piano accompaniment, and a 'Balinese' song called *Wayang,* which had nothing Balinese about it except the title. He told an amusing but rather unkind story of the behaviour of Dilip Kumar Roy at the *asram* at Pondichéry, when he had gone there to sing. He described the Darshan, and Sri Aurobindo sitting crouched in a corner, a very weak-looking, shrunken old man, who gave out, according to him, no life. The picture of a rather spoilt, plump Dilip was not altogether untrue to life. But it is hard to imagine him jealous of Hubert Rajapaksa, though he may perhaps not have welcomed competition at the *asram*. Dilip is a generous character, though somewhat naïve and childish.

A rather grim and mottled old Burgher who was also at lunch spoke about the splendid government of the Dutch, their schools, their policy of not interfering with the culture of the country. The English, he said, suppressed the vernacular schools, which meant that they suppressed Buddhist teaching. In effect, only English-speaking people got jobs, and so gradually Sinhalese was shouldered out. The substitution of English for Sinhalese history completed the rot. I do not feel so confident as Dr. Reimers that 'Independence' will really restore the old culture. It seems sad that a man like Hubert Rajapaksa should not be really interested in the prodigious musical culture of Ceylon, and only in folk-songs in so far as they can be turned to his purpose.

It appears that the Dutch did not allow natives to put up an

Kolan masks at Ambalangoda

Maker of masks

Animal masks by the same maker

umbrella in their presence. This was perhaps because they realized the ritual importance of the umbrella and the dignity it confers, which the English had apparently not jumped to.

11th October. The car came early to start to Yala. Only unfortunately it would not move. No power on earth would induce it to stir. It was a Ford specially adapted for jungle work! And now another—unadapted—had to be fetched, and I was very angry, particularly at the attempt to persuade me that it was a much better car. We drove with infinite precaution along Yala Road, already full of traffic, but contrived to reach Tangalle by 12.30. I am rather sick of the South Coast road, lovely though it is. From Tangalle the country changed. There were salt lakes and a very dry country, relieved by distant mountains. The driver turned out to be a gay and charming person. Soon after Hambantota the jungle began, and we turned off by a jungle road which at first was like a billiard table, and then like the pockets! We picked up two men at a forestry station. On the way many peacocks ran across the path, and we saw two large family parties of wild boar—deer on the horizon—four jackals very near, heads very doglike, who were not at all perturbed by us; and a large solitary elephant, who crossed the road with infinite deliberation and stood in the thicket. His tail was very short, and all declared he was dangerous, and had pursued cars on various occasions. It struck me as irritating that just as one came on a jungle monster one was obliged to retire from looking at him. Naturally he disliked cars invading his domain.

The road rose and fell and often became a ditch. It is very dry, and the waterholes are dried up, which makes the animals, fortunately, come to the Menikganga—our river below the circuit bungalow—to drink. It stands on a bluff overlooking the river and jungle—a great stretch of the river over which the moon and sun rose, and a northward curve—where the deer came down to drink and peacocks to bathe in the early morning. We heard the sad cry of a deer at dusk, caught by a leopard. A black bear is about here too, but we have not seen him.

The sunset was superb behind a group of strangely-shaped high rocks, on one of which is Akasa Cetiya—sky temple—a small dagoba. To the north lies Kataragama; to the south and very near to us, the sea behind a sandy ridge. We hear it all the time. It is a most lovely place. The bungalow has a long veranda, wired in, so one can sleep on it in large camp beds—the broadest I have seen—and watch the moon rise, and the jungle and starry sky almost without impedi- ment—like looking through a finely meshed veil.

We drove to Buttuwa, the other and grander bungalow; on the way walked along an elephant-coloured rock with a nearly dry water-pool; passed several great plains where herds congregate. Saw wild water-buffaloes, a jackal, two herds of wild boar, one of which ran very comically across a stream, with a see-saw motion in single file—in fact they always seemed to run in single file. Buttuwa is quite near the sea, and on the edge of a very wonderful bay with great rocks, yellow sand, hyacinthine water, and from the rocky promon- tory a fine view of the Haputale range, and in the foreground Katara- gama. It is an enchanting spot, and the stretch of sandy shore border- ing a sea inlet is covered with the tracks of animals' feet. It was here we saw more jackals, and last a family of wild boars. When we got back, the tree on the opposite shore was full of monkeys of all ages and sizes, gambolling on the bank and swinging in the boughs. They look like langurs—grey bodies, long legs and black heads. Stags and deer also came down to drink, and several peacocks: one of them (or is it a cormorant?) has stood for ages on what looked like a white log in the river, motionless, except for a turn of the neck from time to time. I went to sleep, and each time I woke he was still there, but now has escaped without being identified. It is 11.30, and all the creatures seem to be resting, as none is on the river bank. Last night the stars were indescribably brilliant. One firefly of huge size flew among the trees, and finally rose above them and disappeared. I saw the sun rise over the river, but missed the herd of deer who were camped on the plain. The river at this hour looks very lovely under a clear blue sky, with milky white sailing clouds. But crocodiles are hidden under this green, opaque water.

Walked to the sandbanks at 4 p.m. Deer passed rapidly through the trees and an elephant's huge footprints went straight along a nar- row path to the river. It is an exquisite shore, very broken by woods and ponds and sand-drifts. The high sandbanks overlook the whole glittering jungle to the mountains.

Drove at sunset a short way towards Kataragama; saw a herd of deer and a deliberate procession of wild boar, also many water-buffaloes. Marvellous sunset flaming behind the Akasa Cetiya. A leopard was seen, but not by me, crossing close by the car. Sheila is extremely timid of her beloved animals, and drinks in greedily every tale of their depredations.

13th October. Exquisite patterned shadow of the suriya-tree outside on the terrace from the still-bright moon. I got up early, long before Sheila allowed the sun to rise. But the sun actually rose three-quarters of an hour before she allowed it to! Watched for animals while the sky brightened and the earth grew rosy. Only wild boar and a distant deer and a jackal; I heard stags cry in the night. This sudden lighten-ing of the earth is very lovely. Came back by the sandbanks, to find my *Bhagavad Gita* burnt to ashes by a candle which had been left burning. It was given me by Monod Herzen, who translated it. Am lying out now on the river bank watching great white cranes and orange-beaked, long-necked black birds of the crane variety, and many others fly and perch above the river. There are innumerable birds, great and small. A party of peacocks and hens came saunter-ing along the bank from a sunny opening and went into a huddle under the bank, then rose by common consent and returned in single file. A buffalo is now grazing and drinking, watched by a peacock, who appeared suddenly on the bank. The appearances are all very sudden and the tempo, once arrived, very slow. Suna, the caretaker, has given me an old coin found on the shore, of 1750. It has a crown above a harp, and on the reverse a small crown at the top.

The peacock stays quite still watching the buffalo, who is in full sunlight. I should like to stay here now all day. Every beast has its stated time for visiting the river, and the young monkeys are only brought down to play perhaps about midday for an hour. Why is the peacock so motionless? As I ask this he advances from the shadow towards the buffalo. It is too much to hope that he will dance for him.

(I dreamed of Ninette de Valois with a peroxide blonde coiffure. She was with a little girl whom she introduced as the last word in dancing. She told me Martin Guldenburg would tell me where to see her dance.)

Now the buffalo is grazing towards the peacock, and now is eyeing him. But he has turned off to drink, and the peacock—the green pillar of his neck facing me—sits motionless. There was a great plunge of something in the river—perhaps the crocodile. The buffalo came and eyed the peacock, but now has moved quickly away to the sunny glade he came from.

It is missing that week with Mr. Nicholas that I most regret.

We drove off at 8.30—saw more herds of wild boar, a deer in the thickets, also a very large wild buffalo and the famous leopard, which slunk across the track just in front of us. His movements were clearly somehow connected with the deer. Wonderful drive, bowling across a salt plain before we reached the road, and then between lagoons of exquisite colours, and the pale blue, sky-blue mountains. I went to look at some sculptures of Anuradhapura times in a very old dagoba —of which the cement covering had disappeared. Dvarapala and Buddha and a Hindu god, with *Kathakali* crown. There were many stone pillars betokening a palace. Lunch at Hambantota, in a dreary position but very nice and clean rest-house.

At Ekessa we turned north on the Ratnapura road—a most beauti-ful drive, hardly passing a car. A great relief from the crowded Galle road, which I am heartily tired of. The road wound continually, through cultivated fields, heavily deforested rocky hills and dense tree jungle. Here there are elephant kraals: we saw one working ele-phant; also Rodiyas[1] live here. All the time the mountains were in front of us, and gradually the wooded hills closed round us, also rubber plantations. At Madampe the Hayes-Lauderdale winding road from Deniyaya joined our road, and we went on to Ratnapura, teaing in the rest-house, which has an enchanting and very peaceful view over the mountains, though the rest-house itself is not nice— too much hung with advertisements. Along the road after we turned off, a river wound for a long while. It was rather like an English lane. This is one of the loveliest roads in Ceylon, and as it is no longer than the Galle road I can't understand why it is not more often taken, except that one cannot go so fast, which in any case I hate.

14th October. Dined with Thornley and a nice couple called (I think) Armitage, who always began to talk at the same moment, and then withdrew with many mutual courtesies. A curious conversation with-

---

[1] See p. 80, note.

out much cohesion—about the British Israelites, the keeping of the Sabbath, the measurements of the Pyramids, etc. Thornley is just off to Kenya, and thence by road to Cairo, where his brother is Education Officer—also to Fez. He takes remarkable photos, also showed me Lionel Wendt's, which display every kind of ingenuity and photographic device, but are also very beautiful; nudes, landscapes, architectural compositions, reversals of light and shade: there were innumerable prints of the same photo, treated in various ways.

Thornley said that north of Kankesanturai in the extreme north of Ceylon, is a village of smugglers of a particular cocaine-like drug, which the smugglers fetch by speedboat from India. The village street is full of showy garages, filled with Hudson cars. The smugglers make enormous profits. Recently a Minister was stranded up there and had to get quickly to Colombo. He was told there was no difficulty—a car would be placed at his disposal, and he drove in a magnificent Hudson to Colombo with quantities of the forbidden drug under the seat.

Malalasekara called for me very late, i.e. about eleven, instead of 9.30, and we drove to the ferry at Hanwella, which I only then recognized as the place where I had come my first Sunday with the Mendez, also the ferry we crossed to the best *Gam Maduwa* I ever saw. Malala explained the role of the secondary devas. We are as ants to the great gods; they cannot feel for our sorrows. But to the lesser gods, the devas, we are as dogs are to us. They feel for us and protect us. This gives a good image of the role played by the lesser gods. Aiyyanar (Sasta), Vishnu's doorkeeper, is one of these. They are really Rakshasas (demons) who, to propitiate them, are called devas (gods). Alutnuwara Temple (new capital) near Kandy is presided over by Aiyyanar. It is here the elephants come to do obeisance. It was only 300 years ago that the South Indian mythology infiltrated into Ceylonese folklore. It was Sanghamitta who brought the bo-tree to Ceylon. Uppalavanna (wholly coloured one), i.e. the blue lily, was appointed the guardian of Buddhism in Ceylon. He later got mixed up with Vishnu in Buddhist temples, Vishnu taking the place of Uppalavanna. Only one temple, at Dondra, is actually dedicated to Uppalavanna. He is the brother of Sakra, i.e. Indra, chief of the Vedic gods.

The gods he said tended to become confused, and thus it is that the blue-faced Uppalavanna becomes interchangeable with Kalu Kumara, who is the lascivious black-faced demon, much addicted to women.

The Protestant idea of One God and one devil confuses the issue. There are various supreme gods and many assistant devas, who correspond to patron saints in the Catholic Church.

The Jains, he told me, believe in a Creator and also in original sin, which has to be expiated or got rid of. So man must do penance, and get free from all ties, even clothes, and must not take the life of the most obnoxious pests. Later the Digambara reacted to this Puritan-ism, and developed Tantric practices.

I understood Malala's position much better after this talk. He is an ardent Buddhist, partly because he is an ardent patriot. At fourteen he founded a Buddhist school, as a set-off against the Christian mis-sionary efforts in his village. It now has 750 pupils and is Govern-ment supported. He says I made a contribution to it in 1935, for which I am glad. He is uncompromisingly frank in the expression of his views and they are very definite.

16th October. On the plane bound for India. The light over Ceylon was marvellous. I saw Sri Pada plain for the first time. The mountains were exquisitely clear, but I had chosen the wrong side of the plane, and the indifference of the passengers to this beauty is expressed by all the blinds being drawn, even though there is no sun. I have never seen Ceylon look so lovely. There seemed far more ranges of moun-tains than usual, their feet bathed in mist, which rose like a thin veil between each line of hills. Now the smooth sea is traversed by endless ice floes, which pile up on the horizon into great bergs lit faintly by the sun.

I remember an old man bathing in the Kelaniganga at Hanwella ferry. He dipped continually up and down, and each time clapped his hands under the water, which gave a hollow sound like a drum or water-pot. Perhaps he did it for sheer pleasure in the sound. The paddy-fields were all most brilliant emerald touched with gold.

Now a chain of sand islands, lapped by little silver waves, stretches to an India-shaped continent of sand. The islands are luminous.

9.20. White clouds like a chorus of Furies over India. We are immediately above the coastline, but so are the Furies, so that there is again no hope of seeing Pondichéry or Mahabalipuram. The clouds rear themselves into magnificent shapes, and the highest gesticulate wildly to each other.

9.45. The clouds are massed now in dreamy radiance above the land, riding over it like chariots. Their pearl reflections dip into the sea.

Pondichéry! Very clear and neat between lagoons and coco-palms and sea. Its streets very straight and clearly defined: the harbour is fine. Round here the earth is red, but passes later into grey, green and brown as we move north. The clouds—now much less dense—cast long black shadows over the land. There are many lakes, perhaps floods, and I have hopes of Mahabalipuram. Alas! the coastline was hidden by the plane itself. I only saw the estuary and the temple on the rock, where vultures (or are they crows?) arrive punctually every day to feed at twelve. A huge green cloud-dappled world spreads out, and we are losing height.

After Madras: A great lake which I had forgotten, vast variegated plains interspersed with lakes or tanks, and long ranges of hills. The clouds have packed themselves into closely curled masses, forming a shining wall on the horizon. Sometimes one envelops us for a moment, blotting out the day, and we bump about.

12.45. Over the Nottamal range we got into a region of storm, sometimes blotting out the sky and earth, but often revealing stupen-dous scenery and Promethean clouds, wrestling and counterpointing above densely-wooded mountains under an intensely blue sky. Two Americans—a solid man and husky boy—armed with tripod and every sort of camera, are here with a newly purchased book on India. Now there are glimpses of golden earth—wiped out by a blanket of cloud. It is extremely dramatic. The flat earth, freed from storm clouds, is broken by huge cloud-shadows, and swiftly driving vapours move against luminous battalions of Correggiesque clouds, backed by a vast Olympian golden wall. The ground is rocky, but we are too high to realize the height of the hills. I see towers and crags.

1 p.m. All the great cloud architecture has vanished, but a grey roof lowers, and the red and green earth is mottled with violet lakes of shadow. A great city is spread out beside a lake—Hyderabad?

From Hyderabad we flew into a region of fearful night, and it seemed as if we must be submerged, but somehow we have skirted it and come out into misty sunshine—very calm.

The earth is lapis lazuli, with pools of reddish water. Shafts of rain drive down from a long rift of cloud. But here all is calm. Spectacular wrack of sultry clouds lying motionless and sunlit across the sky. A swarm of dolphin-like cloudlets—very bright against the dark earth; and advancing from the south a dense curtain, blotting out the earth, but perhaps it will not reach us. It did, and we have been tossing in the clouds, but now above them we see glimpses of a turquoise sky, very smooth and calm, and a stupendous landscape of cumulus clouds. We are just driving down into another valley of obliterating vapours, hiding the wonderful promise of the sky. Far below the green earth lies serene, while we jolt among the rain clouds. Now we look through strata after strata of dazzling clouds to a titanic horizon of brilliant peaks piled one above the other in Himalayan splendour under the hot blue sky. The earth is a strange black and green chessboard in contrast with the golden altitudes of the clouds. From time to time storms drive forward under the bright horizon and steal over the land. We sail on through the most sublime and ever-changing shapes, bewildering in their fantasy. Sometimes they draw quite near —sometimes withdraw to show a red river coiling through the land. Only Prospero could describe it. The clouds seem now to have come down to earth and to be sitting on the land. They give the excitement of a wonderful pageant, in which every tempo and form are mingled. Chariots go sailing by. Icebergs form and dissolve. One is crushed by giant rocks, or soothed by flower-like forms. Has anyone praised in verse this incredible beauty which can only be seen from the air? I welcome the hot sun shining in.

3.30 p.m. The earth is dark. Ghostly clouds encompass us, without form, but with strangely serrated edges, very threatening. The sky is hidden, the bright sun gone, but vaguely lights calm areas to the north. We are sinking into a Polar sphere, dense and woolly. We have come out now into a strange green world, where water lies like fiords between the woods and fields.

A high plateau on the top of a mountain range, densely wooded, with level strata of rock, very beautiful, and rather sinister in this light. Above it rise higher mountains. From it waterfalls drop to the plains—I see no sign of a habitation. A dense cloud covers the further range, but to the south-west range after range of rugged hills stretch away to higher mountains. These near hills are like great bastions, with paths along their battlements. They fall jaggedly in all directions, but alas are now again obliterated by the cloud in which we are wallowing—rain streams along the windows, and now and then a high green mountain rears its head.

We are coming through a rain-swept world—an estuary—a golden sea—and many little boats in harbour. There are islands, promontories, peninsulas—a watery lunar world. Now pale blue sky crossed by pink clouds is spreading. Alternation of rainstorms and fine—till we approached the harbour of Bombay, and skirted the lovely waterways, with inlets, peninsulas, islands.

Epilogue

This was not the end of my Ceylon adventure. I had much still to discover about the background of the people of Ceylon and their dances. Some may even succeed in saying the last word about the origins of the magic dramas of Ceylon and their significance. This is perhaps of less interest to the poet. So I would have preferred a more evocative title—and thought I had found it in the letters of my favourite poet John Keats during his walking-tour in the Lakes the year before his death. This tour may have hastened his death by its unaccustomed rigours, but so extraordinarily enriched his imagination that he felt a new era of poetry was opening for him. I can only quote here one image of a waterfall which—rejected by my publishers as the title—will I hope evoke for those who have read so far—the thunder of the drumming in that hour of dawn when the scent of flower-offerings spreads through the cool courts of the Dalada Maligawa—*The Thunder and the Freshness*.

APPENDIX I

Captain Thomas Skinner

Captain Thomas Skinner's life was compiled by his daughter, from his own journals after his death. It is entitled *Fifty Years in Ceylon,* and is the record of a precocious and admirable young man, who had a poet's eye and ardently humane heart, which taught him all kinds of things, usually undreamed of by British colonial officials, civil or military. He had been sent for by his father, an army officer stationed at Trincomalee, when he was about fourteen; but the father was so shocked by his son's ignorance of academic subjects that he would have been packed off home immediately to complete his education, had he not been begged off by the commander of the British army stationed at Colombo, who happened to meet the boy at a dinner. He was struck by his unusual intelligence, pleaded for him, and offered to take him under his wing. Poor Thomas had no wish to be a soldier, but it was better than being sent off ignominiously to finish his education; and though he had set his heart on the Navy, he made the best of it, and immediately distinguished himself, by taking a regiment across country to Colombo, which he reached in record time and without mishap. He thought it unworthy of an officer not to share all the hardships of his men, and went barefooted on all occasions, having discovered that it was better to allow leeches to fall off of themselves when replete, and leave no dangerous remains. When his native corps fell victims to smallpox, Captain Skinner tended them with singular devotion, and even kept all night, in his own bed, the small son of his sergeant, hoping by warmth to save his life.

The record of Thomas Skinner is indeed remarkable. His extraordinary health was no doubt due to his great abstemiousness. He lived hardily, and found it difficult to understand the wasteful self-indulgence and drunkenness of his fellow-officers. Skinner was a

218

demon for work, one must confess. If he could not finish the job he had set out to do in the time planned, he stayed on till it *was* finished, sometimes living almost entirely on salt for several days, as many beasts do in the desert. There were no bearers to bring relays of food; nor would it have occurred to him to employ them for such a purpose. He paid for whatever he was obliged to requisition from the villages his regiment passed through; but his chief pleasure was in those solitary watches, when the poet in him found expression.

It was in 1833, when he was nearly thirty, and had been distinguishing himself by diligence and invincibility since the age of fifteen that he wrote that wonderful description of dawn on Adam's Peak, which I quote below. He acquired the science of mathematics simply because it was required of him by a superior officer who believed in him; he could not bear to fall below that standard. So without any previous training in mathematics—for you must remember his father thought his education too scrappy to be tolerated in a gentleman, he taught himself the use of a theodolite, and became *malgré soi*, a surveyor. He taught himself to sketch, a gift in which he was as he thought, wholly lacking. I can imagine no better definition of the art of drawing than 'sympathy between the eye and hand'. This sympathy, he declares, became at last so perfect, that he found no difficulty in setting down what he saw. The one-inch map of the Kandy province, and the general map of Ceylon, were the result. 'I used often to see the most wonderful effects when thus camping out. On one occasion my sojourn on Adam's Peak lasted for a fortnight on the top of the Peak, where I was waiting for fine weather, which I did not get, to admit of completing my operations. One morning as the sun was rising, the shadow of the mountain was thrown across the land and sea to the horizon, and for a few minutes the apex was doubled, and so clearly marked, that the little shed over the impression of Buddha's Foot, was perfectly distinct in the shadow. Another most curious effect was when the mist had lain deep in the shadow below, between the Great Peak, and the opposite range of Rackwanie, it was an exact representation of the sea; the clouds rolling against the base of the mountains, resembling the surf beating against the cliffs which seemed to project into the sea, the points of the hills peeping through the mists, appeared like beautiful little islands. At another time looking down from the cone, a small white cloud, the size of a man's hand, might be seen floating upwards, about midway between the mass of vapour-sea below, and the top of the Peak. Sometimes, under certain conditions of the atmosphere, this little cloud of fleecy vapour would suddenly expand into a huge dark cloud, and come rolling up the cone, apparently lashing it as if with its utmost fury, and then suddenly envelop it with a dark mantle, a strange contrast to the clear atmosphere through which but a few minutes before, objects might have been seen sixty or seventy miles distant.'

For me, I admit, the most interesting episode in his career was his visit to Java, presumably not long after the great Sir Stamford Raffles had been obliged, by one of those immoral arrangements beloved by diplomats, to hand over Java to the Dutch, and build anew in Singapore an outpost of Empire. His name is little known in Eng-land, though his birthday used to be kept by the Dutch in Batavia, and the Indonesian Republic carries on the tradition of honouring a great man.

The actual purpose of Skinner's visit to Buitenzorg was to ask that the Javanese sailors who had presumably been serving under the British flag should be allowed to return to their homes. By tact and patience this was finally accomplished, though of course there was no question of allowing them to re-enlist. It would be cheaper and better, said the Governor, to buy some slaves in Bali from the Sultan. Skinner explained that this was not countenanced by his govern-ment; but he continued to be treated with the utmost courtesy, and was astonished by the hospitality and kindness of the Dutch, which he contrasted favourably with that of the British abroad. The Governor invited him all the same to visit Bali, and offered transport through Java, under the most favourable circumstances. Oh, how tempting! But the dutiful Captain Skinner would, had he accepted, outstayed his leave. If only he had for once disobeyed orders!

APPENDIX II

Hugh Nevill's Description of Ella, the last Stronghold of Ravana

Taprobanian, December 1888.

'Maligawana, ancient capital of Eastern Ceylon, was on the edge of the East plain of Bintenne, and on the bank of the Maha Walli Ganga, which winds parallel to the towering wall of mountains forming the Eastern border of Central hill country. Immediately to the West, an ancient path creeps up the abrupt ascent, passing into Dumbara over the crest of the hills. Proceeding, however, some six or seven miles north of this path, along the western bank of the river, we reach an angle of barrier hills flanked by a precipitous mountain, called Bambara Gale. Down the slopes of this forest-clad recess rush several purling streams, while beneath the densest shade of night old trees growing among blocks of rock-boulders everywhere scattered in picturesque confusion, amidst sombre gloom, with murmuring babble of waters, are hidden the mysterious ruins called Sita Kotuwa, or Sita's prison. Packed on the side of the hills, a mile or so above, is a little plain, with a few rice fields, and the hamlet of Guruluneta.

'Near this same jungle-covered land was once the site of an ancient village, with varieties of broken crockery of early design scattered in the soil, as well as refuse of iron ore. Above this again, a secret path wound up the wooded cliffs, and passing into the dense forest in their ravine, skirted a rock whence one has a magnificent view over all the plains from the North East to the South West. This rock is called Bellin Gata, or Watch Rock, and this path is said to have been of old jealously kept secret. From this point the track leads over the crest of the range down to the village of Maedawaka, passing the whole way for miles through what was once the densest forest, until the rage for coffee gardens caused its lower portions to be felled. On reaching Maedawaka it rejoined the road to Dumbara. This secret stronghold therefore afforded unsurpassed opportunity for escape among the pathless recesses of the forests and hills, and was by its position exceedingly unlikely to become known to an invader.

'My imagination had been greatly excited by the talk of this myste- rious fort, for the villagers assured me that one might search for it for days without success, or again stumble upon it at the first search. For here were legions of Yakas, spirits of vast power who rendered it invisible to the unwelcome intruder. Above the ruins is a waterfall; and the rock concealed by the volume of the stream, is said to contain a cave in which treasures, as of the Nibelungen, are stored. It is said that if a man can find the entrance, and take with him candles to light him at every third fathom as he proceeds, he will reach the treasure-chamber. Here are golden beds, gem-set vessels of quaint device, glittering with rainbow hues, and made of the soft gold now unprocurable. From the walls hang creepers made of silver and gems, bearing golden pumpkins wrought of burnished gold. Ropes of pearls and rubies hang about. No king could picture any treasure which he would not find there.

'Eagerly the trembling adventurer loads himself with those glitter- ing spoils, but alas, as he passes out of the mouth of the cave, the Yakas render all invisible. Impalpable they glide from his grasp back to their original position, to await the day when the pre-destined prince shall claim them.'

Nevill is relating the gossip, as given in deferentially stilted but impressive language by one of the guides, leaving out, as he says, the more tedious details.

He continues: 'At the village above these ruins, we reach what I distinguish as tradition. Broken crocks of refuse ore mark the site of the camp of the workmen who built the ruined buildings below, and who laboured at the treasure cave. Present day villagers do not know how to find the entrance to the cave, but their ancestors did. It is said all was damp and gloomy, yakas had closed the rock over the treasure. This treasure may easily have been that of the Kandyan kings.'

Robert Knox's story shows how easy it was to remain hidden in the jungle; a fact of which the unfortunate Captain Johnson and his redcoats was, centuries later, to become only too well aware.

'Proceeding up the valley beside the stream, we reach a point of land enclosed between two of its branches, where are stone posts and traces of buildings; crossing to the north, a ruined causeway with stone posts and pavement, we reach a point of land enclosed between two of its branches, where are stone posts and traces of buildings; crossing to the north a ruined causeway with stone steps and pavement passes up the ravine. To the north of this and close to it is the site of a large building, indicated by an outer wall of stylobate, and the posts that supported the upper floor or floors. Further up the causeway we pass again a small ruin, probably a temple or altar, perched on the rock to the north of the path, the causeway ascending the lower shoulder of the rock by a flight of steps now fallen away. Beyond we reach a narrow rocky stream with steep banks, over which a bridge formerly passed, its stone supports now lying in ruins in the bed of the stream. Further on we reach the last building of the group, the stone stylobate showing its importance.

'The stones were well dressed with simple mouldings, and no attempts at ornaments of a florid nature. Arrangement and position of buildings reminds one of the pre-historic city of Riti Gala, and also resembles older ruins at Pulu Kanaka, doubtless also once a Yaka capital. There is nothing to indicate so early a date as 1000 B.C.; it may equally be 200 B.C. or even later.'

Index

Index

Buddhism, 12, 44, 47, 64–5, 83, 86, 88, 91, 97, 103, 106, 126, 149, 150, 152, 165, 171, 195, 196, 208, 213, 214

Buitenzorg, Botanical Garden, formerly official residence of the Dutch Governor-General outside Batavia, 76, 220

Butterflies, a dance episode in the *Tale of Genji*, 30

Buttuwa, one of the circuit bungalows at Yala, 210

Calcutta, 72

Caldecott, Colombo, 32, 38, 107, 145, 146, 181, 182–3

Cambodia, 36

Canaria Zeylana, a Ceylonese variety of *Canaria*, 70, 86

Cannon-ball tree, in Peradeniya Botanical Gardens, 69

Capetanakis, Demetrios, a famous Greek poet, who died in London at the age of thirty and is buried in Norwood Cemetery, 128

Carroll, Lewis, *Alice Through the Looking Glass*, 15–16

Catamaran, flat native boat, 42, 77

Ceylon Daily News, 28

Ceylon (Trant), 19 n.

'Ceylon Tours', 127

Chamara, ceremonial fly-whisk made of 'feathers' of palm fronds, representing *sabada*-bird feathers, 49

Chitra, Malalasekara's eldest daughter, a pianist, 72

Chitra Sena, a Sinhalese dancer, pupil of Lapeya, 148, 150, 155, 157, 159

Churchill, Sir Winston, 76

Clark, Sir Kenneth, 146

Colombo, 17 n., 19, 23, 27, 28, 32, 36, 39, 40, 65, 71, 76, 89, 104, 107, 110, 119, 125, 128, 157, 159, 161, 165, 166, 175, 182, 190, 204, 205, 207, 213, 218

Colombo Archaeological Museum, 112, 125

Colombo Arts Festival, 17 n., 60, 125, 138 *seqq.*

Colombo Museum, 37, 38, 60, 65, 140

Colpetty, a suburb of Colombo on the Galle main road, 28

Conch-shell dance, 71, 183

Cooke Brothers, clients of Leston Fernando in Jaffna, 64

Culavamsa, small chronicle, 75, 103

Dagoba, a round beehive Buddhist temple containing offerings, 36, 69, 103, 105, 119, 121, 128, 129, 132, 136, 176, 178, 198

Dalada Maligawa, Temple of the Tooth in Kandy, 116, 122, 217

Dambulla, frescoed cave temple, 120, 133, 157, 168, 188

Darshan, literally 'viewing', 73, 208

David-Neel, Madame, famous Tibetan traveller, 114

Davis, Mr., London Library librarian, 15

Davy, an early writer on Ceylon, 115

Dawul-Gale, drum rock, 118

Dawula, drum, the same name is applied to a famous drum of Uzbekistan, 124, 136, 185

Degaldoruwa Temple, 121, 123

Dehiwala, 183

de Koninck, Dutch landscape painter, 185

Delgoda, E. A., a landowner who has devoted his life to music and dance, 14, 110, 130, 131, 146, 153

de Mel, Lakdasa, Bishop of Kurunegala, 14, 145, 204

Deniyaya, 212

Deraniyagala, Justin, 38, 180, 181

Deraniyagala, Paul, 38

Deraniyagala, Mrs., 109

Dervish dancing, 22–3, 51–3, 114

de Silva, Austin, 140–1, 180, 205

de Silva, G. L. S., 14, 203

de Silva, George, one of the most remarkable personalities in Ceylon and my host at Kandy, 14, 86, 87, 89, 94, 97, 125, 142, 161, 163, 169, 170, 201, 207

de Silva, Mrs., 87–9, 161, 171, 189, 195

de Silva, Minnette, younger daughter of the de Silvas, the first woman architect in Ceylon, a pupil of Corbusier, a very able

Index

Kotte, former kingdom in south Ceylon, 91, 147, 165

Kottegoda, Mr., in rubber control department, learned in folksongs of Ceylon, 74, 77

Krishna, most beloved of Hindu gods, 139, 192, 193

Kujela, a poor Brahmin enriched by Krishna, 193

Kunju Kurup, finest living teacher of *Kathakali*, 13, 192

Kurugalle, wild boar rock, 115, 119, 120

Kurunegala, a small but famous town, seat of a bishopric, 14, 39, 65, 75, 107, 115, 127, 128, 132, 135, 145, 157, 173

Kuruvanse Caste, originally a warrior tribe of North India, 191

Kusa, one of the sons of Rama, 193

Kuveni, abandoned Yakka wife of Vijaya, 159, 160, 161

Lakdasa—*see* de Mel

Lake House, 152

Lake Road, 167

Lakshmi, Hindu goddess of Fortune, wife of Vishnu, mother of Kama (love), 119, 198

Lamuwa, famous old teacher of Kandyan dancing, 71-2

Lanka, Ceylon, 17, 22, 138

Lankatillaka, temple, 119, 120, 122

Lapeya, one of the great teachers of Kandyan dancing, 35, 148, 155, 157, 158, 173

Lava, one of Rama's sons, 193

Legong, the Balinese dance best known to tourists, 185

Lingam, male organ, 84

Lion Bath (Mihintale), 178

Lipton, Sir Thomas, 81

London Library, 15

Ludowyk, Lyn, 152, 190

McBean, Angus, a famous photographer, 145

Mace dance, 53

Madampe, 212

Madras, 35, 65, 215

Madras University, 13

Maduwa, pavilion (*see also Mal maduwa*), 41, 43, 46, 51, 52, 65, 67, 120, 122, 140, 142, 145, 186, 187, 188, 207, 208

Maedawaka, 221, 222

Magulbera, 140

Maha devale, 164, 170, 171, 172, 173, 193

Maha San Yakka, 41

Maha Sona, 46

Mahabali, King, 192

Mahabalipuram, 175, 215

Mahabharata, immense Sanskrit epic in which occurs the *Bhagavad-Gita*, 139

Maharishi, 73-4

Mahavamsa, 'Great Chronicle', the oldest Ceylonese Chronicle, 75

Mahaveliganga (Maha Walli Ganga), 'Great Sand River', 97, 106, 125, 145, 172, 195, 221

Mahincante, 92

Maho rest-house, 129

Makara Sankavanti, 117

Malabar, 11, 88, 91, 192, 198, 199

Malagamana, J. C., 97, 98, 99, 101, 117, 143-4, 148, 174, 187

Malalasekara, Professor G. P., Professor of Pali in the University of Ceylon, 17, 20, 32, 33, 72, 85, 107, 108, 110, 125, 126, 133, 138, 148, 149, 178, 213, 214

Maligawa (Temple of the Tooth), 95, 105, 107, 124, 138, 143, 167, 168, 196, 198

Mal-Bali, flower-offering, 54

Male Raja, King born of a flower, 63, 189

Mal-maduwa, flower pavilion, 46, 51, 52

Mal-yahana, floral altar, 205

Mandalay, Burmese royal city destroyed by the British, 96

Mandapa, a shed or shelter, 75

Manipuri, 150

Manjusri, a painter friend of Harry Pieris, 107

Mantras, spells, 41, 47, 48, 53, 93

Marg, an excellent illustrated journal edited in Bombay by Malk Raj Anand, 127

Margosa tree, 61

Maria Estate, Wattegama, 168

Marinelli, Italian impresario, 89

Index

Index